Heralding the Loud Cry

Progression of Light from 1888

Camron Schofield

HERALDING THE LOUD CRY

Progression of Light from 1888

by

Camron Schofield

Co-edited by

Kerensa Grigson

Published by

Eternal Realities

For more resources please visit the author's website at:

www.eternalrealities.com

This book is dedicated to the three dignitaries of heaven – the Father, the Son, and the Holy Spirit – for the promotion and propagation of the "most precious message" of *Righteousness by Faith*.

CONTENTS

FOREWORD

Heralding the Loud Cry is a precious book, containing progressive light and truth for our time in relation to the Loud Cry of the Fourth Angel. Each chapter of the book reveals newer and deeper spectrums of this multifaceted diamond of truth – as if one were holding the diamond up towards the sun, light permeates off its illuminated sides in every direction, radiating outward, upward, downward and inward. In beautiful simplicity, Camron Schofield shares the eighteen gems of wisdom he has collected on Righteousness by Faith from his personal sojournings out of spiritual Egypt to the Red Sea shore. Consider each one of these sermons on Righteousness by Faith a unique and precious stone that you can yet polish and beautify further in the experience of your own life.

Perhaps as you proceed through the studies, you will hear the voice of Jesus saying to you in a gentle whisper: "Take my yoke (doctrine) upon you. For my yoke (doctrine) is easy, and my burden is light." (Matthew 11:29-30). This message of a personal, living Saviour, who has become at-one with us in our experience, to give us complete victory over sin, and power to obey the gospel, could not be more dear to the Christian pilgrim who hungers and thirsts for Christ's righteousness in a time where pure truth is not widely found.

'Tis true the message of Righteousness by Faith is an old message! From the commencement of the reformation until the early 1900's it has spilled forth from the lips and pens of Martin Luther, John Bunyan, Charles Spurgeon, Ellen G. White, Ellet J. Waggoner and Alonzo T. Jones and many others. However, the reality is that this message has never been properly understood by Christendom at large. So God in His providence has provided yet a clearer message in the pages of this book, to open up this understanding to the minds of His people so they cannot miss it this time around in the closing scenes of earth's history!

The prophetic theme of this book is the Loud Cry of Revelation 18:2, which is the warning message given to the world, by a company of people here on earth (represented by an angel in prophecy) to "come out of Babylon". The problem is, many Christians do not realise that the Loud Cry itself is a message that is designated to fit a people in righteousness (Christ's perfect obedience) before God without an intercessor, so they can give the final message to the world to come out of Babylon.

The world's most accomplished female writer, Ellen Gould White, who penned the

Spirit of Prophecy, clearly identified the Loud Cry was in fact the message of Christ Our Righteousness or Righteousness by Faith which she had been presenting for forty-four years prior to the Minneapolis General Conference of 1888.

The message is certainly a common thread in all her prophetic writings but as with past generations the people were spiritually blind and could not discern it. Henceforth God, out of necessity, raised up two new messengers in the succeeding generation to voice and pen the message in even clearer tones.

The book, *The Everlasting Covenant* was a brilliant literary work by Ellet J. Waggoner. At the 1888 Minneapolis Meeting he communicated the message of Righteousness by Faith in the simplest language from draft notes that would later compile the chapters of his book. In the proceeding years Ellet J. Waggoner and Alonzo T. Jones had the full support of Ellen G. White, who travelled far and wide across the country to be at the very side of the messengers as they spoke to Christian congregations.

Despite God's extenuating efforts to communicate the Loud Cry message more simply through His servants, to prepare a people to give the Three Angels Messages to the world, the message was again misunderstood, unheeded and rejected by the majority of people.

Ellen G. White states in several places in the Spirit of Prophecy that had the people understood the message of Christ Our Righteousness and been faithful in proclaiming it, the Lord would have come in only a few years from that time (1888). But as a consequence of the ministers and the people rejecting the message, the sealing time was delayed and the Church was sent back into the wilderness, spiritually speaking.

In the *1895 General Conference Bulletins*, Alonzo T. Jones gave the address to the ministers that we cannot call a people out of Babylon (out of the world and the fallen churches), if we are not out of Babylon (sin) ourselves. He reiterated the point: how can you call people out of sin if you are still sinning – it can't be done.

This was the dilemma of a sister in 1888, who did not feel she was making progress fast enough to be ready for Christ's soon return. A brother in the faith expresses her sentiments in the following quote:

"A sister told me not long ago that before that time four years ago she had just been lamenting her estate and wondering how in the world the time was ever going to come for the Lord to come if He had to wait for His people to get ready to meet him. For she said the way she had been at it--and she had worked as hard as anybody in this world, she thought--she saw that she was not making progress fast enough to bring the Lord in any kind of reasonable time at all, and she could not make out how the Lord was going to come.

"She was bothered about it, but she said when the folks came home from Minneapolis and they said, 'Why the Lord's righteousness is a gift; we can have the righteousness of Christ as a gift, and we can have it now.' 'Oh,' said she, 'That made me glad; that brought light, for then I could see how the Lord could come pretty soon. When He Himself gives us the garment, the clothing, the character, that fits us for the judgment and for the time of trouble, I could then see how he could come just as soon as He wanted to.' 'And,' said she, 'it made me glad, and I have been glad ever since.' Brethren, I am glad of it too, all the time.

"Now there is sense in that thing today. You know we have all been in that same place. You know the time was when we actually sat down and cried because we could not do well enough to satisfy our own estimate of right-doing; and as we were expecting the Lord to come soon, we dreaded the news that it was so near; for how in the world were we going to be ready? Thank the Lord He can get us ready. He provides the wedding garment. The master of the wedding feast always provided the wedding garment. He is the Master of the wedding supper now, and He is going to come pretty soon, and He says, 'Here is the clothing that will fit you to stand in that place.' Now there will be some folks that cannot attend that feast, because they have not on the wedding garment, but the Lord offers it as a free gift to all and as to the man who does not take it, who is to blame?" Alonzo T. Jones, *1893 General Conference Bulletins.*

Have we not all felt in the position of this sister, that we do not feel ready for Christ's return? Well the message of Righteousness by Faith, if heeded by God's people, is a message that will perform a quick work in righteousness, at a time when the world has made void God's holy law (Romans 9:28, Psalms 119:126).

God in His precious love for humanity is breathing life back into this well worn message of Righteousness by Faith that promises to perform the very thing God's word says it will perform in the life. It will produce a people who have the faith of Jesus, for it is only those that have the faith of Jesus that will be fitted in His righteousness to obey all the commandments of God and go through the time of trouble in the last days without an intercessor.

In Luke 18:8 Jesus asks the question: "Will I find faith on the earth when I return?" He is looking for His faith to be reproduced in His people and this book is the key to unlocking the mystery of that faith of Jesus as a living reality in our lives. Do we want it friends? I pray so. Amen!

The Co-editor

Publisher's Note

The following pages are transcripts from the spoken word and we have made minimal changes to the grammar and flow of the words in order that we might preserve the original pathos. We ask that you will therefore not read this as you would a normal book, but that you will bear in mind that it was delivered as a verbal presentation.

At the end of each quotation, we have also provided a footnote reference number. The full reference is found in the back pages of the book with the actual paragraph specified from which the statement was taken. We hope that this may assist those who wish to read the quotes in their fuller context in their original setting.

THE SWEETEST WORDS ON EARTH

May 29, 2010

He speaks and the sound of his voice is so sweet,
the birds hush their singing.

THE voice of Jesus is so sweet that even creation stops to listen. Are we His creation? Do we stop to listen to His voice? There is a time coming when there will be a voice spoken and those who have not *now* stopped to listen to His voice will then be forced to hear it. The words will be spoken, "My grace is sufficient for thee." That voice will glorify the redeemed and raise the righteous, but it will be a different experience for the wicked. In *The Great Controversy*, p.642, Ellen White writes here:

> That voice which penetrates the ear of the dead, they know. How often have its plaintive, tender tones called them to repentance. How often has it been heard in the touching entreaties of a friend, a brother, a Redeemer. To the rejecters of His grace no other could be so full of condemnation, so burdened with denunciation, as that voice which has so long pleaded: "Turn ye, turn ye from your evil ways; for why will ye die?" Ezekiel 33:11. Oh, that it were to them the voice of a stranger! Says Jesus: "I have called, and ye refused; I have stretched out My hand, and no man regarded; but ye have set at nought all My counsel, and would none of My reproof." Proverbs 1:24, 25. That voice awakens memories which they would fain blot out-- warnings despised, invitations refused, privileges slighted. [1]

This sweet voice is not sweet to the sinner. It is a voice which speaks condemnation even though it has come to them in entreaties and in calls to repentance. In it all they saw condemnation. And there, when it finally comes, they will have none of it. They know the voice, they have heard it before but "Oh, that it were to them the voice of a stranger!" The words of Jesus Christ are not sweet to the sinner.

I would like for us this morning to examine: what are the sweetest words on earth? What are they? If we turn to Philippians 3:4-6 we commence our study from an interesting viewpoint:

> Though I might also have confidence in the flesh. If any other man thinketh that he hath whereof he might trust in the flesh, I more: Circumcised the eighth day, of the stock of Israel, of the tribe of Benjamin, an Hebrew of the Hebrews; as touching the law, a Pharisee; Concerning zeal, persecuting the church; touching the righteousness

which is in the law, blameless.

Apostle Paul had read the word of God and he had heard this word and it had filled him with zeal. He thought it was sweet, he thought it was satisfying. And indeed, as that law of God, the Ten Commandments, stood before him, he looked at them and he said, "According to that – I'm blameless. I've done this right, I've done that right, I've done it all right." The Pharisee looks at the law of God and His words and says, "They are sweet. They make me to feel very sweet myself." And indeed, Luke 18:11, Apostle Paul says, "a Pharisee":

> The Pharisee stood and prayed thus with himself, God, I thank thee, that I am not as other men are, extortioners, unjust, adulterers, or even as this publican. I fast twice in the week, I give tithes of all that I possess.

He looked at this letter of the law and he compared himself with it and he said, "Hey, it's pretty sweet. Look at what I've done right – I fast twice in the week, I give ten percent of everything of even the cumin and the mint, and look, I haven't committed adultery, I'm fair and just in my dealings, I haven't extorted people and I'm not a publican!" He looks at this word of God and he says, "It's good. I like that. It makes me feel good." But Jesus Christ, when He was asked in regards to the law, He said, "How readest thou?"

Apostle Paul claimed to be, according to the law, blameless, but he met Jesus Christ. He saw the law of God as it really stood toward the sinner. And if we come there to Romans 7:7-13 we read of his experience, and this particular experience is a profound experience. And as I have considered what it is that I am sharing with you this morning, I have come to realise how few have actually made this experience in its *entirety* as it is really meant to be made. Apostle Paul loved the law, he thought he had kept it, but when he saw it as it really was, he said:

> What shall we say then? is the law sin? God forbid. Nay, I had not known sin, but by the law: for I had not known lust, except the law had said, Thou shalt not covet...

He had read the law but he hadn't seen how far reaching the law actually was. He had seen the law, "Thou shalt not covet," but he hadn't discerned in it, "Don't *lust*," until he saw it as it really was.

> ...But sin, taking occasion by the commandment, wrought in me all manner of concupiscence. For without the law sin was dead. For I was alive without the law once: [AND I THOUGHT I WAS BLAMELESS. I THOUGHT THAT ACCORDING TO ALL OF ITS PRECEPTS I WAS QUITE WELL, THANK YOU] but when the commandment came, sin revived, and I died. And the commandment, which was ordained to life, I found to be unto death. For sin, taking occasion by the commandment, deceived me, and by it slew me. Wherefore the law is holy, and the commandment holy, and just, and good. Was then that which is good made death

unto me? God forbid. But sin, that it might appear sin, working death in me by that
which is good; that sin by the commandment might become exceeding sinful.

He read the law as it was meant to be read and it killed him. He came to realise that
what he thought he had been keeping was not what he had been keeping. According to
the letter of the law – perhaps he was pretty good – but when it came to the spirituality
of the law, it slew him. "When the commandment came, sin revived and I died."

As you continue reading through Romans 7, he makes a precious experience. He
finally says in verse 25:

I thank God through Jesus Christ our Lord. So then with the mind I myself serve the
law of God; but with the flesh the law of sin.

What does he thank God for? The Ten Commandments? The law as we know from
Galatians 3:24 is a school master. And when I read that particular Scripture, I don't
think of me there sitting at a desk listening to a teacher, I actually think of me getting
the cane. That is the school master I have always considered the law to be. It chastens. It
comes to us and it says, "You think you have done that right? You *haven't* done it right!"

Have you kept the law? Can you say, "I have kept the law"? To keep the law would
be to do what is right. Have you done that which is right? Children, have you been a
good boy or a good girl? Adults, have you been good this week? Do you *think* that you
have been good this week? Has someone come to you and said, "How are you today?"
and you said, "I'm good"? You haven't been good. Only God is good, as Jesus Christ
said (Matthew 19:17). The law comes to us and it says, *"I want righteousness.* I want
right-doing. Here are my ten precepts and I want you to obey them." It will accept
nothing short of that. Nothing short through your whole entire life. You can live for
eighty or ninety years and if you sin once in your whole entire life you have broken the
law of God and you must pay the wages. A *whole entire life of obedience* is what the law
demands. Do you have that? "When the commandment came – I died." I came to realise
how far short I actually am. I can do everything right but I didn't do it right yesterday. I
didn't do it right ten years ago or twenty years ago. The law *will not* be satisfied.

What does the law *really* demand of us? What is the law? It is the transcript of
the character of God. It is a declaration of *His* righteousness, *His* right-doing. This
is the truth of the law that slays. It wants perfect righteousness, but whose perfect
righteousness does the law want? God's perfect righteousness. It is *His* character,
it is *His* righteousness, it is *His* law, therefore it wants *His* right-doing. It wants the
righteousness which God does, the righteousness which is manifested in *His* life. It
wants the right-doing which is done in *His* life. And it will accept nothing short of that.

When you look at the law from that perspective, how readest thou? When you
come to see that the Ten Commandments actually require the very righteousness of God
Himself in your life, does that law slay you? Do you have that to offer to the law?

When you look at the law like that, does it not work in you all manner of concupiscence? How can I attain unto that? But you know, there is actually no excuse for sin. As much as this is what righteousness is, if you are lacking it you have no excuse. *You have no excuse.*

Have you ever said to someone you should have done this or you should have done that? Have you have heard it in the church where we place expectations upon one another and get disappointed when those expectations fail? We expect this person to be doing this, and that person to be doing that, and then we get annoyed when they don't. They can't do it! They can't! "There is none righteousness, no not one," it says. "There is none that seeketh after God. They are all become unprofitable" (Romans 3:10-12). That is you and that is me. We put expectations upon one another which they cannot meet and we get disappointed. So in our dealings with one another, if you don't want to be disappointed, *don't expect.*

Yes, we think we are alive, we think that we are doing things really well and that God will be happy with my efforts, but when the law comes as it really is, *gulp*, sin revives, and what do I have to offer God? *What do I have to offer God?* We have nothing to offer God. He wants *His* right-doing. Do you have that to offer? No. We don't. Romans 7:13:

> Was then that which is good made death unto me? God forbid. But sin, that it might appear sin, working death in me by that which is good; that sin by the commandment might become exceeding sinful.

So now we have a problem. I wasn't just sinful, doing some things right here and OK, I was a bit slack on some things there. But we are seen to be now exceedingly sinful. Or as Romans 5:20 puts it: an *abundance* of sin:

> Moreover the law entered, that the offence might abound. But where sin abounded, grace did much more abound.

And the word *abound* means to have or possess in great quantity. Do you have and possess sin in great quantity? – to be *copiously* supplied? That word 'copious' is a very descriptive word of an abundance of sin or to be in great plenty and for it to be very *prevalent*. What's a prevailing wind? It's a wind that has it's way. It has force in it and carries everything with it. Our sinfulness *prevails* within us and we get carried away with it, as it says there in Isaiah 64:6:

> But we are all as an unclean thing, and all our righteousnesses are as filthy rags; and we all do fade as a leaf; and our iniquities, like the wind, have taken us away.

That is the law of God as it comes to the sinner. This is the law of God, the word of God as it comes to the sinner. But, it is a school master and it leads us to Jesus Christ. Do I have that which I can give to God, to the law? I do not. *Now* I know it. And if I have let this really sink in as it did with Apostle Paul, I will have a *great* sense of need.

Where do I get it? I want it, I don't want to die. I want to please God, as apostle Paul says in verse 22, "I delight in the law of God after the inward man." I love it! I consent to the law that it is holy, and just and good, but I see within myself this prevalent abundance of sin.

But where sin abounded, grace did abound? *Much more* abound! Where sin abounds, grace did *much more* abound. So here we find ourselves with an abundance of sin, a copious amount of transgression, of unrighteousness. But what do we find there as well? *Even more grace!* But if we don't find that sin is abounding, can we find an abundance of grace? We cannot. We have an unrighteousness which is as an unclean rag – a filthy, dirty rag. Have you been in a mechanics workshop and looked in their bag of rags? That's you, that's me. The next time you look in a bag of rags, think of our church.

All our unrighteousness is as filthy rags. We do not have the righteousness that God wants. We do not have that which the law demands. But where sin abounded, grace much more abounds.

Isaiah 54:17. What is an abundance of grace? If I have an abundance of sin, in its place is an abundance of grace. Yea, much more. Here in the last part:

> This is the heritage of the servants of the Lord, and their righteousness is of me, saith the Lord.

Whose righteousness? *Your* righteousness. But does it come from you? NO. You can't produce it. But God says, "I will give them righteousness, I will give them that which will satisfy the law."

This giving of righteousness and this abundance of grace – how do we gain it? Through what way does it come? Romans 3:23-27:

> For all have sinned, and come short of the glory of God; Being justified freely by his grace through the redemption that is in Christ Jesus:...

The abundance of grace now justifies us freely through the redemption that is in Christ Jesus.

> ...Whom God hath set forth to be a propitiation through faith in his blood, to declare his righteousness for the remission of sins that are past, through the forbearance of God; To declare, I say, at this time his righteousness: that he might be just, and the justifier of him which believeth in Jesus. Where is boasting then? It is excluded. By what law? of works? Nay: but by the law of faith.

This abundance of grace in the the place of an abundance of sin justifies and it sets forth Jesus Christ as a propitiation. In other words, Jesus Christ takes my place in respect to the demands of the law of God. Where I have failed, He takes that failure upon Himself and He appeases the justice and wrath of that law. He stands in my place. And that redemption is where? It is in Jesus Christ.

Let's look at this a little more closely. John 15:5. When we are in Christ, what is the blessing?

> I am the vine, ye are the branches: He that abideth in me, and I in him, the same
> bringeth forth much fruit: for without me ye can do nothing.

The laws needs to work to bring me to Jesus Christ, because without Him I can't do anything right. But now, when that school master has brought me to Jesus and He abides in me, now there can be brought forth fruit which satisfies; but He says, "Without me you can do nothing."

John 5:30:

> I can of mine own self do nothing: as I hear, I judge: and my judgment is just;
> because I seek not mine own will, but the will of the Father which hath sent me.

He says, "Without Me you can't do anything." But then He says, "I can of My own self do nothing."

John 14:10:

> Believest thou not that I am in the Father, and the Father in me? the words that I
> speak unto you I speak not of myself: but the Father that dwelleth in me, he doeth
> the works.

Jesus Christ laid down Himself. He put Himself aside and took upon Himself the garb of humanity. And of His own self He could do nothing. That which He did which was right was not His own works. It was the works of the Father in Him. Jesus says, "Without me you can do nothing. Except you abide in me and I in you, you cannot do the works of God – you cannot meet the righteousness which the law demands." But if we abide in Him, we can, because He emptied Himself and was filled with the fullness of God and God worked in Him perfect righteousness. So as we abide in Christ and Christ abides in us, and Jesus Christ works in us and the Father worked in Jesus Christ, we work the works of God. That righteousness which the law demands is satisfied.

As Christ was set forth as our propitiation, and we receive that and believe that and we come to Him and hide there in His bosom, the Father only sees His Son. When He looks upon you and me, we are hiding in Jesus Christ and He does not see our sinfulness. He only sees the perfect right-doing of Jesus Christ, which is His own perfect right-doing. So when He looks upon us, He is very happy because He sees *His* righteousness. Where there were miserable failings, where there is only a wretched, poor, blind and naked being, He sees a perfect life. He sees a life that is as perfect as His own, because *it is* His own. And that life is from everlasting to everlasting. And the law is very happy because that law is that thing itself – perfect righteousness from everlasting to everlasting.

And therefore, Romans 7, if we come back there, we understand how it is that

Apostle Paul can be so happy to have found Jesus Christ. He found this law but all it did was give him a real state of discomfort and concupiscence and a sense of burning and roasting. "Here I am and all I see is I can't do anything right. There is nothing in me to feel good about." And there *is* nothing. Have that sense, keep that sense of roasting, because it leads us to Jesus Christ. It makes us appreciate Jesus Christ, the propitiation for my sin. Romans 7:25-8:1:

> I thank God through Jesus Christ our Lord. So then with the mind I myself serve the law of God; but with the flesh the law of sin. There is therefore now no condemnation to them which are in Christ Jesus, who walk not after the flesh, but after the Spirit.

Now that you are in Jesus Christ, you have believed His propitiation, you have believed that He now stands in your place and you are believing it everyday – there is *no condemnation*. How perfectly do we believe these words? How perfectly do we believe that we are not condemned? *There is no condemnation.* And in Psalm 119:89 it says:

> For ever, O Lord, thy word is settled in heaven.

God means what He says. You are not condemned if you have been killed by the law and are now hiding in Christ. Satan can tell you otherwise until the cows come home, but if this is what God's word says, then we must believe it. There is no condemnation to those who are in Christ Jesus. Absolutely none.

And now that we have reached the point where the law has killed me, and as the Scriptures say you are no longer under the law but under faith, do we make void the law? Does that particular word of God have any more relevance in our lives?

Jesus Christ comes and He declares "righteousness". What is *righteousness*? Psalm 119:172:

> My tongue shall speak of thy word: for all thy commandments are righteousness.

Is the law done away with when you are in Jesus Christ? No. It is that very word that Jesus speaks. He speaks His Ten Commandments.

"How readest thou?" were the words of Jesus Christ. How do we read the word of God? To the sinner it condemns, but if they have permitted that condemnation to slay them, and they have found a propitiation, how readest thou *now* the Ten Commandments? Christianity wants to do away with them. Do you want to do away with the Ten Commandments? God said, "Thou shalt have no other gods before me, Thou shalt not make any graven images." We are familiar with the Ten Commandments as it reads.

But did you know that in 2 Corinthians 4:6 it says that God commanded the light to shine out of darkness? In the beginning there was darkness and God said, "Let there be light" and there was light. He *commanded* the light to shine out of darkness. Did that light produce itself? It didn't. But God commanded it. And we have before us the Ten Commandments and we read them as God saying, "You should do this. You should do that." That is how we consider the commandments of God. But reading line upon line we see that the word which God speaks, *it* will produce what it wants. So when God comes to us and He says, "Thou shalt have no other Gods before Me," how readest thou? Do you read it is as *you* are not to have any Gods before me? Make sure *you* don't go and bow down to any idols?

No. It is the same word which was spoken in the beginning. That word *itself* will produce *itself*. If we receive the word of God in *this* manner, then not only will Jesus Christ stand in the place of our failures but the very word that He has spoken will produce His own righteousness within our own lives. *It* will create it. When the Israelites received the Ten Commandments what did they say? "All that the Lord has said we will do it." "I will do it. Yes God, that is what you commanded and that is what you want so I'm going to go and do it now." That is *not* what God wants. That is not what the law wants. It doesn't want *your* right-doing. It doesn't want *your* obedience. It wants *God's obedience*. The word of God must be permitted to produce its own fulfilment.

2 Peter 1:4 – how readest thou the word of God?

> Whereby are given unto us exceeding great and precious promises: that by these ye might be partakers of the divine nature, having escaped the corruption that is in the world through lust.

What are the Ten Commandments? They are promises, but not just promises. They are *precious* promises. Are we receiving the word of God like that? Are we receiving all of His requirements like that? We look at His demands – what *we consider* to be His demands – with our mind which naturally places upon the words of others an arbitrary requirement. God is not arbitrary; but we see His law, we see the principles of a changed life and we think I have to go and do that; I have to go and do this. That is not what God wants. When the Israelites stood at the foot of Mount Sinai, they should not have said, "All that you have said, we will do it."

They should have said, "Amen! Let it be so. Thy word, O Lord, it will fulfil itself. Thou hast said that it will not return void, it *itself* will accomplish the thing." When God comes to us with His law, or any of His other requirements, say "Amen!" Let God fulfil it in you. Don't go about like the Pharisee trying to set up your own way of doing things. Don't take the principles of God saying, "I've done that right, and I've done this right." You *haven't* and you *can't*. But I *can* do all things through Christ which strengtheneth me. *He* will work in you both to will to do of His good pleasure, *if* you will receive the word, *then* it will work and produce. But you have to be dead. You have to *let* it abide in you.

We return to Romans 3. Now this word is received, not as something arbitrary, but as it says there in 1 John 5:3: "This is the love of God that we keep His commandments." The love of God will keep His commandments in you – that is where the love of God is. He will work in you to keep His commandments – that is what God's love is.

Now, Romans 3:19-22:

> Now we know that what things soever the law saith, it saith to them who are under the law: that every mouth may be stopped, and all the world may become guilty before God...

Those who are under the law are those who think that they can keep it; they are those who say, "All that the Lord has said I will do it." But every mouth will be stopped because they can't and the whole world will become guilty before God.

> ...Therefore by the deeds of the law there shall no flesh be justified in his sight: for by the law is the knowledge of sin...

All your right-doings are not good enough. *It is not good enough.*

> ...But now the righteousness of God without the law is manifested, being witnessed by the law and the prophets; Even the righteousness of God which is by faith of Jesus Christ unto all and upon all them that believe: for there is no difference.

So now in your life, *God's own doing* will be manifested. There will be no more boasting because you have become guilty before God and you have realised that where you thought you had got it right you had not, and you cannot. But now you have yielded and that word works within you and produces *your* righteousness? No. It produces the *righteousness of God*. That is what is manifest in you, in your earthen vessel.

So one final appreciation then of God's law.

We have seen how it leads us to Jesus Christ. It shows me up. It gives me a sense of need and now I come and I find in Jesus Christ that which satisfies the demands of the law. And then I receive that word itself which previously condemned me. I now receive it and it *itself* works in me to produce that which the law wants. Romans 3:21 again:

> But now the righteousness of God without the law is manifested, being witnessed by the law and the prophets.

The law now is *not* done away with. In fact we see all the way along that to do away with the law is to do away with eternal life. But now that law is a *witness*.

And I cannot put it any better than Alonzo T. Jones does in the *1893 General Conference Bulletins*, Study No. 18:

> The law gives a knowledge of sin, in order that we may have the knowledge of the abundance of grace to take away the sin, then grace reigns through righteousness

unto eternal life by Jesus Christ–and this righteousness of God by faith in Christ is our own through the working of the law, and this knowledge of sin has brought us to Christ, and we have Him, and the law is satisfied in all its demands that it has made upon us.

Now when it is satisfied in all its demands it has made upon us, then will it stick to that and keep on saying that it is satisfied. That that is all right? When the law has made demands upon us that we cannot satisfy by any other possible means except by Jesus Christ being present in ourselves, then, will the law of God, as long as we stay there, stand right there and say, "That is right, and I am satisfied with it"? [Congregation: "Yes."] Then if anybody begins to question it and says, "It is not so," then we have witnesses to prove it, have we?

Now you see this: that it is necessary for several reasons that we should have witnesses. One in our own connection and in our own personal experience is this: When God speaks and we believe it, then we know, each one for himself that the righteousness of God is our own, that we are entitled to it, that it belongs to us and that we can rest in perfect peace upon it...

There is the law and we can read the Ten Commandments and receive them as that promise – that promise that God is satisfied. Because in us He sees His Son and in His Son was the satisfaction of the law.

But there are other people that need to know this, too. Can they know it by my saying so? [Congregation: "No."] Can they know it by my saying that I assent to this and that I say that is so and therefore it is so? Will that convince them? Is that proof enough to them? [Congregation: "No."] They need something better even than my word. Don't you see, the Lord has met that very demand and has given us witnesses to which they can appeal and they can go and ask these witnesses whenever they please whether this that we have is genuine or not. Is that so? [Congregation: "Yes."]

"In Jesus Christ I am righteous. If you don't believe it read Exodus 20 and it will tell you that in Jesus Christ I am righteous." This is what Alonzo T. Jones is saying here.

They need not come and inquire of us; if they inquire of us, of course we can tell them what the Lord has told us to say and if that is not enough, they can go and ask those witnesses. We can say, There are some friends of mine...

Have you ever considered the Ten Commandments to be your *friends*? They are your friends.

They know me from my birth till now. They know me better than I do myself and if you want any more than this that I say, go and ask them. They will tell you. How many of them are there? [Congregation: "Ten."] is their word worth anything? Do they tell the truth? Ah, they are truth itself. They are the truth. Psalm 119:142. Well then it is impossible for them to testify otherwise in bearing witness than that. When they say that that demand is satisfied, "This life is well pleasing to me," that is enough for anybody in the universe, is it not? [2]

Can you understand how it is that David says, Oh how I love thy law? It is my meditation all the day? It has killed him, but through being slain he has found peace with God. He has found something which will satisfy, which will cover for his entire existence, from his childhood right the way through to eternity. And now it is working itself to fulfil itself in him. And there it stands and that very thing which slew him, says, "He is worthy of everlasting life." This is amazing! How readest thou? How have we been receiving the word of God in our own lives? How?

Alonzo T. Jones speaks of the last day when God brings everyone up to judge them. And I have to share this with you because it is so heart touching. It is so revealing of the law of God as *love*.

> And in that day there are going to be two parties there. There are going to be some there when the door is shut, and they will want to go in, and they say, " Lord, open to us. We want to come in." And someone comes and asks, "What have you done that you should come in? What right have you to enter the inheritance here? What claim have you upon that?" "Oh, we are acquainted with you. We have eaten and drunk in thy presence, and thou hast taught in our streets. Yes, besides that we have prophesied in thy name. In thy name we have cast out devils and in thy name we have done many wonderful works. Why, we have done many wonderful things. Lord, is not that evidence enough? Open the door." What is the answer? "Depart from me, ye that work iniquity.

But didn't they preach in His name and cast out devils in His name? They did all that which the law required!

> "What did they say? "We have done many wonderful works. *We* have done them. *We* are all right. *We* are righteous. *We* are just. Exactly right. Therefore *we* have a right to be there. Open the door." But "we" does not count there, does it?

Are we learning that?

> There is going to be another company there that day–a great multitude that no man can number–all nations and kindreds and tongues and people, and they will come up to enter in. And if anyone should ask them that question, "What have you done that you should enter here? What claim have you here?" The answer would be:

> "Oh, I have not done anything at all to deserve it. I am a sinner, dependent only on the grace of the Lord. Oh I was so wretched, so completely a captive and in such a bondage that nobody could deliver me but the Lord Himself; so miserable that all I could ever do was to have the Lord constantly to comfort me, so poor that I had constantly to beg from the Lord; so blind that no one but the Lord could cause me to see; so naked that no one could clothe me but the Lord Himself. All the claim that I have is what Jesus has done for me. But the Lord has loved me. When in my wretchedness I cried, He delivered me. When in my misery I wanted comfort, He comforted me all the way. When in my poverty I begged, He gave me riches. When

in my blindness I asked Him to show me the way, that I might know the way, He led me all the way and made me to see. When I was so naked that no one could clothe me, why, He gave me this garment that I have on, and so all I can present, all that I have to present as that upon which I can enter, any claim that would cause me to enter, is just what He has done for me. If that will not pass me, then I am left out, and that will be just too. If I am left out, I have no complaint to make. But, oh, will not this entitle me to enter and possess the inheritance?"

But he says, "Well, there are some very particular persons here. They want to be fully satisfied with everybody that goes by here. We have ten examiners here. When they look into a man's case and say that he is all right, why then he can pass. Are you willing that these shall be called to examine into your case?" And we shall answer, "Yes, yes, because I want to enter in, and I am willing to submit to any examination, because even if I am left out I have no complaint to make. I am lost anyway when I am left to myself.

"Well," says he, "we will call them then." And so those ten are brought up and they say, "Why, yes, we are perfectly satisfied with him. Why, yes, the deliverance that he obtained from his wretchedness is that which our Lord wrought; the comfort that he had all the way and that he needed so much is that which our Lord gave. The wealth that he has, whatever he has, poor as he was, the Lord gave it, and blind, whatever he sees, it is the Lord that gave it to him. And he sees only what is the Lord's. And naked as he was, that garment that he has on, the Lord gave it to him. The Lord wove it, and it is all divine. It is only Christ. Why, yes, he can come in."

And when Jones shared this back in 1893, the congregation started singing:

"Jesus paid it all,
All to him I owe;
Sin had left a crimson stain:
He washed it white as snow."

And then, brethren, there will come over the gates a voice of sweetest music, full of the gentleness and compassion of my Saviour–the voice will come from within, "Come in, thou blessed of the Lord." [Congregation: "Amen."] "Why standest thou without?" And the gate will be swung wide open, and we shall have "an abundant entrance into the everlasting kingdom of our Lord and Saviour Jesus Christ." [3]

How readest thou? How *receivest* thou?

We read it in our Scripture Reading. What was the word? Psalm 119:103:

How sweet are thy words unto my taste! yea, sweeter than honey to my mouth!

Can you taste them? Are they sweet? Thoroughly masticate it. Don't be fast with your food. Chew it; taste it; enjoy it; soak it in! As God brings to you His requirements, *let* them be sweet.

May God help us, and I mean may God really, really help us, to receive His word *as* He intends us to receive it – to do and say exactly that which Jesus Christ said in Psalm 40:7-8:

> I come: in the volume of the book it is written of me, I *delight* to do thy will, O my
> God: yea, thy law is within my heart.

AMEN.

God's Abounding Grace

Part 1
WAKING UP TO THE REALITY
June 19, 2010

IN the few opportunities that I have to speak I would like to share with you a series. A few weeks ago I shared a divine service and there were requests from several that I break it up in its simplicity and get every step that we went through clear in our mind. So I have intended on presenting a series called *God's Abounding Grace.*

The first part that I want to share with you tonight is called *'Waking up to the Reality'* or *'Slain by the Law.'* As we go through, you will realise that both these titles are both one and the same, that to wake up to reality is to recognise that I am slain by the law. As we go through our study, our key text will be found here in Romans 5:20:

> Moreover the law entered, that the offence might abound. But where sin abounded, grace did much more abound:

Here in this simple text is the story of salvation, from the beginning of sin, right the way through to the immortal inheritance. The abundance of grace follows the abundance of sin.

"The law entered that the offence might abound." This in God's program of grace towards man is the first step of his restoration. The law enters.

Now read Romans 3:20:

> Therefore by the deeds of the law there shall no flesh be justified in his sight: for by the law is the knowledge of sin.

Why does the law need to enter? The law needs to enter because man is ignorant of something and what is it?

Man was just walking along in his own happy little way not realising that sin abounded, not realising that he was in sin, in *death*, because the wages of sin is death. So the law entered to bring to man a knowledge of sin, to bring to man a realisation that he's in a predicament – there is a problem and that problem needs to be resolved.

Without the entering in of the law there is no realisation of the problem. And in Mark 2:17 we read the very words of Jesus Christ Himself:

> When Jesus heard it, he saith unto them, They that are whole have no need of the physician, but they that are sick: I came not to call the righteous, but sinners to repentance.

It's a very basic principle. If you don't know that you're sick, will you go to the doctor? Will you obtain and apply a remedy for something if you don't think you have it? You won't. You won't go through the pains of trying to deal with the issue if you think there's no issue. So Christ says, "I came not to call the righteous, but sinners to repentance." He was speaking to the Jews if you remember and the Jews thought they were pretty good; they thought that according to that law – as Apostle Paul says, he was blameless – they all thought they were blameless.

Christ came to call the sick and in order for Him to effect that call, He must set in action the law. He must give the law in order to create a sense of need. Let's read of it in Galatians 3:24:

> Wherefore the law was our schoolmaster to bring us unto Christ, that we might be justified by faith.

The law was a schoolmaster to bring us to Christ. We had to come to Christ because we were not there at Christ. So He gave the law. The law entered to make man realise: *Hey, I'm sick, I'm a sinner, I need to repent.* And what is repentance? Repentance is a change of mind. And this here in Isaiah 1:4-6 is exactly the situation that man finds himself in:

> Ah sinful nation, a people laden with iniquity,

A few weeks ago we looked at the word *abounding*: abundant, sin abundant, abounding. Abounding means it is in a large quantity; it is a copious amount. In fact the word was used, it was *prevalent*, it was *controlling*. And here they are, "a sinful nation, a people laden with iniquity," there's a huge amount of sin that they have.

> …a seed of evildoers, children that are corrupters: they have forsaken the Lord, they have provoked the Holy One of Israel unto anger, they are gone away backward. Why should ye be stricken any more? ye will revolt more and more: the whole head is sick, and the whole heart faint. From the sole of the foot even unto the head there is no soundness in it; but wounds, and bruises, and putrifying sores: they have not been closed, neither bound up, neither mollified with ointment.

Sick! Isn't that a description of someone who is *grossly* sick? He is repugnant. David says, "I stink because of my foolishness and no one wants to come anywhere near me" (Psalms 38:5,11). This is the sinfulness that man finds himself in. This is our situation. Those who will recognise this are those who will say, "I need a physician."

But the Pharisee looked at the law, he took it according to its words and he said, "I haven't committed adultery, I haven't been profane, I haven't been like this publican," – you know the story there of the parable that Christ told. (Luke 18). According to the outward forms of the law, we can look at it and we can say, "I've done everything right, what's the problem?" But what is it that the law identifies? It identifies that the *head is sick*. Now this is the part of the law that slays.

We come to a realisation that as this law enters, it's not just talking about the outward life – it's talking about the inward thoughts, the inmost desires. And Apostle Paul defines this very clearly for us in Romans 7. And over the years we have spent time delving into Romans 7 but let's do it again and see if we can gain more depth out of it. It pays to go back over these Scriptures again and again because as we are on our journey we make deeper experiences, so we go back, and we read something deeper out of it, because now I can understand more of what's being conveyed there. So if we start here in verse 7:

> What shall we say then? is the law sin? God forbid. Nay, I had not known sin, but
> by the law: for I had not known lust, except the law had said, Thou shalt not covet.

Now when Christ spoke of the law, do you remember He brought the spirituality into the law? He brought the depth into it. The Ten Commandments say, "Thou shall not kill." When Christ came, He revealed to man what the law really was. To *"kill"* is if you are ever angry at your brother. If you are angry at your brother, you are guilty of murder. To look upon a woman is to commit adultery if even just in your mind you lust after them.

This was the depth of the law that Apostle Paul came to realise. He knew the law. According to it, he was blameless. But there came to him a realisation that it reached right into his head, right into the very desires of the mind. He says, "I had not known lust, except the law had said, Thou shalt not covet." The Pharisee said, "I haven't committed adultery," but now the law said, "Thou shalt not covet," and he came to realise that to lust is to covet. Verses 8 and 9:

> But sin, taking occasion by the commandment, wrought in me all manner of
> concupiscence. For without the law sin was dead. For I was alive without the law
> once: but when the commandment came, sin revived, and I died.

There is something in these Scriptures that we want to understand a little more clearly. Without the law, sin was dead. But when the law came – this right appreciation – suddenly it came to the apostle's mind a realisation that his whole head was sick! And note this: "Sin wrought in me all manner of concupiscence." Do you know what the word concupiscence means?

It's amazing how often we can read these Scriptures and think we understand what it is saying, when the dictionary lies at hand and we don't go and read it. I'm going to read to you the meaning of *concupiscence* and I can assure you, friends, that this will bring an entirely new appreciation of the law to you and what it does in slaying you.

This is from an 1824 Webster's dictionary so it's very old English and this is what would have been meant when it was being used:

> *Concupiscence, n.* [L., to covet or lust after, to desire or covet.] Lust; unlawful or irregular desire of sexual pleasure. In a more general sense, the coveting of carnal things, or an irregular appetite for worldly good; inclination for unlawful enjoyments.

The law came to him and as it came to him it showed to him sin and as that sin came, it actually wrought in him *unlawful* and *irregular desires*. There suddenly awoke within him a coveting of carnal things, desires to do wrong, to please the flesh. It *abounded* within him. It became *prevalent* within him.

Do you understand what you've just read? The commandment came and sin revived. When the commandment came, suddenly within his being was a revival of all the works of the flesh and what beforehand seemed to be subdued and not even known that it was there, suddenly there came to him all these drawings and desires for something he had never wanted before, that he didn't think he wanted before. When the law came, he found who he really was. He thought that he had done everything well and that his head was pretty good but suddenly it was all stirred up, and, Whoa! Is this who I am? I will continue reading now Romans 7:9-15. Bear in mind this person's experience:

> For I was alive without the law once: but when the commandment came, sin revived, and I died. And the commandment, which was ordained to life, I found to be unto death. For sin, taking occasion by the commandment, deceived me, and by it slew me. Wherefore the law is holy, and the commandment holy, and just, and good. Was then that which is good made death unto me? God forbid. But sin, that it might appear sin, working death in me by that which is good; that sin by the commandment might become exceeding sinful. For we know that the law is spiritual: but I am carnal, sold under sin. For that which I do I allow not: for what I would, that do I not; but what I hate, that do I.

So there awoke within him a desire to keep the law of God. "I love the law, and consent to it that it is good and holy and just." But he suddenly found that within him was a contrary working to that law. It *awoke* within him. "What do I do? What I want to do, I can't do it and what I don't want to do, before I even know it I've done it!" Verses 16-24:

> If then I do that which I would not, I consent unto the law that it is good. Now then it is no more I that do it, but sin that dwelleth in me. For I know that in me (that is, in my flesh,) dwelleth no good thing: for to will is present with me; but how to perform that which is good I find not. For the good that I would I do not: but the evil which I would not, that I do. Now if I do that I would not, it is no more I that do it, but sin

that dwelleth in me. I find then a law, that, when I would do good, evil is present with me. For I delight in the law of God after the inward man: But I see another law in my members, warring against the law of my mind, and bringing me into captivity to the law of sin which is in my members. O wretched man that I am! who shall deliver me from the body of this death?

As the law entered he came to realise: "I'm dead! I love this law, but I can't keep it. I can't." Through that law sin worked to slay him, to kill him, to bring him to even greater temptations and greater trials than ever before. And to clarify this I'm going to read from John Bunyan's book, *Grace Abounding to the Chief of Sinners.* As this law enters, it works all manner of concupiscence and it slays. Now this is speaking of John Bunyan in regard to him wanting to be one of those that are called of God and he was concerned that he wasn't called of God. Remember it was sinners that Christ came to call. So as he was in this perplexity, wanting to be called and desiring to be called, what was his experience? It says here, and listen very carefully here because it clarifies what we've just gained from reading Romans 7:7-9:

> About this time I began to break my mind to those poor people in Bedford, and to tell them my condition, which, when they had heard, they told Mr. Gifford of me, who himself also took occasion to talk with me, and was willing to be well persuaded of me, though I think but from little grounds: but he invited me to his house, where I should hear him confer with others, about the dealings of God with the soul;...

He's listening to this godly man speak about the dealings of God with the soul about how the law has to enter in order to bring man to Christ to bring him that sense of need...

> ...from all which I still received more conviction, and from that time began to see something of the vanity and inward wretchedness of my wicked heart, for as yet I knew no great matter therein; but now it began to be discovered unto me, and also to work at that rate for wickedness as it never did before. *Now I evidently found that lusts and corruptions would strongly put forth themselves within me, in wicked thoughts and desires, which I did not regard before;* my desires for heaven and life began to fail. I found also, that whereas my soul was full of longing after God, *now my heart began to hanker after every foolish vanity;* yea, my heart would not be moved to mind that that was good; it began to be careless, both of my soul and heaven; it would now continually hang back, both to, and in every duty; and was as a clog on the leg of a bird to hinder her from flying. [emphasis supplied]

Did you note the experience there? As he came to an appreciation of the law of God, its spirituality, there awoke within him: "I evidently found that lusts and corruptions would strongly put forth themselves within me, in wicked thoughts and desires, which I did not regard before." Suddenly it wrought in him all manner of concupiscence.

> Nay, thought I, now I grow worse and worse; now am I farther from conversion

than ever I was before. Wherefore I began to sink greatly in my soul, and began to entertain such discouragement in my heart as laid me low as hell. If now I should have burned at a stake, I could not believe that Christ had love for me; alas, I could neither hear Him, nor see Him, nor feel Him, nor savour any of His things; I was driven as with a tempest, my heart would be unclean, the Canaanites would dwell in the land.

Sometimes I would tell my condition to the people of God, which, when they heard, they would pity me, and would tell me of the promises; but they had as good have told me that I must reach the sun with my finger as have bidden me receive or rely upon the promise; and as soon as I should have done it, all my sense and feeling was against me; and I saw I had a heart that would sin, and that lay under a law that would condemn.

Isn't this the experience that we just studied, in Romans 7? This is the experience.

These things have often made me think of that child which the father brought to Christ, who, while he was yet a-coming to him, was thrown down by the devil, and also so rent and torn by him that he lay and wallowed, foaming (Luke 9.42, Mark 9.20).

He wanted to come to Christ but the closer he came to Christ, he suddenly found something else working within him. That which I would, I do not, and that which I would not, *that* I do.

Further, in these days I should find my heart to shut itself up against the Lord, and against His holy Word. *I have found my unbelief to set, as it were, the shoulder to the door to keep Him out, and that too even then, when I have with many a bitter sigh cried, Good Lord, break it open;* Lord, break these gates of brass, and cut these bars of iron asunder (Ps. 107.16). [emphasis supplied]

While he is crying, "Lord, break the door open!" he is getting his shoulder and he is pushing that door shut. He doesn't want to do it, but he finds he can't help doing it.

Yet that word would sometimes create in my heart a peaceable pause, 'I girded thee, though thou hast not known me' (Isa. 45.5).

But while experiencing this concupiscence, this battle with the flesh in awakening and trying to put it down and trying to deal with it:

But all this while as to the act of sinning, I never was more tender than now; I durst not take a pin or a stick, though but so big as a straw, *for my conscience now was sore, and would smart at every touch;* I could not now tell how to speak my words, for fear I should misplace them. Oh, how gingerly did I then go in all I did or said! I found myself as on a miry bog that shook if I did but stir; and was there left both of God and Christ, and the Spirit, and all good things. [emphasis supplied]

O, wretched man that I am! Oh. He's like in the quicksand, the more he struggles, the more he sinks, the more he struggles, the more he sinks.

> But, I observe though I was such a great sinner before conversion, yet God never much charged the guilt of the sins of my ignorance upon me; only He showed me I was lost if I had not Christ, because I had been a sinner... But my original and inward pollution, that, that was my plague and my affliction; that, I say, at a dreadful rate, always putting forth itself within me; that I had the guilt of, to amazement; by reason of that, I was more loathsome in my own eyes than was a toad; and I thought I was so in God's eyes too; sin and corruption, I said, would as naturally bubble out of my heart, as water would bubble out of a fountain. I thought now that everyone had a better heart than I had; I could have changed heart with anybody; I thought none but the devil himself could equalize me for inward wickedness and pollution of mind. I fell, therefore, at the sight of my own vileness, deeply into despair; for I concluded that this condition that I was in could not stand with a state of grace. Sure, thought I, I am forsaken of God; sure I am given up to the devil, and to a reprobate mind;
>
> John Bunyan, *Grace Abounding to the Chief of Sinners*, par. 77-84.

This is the experience of one who meets the law as it really is. I hope you are able to connect these two together and have an appreciation of when the law comes, sin revives, and we die. "O wretched man that I am! who shall deliver me from the body of this death?" The terrible predicament that man finds himself in. Some might say, "I was better off without the law because then I didn't know what I was doing, I had no conviction of sin. But when the law came, sin revived and I died."

This is man's condition under the law and he comes to realise that he is there as Romans 3 describes it, that "there is none righteous, no not one." It says, "All are become unprofitable." And you know in Isaiah 52:3 it says, "Ye have sold yourselves for nought;" so man is *unprofitable*; he is actually not worth anything. You know Isaiah 64:6:

> But we are all as an unclean thing, and all our righteousnesses are as filthy rags; and we all do fade as a leaf; and our iniquities, like the wind, have taken us away.

The prevailing sin takes us away. Filthy rags – everything that we do is like a filthy rag. All our righteousnesses are as a filthy rag. All our right-doings are as a filthy rag because righteousness is to do right, it is right-doing. So the problem that man finds himself in when the law comes – no matter how much he consents unto that law that that law is good – he finds that he cannot keep the law. He *can't*. He tries, but he can't keep it.

He can come to the law and he can say, "But I've done that right, and I've done that right," and the law will look at him very strangely and say, "Well, what are you talking about? It's not good enough!" To do a bit right here and a bit right there is not good enough and to do everything right from today henceforth is not good enough; because the law demands *perfection*, perfect righteousness. That's from the alpha right the way through to the omega of your life. Anything short of that and the law is not satisfied. Do you have that in your life? "Oh but, I've done my best." Again the law says, "What are you talking about? I don't want your best. That's not good enough either!" The law of God does not compromise. The law says, "This is my standard, if you do not meet that standard you're out." It's that simple. As we come to a realisation of that law, I'm out. I'm out! I just can't do it. I just can't do it.

Christ's Object Lessons, p.315 speaks of the law and what the law really is and what the law really wants:

> His law is a transcript of His own character, and it is the standard of all character. This infinite standard is presented to all that there may be no mistake in regard to the kind of people whom God will have to compose His kingdom. [1]

The law is the standard that all must attain to if they are going to enter the heavenly Canaan. But what is the standard? It is the "transcript of His own character." He is the standard. His holiness, His righteousness, is the standard.

So if you did everything right in your whole entire life, will the law be satisfied? It can't be satisfied because your right-doing is not what the law wants. What the law wants is *God's* right-doing, *God's* perfect life and we, in ourselves, do we have it to offer? We don't. Is there any room for you in this picture? Can you satisfy the law? Can you? Have you in your life attained unto the very perfection of God? To do that you would have to be God yourself. Are you God? You're not God!

So man finds himself to be grossly sick. It's like he's got a cancer from the sole of the foot right unto the top of the head eating him out. Are you dead yet? We're going through this very simply. Have you come to a realisation that you're dead? that it doesn't matter how hard you try, you can't, you just can't? As it said, "Sin revived and I died." I discovered that all in me, all that dwelt within me, no matter how great a desire I have; all that dwelt in me was filthy rags, unrighteousness. Nothing of me could attain unto perfect salvation, nothing.

Let us, just by example now, put the nail in the coffin using an illustration from the Scriptures.

Without holiness "no man shall see the Lord" (Hebrews 12:14). No man. If they do not attain unto that standard, then they will not be the kind of people whom God will have compose His kingdom.

The reality that we are to wake up to is that there is nothing that we can do to save ourselves. We often think we can. I've got to do this, I've got to do that. We cannot. There is *nothing* we can do to save ourselves. Is that clear in our minds? Because if there's something you think you can do, then you don't need Jesus or grace; you can do it yourself.

Let us look at the example of Abraham just in closing and here we will seal our appreciation for this evening. Genesis 12:1-3:

> Now the Lord had said unto Abram, Get thee out of thy country, and from thy kindred, and from thy father's house, unto a land that I will show thee: And I will make of thee a great nation, and I will bless thee, and make thy name great; and thou shalt be a blessing: And I will bless them that bless thee, and curse him that curseth thee: and in thee shall all families of the earth be blessed.

In him would all families of the earth be blessed. What does this mean? Ever since the fall of man, they had been awaiting that seed of the woman that would crush the serpent's head. This promise here came to Abraham and God said to him that through your seed will come the promised Deliverer; through your lineage will be Him who will redeem the world from sin. Through Him would come salvation. But if we come to Genesis 15:1-5, Abraham had a problem, or he *thought* he had a problem:

> After these things the word of the Lord came unto Abram in a vision, saying, Fear not, Abram: I am thy shield, and thy exceeding great reward. And Abram said, Lord God, what wilt thou give me, seeing I go childless, and the steward of my house is this Eliezer of Damascus?

His wife never had a child and she was extremely old and to him he thought, Well I can never have a child. I'll never have my own progeny, therefore what about the servant in my house? It is he that will be the heir and the seed will come from him.

> And Abram said, Behold, to me thou hast given no seed: and, lo, one born in my house is mine heir. And, behold, the word of the Lord [came] unto him, saying, This shall not be thine heir; but he that shall come forth out of thine own bowels shall be thine heir. And he brought him forth abroad, and said, Look now toward heaven, and tell the stars, if thou be able to number them: and he said unto him, So shall thy seed be.

He said, "No Abraham, the child will come out of *your own bowels*, he will come from your line." Come to Genesis 16:1-4:

> Now Sarai Abram's wife bare him no children: and she had an handmaid, an Egyptian, whose name was Hagar. And Sarai said unto Abram, Behold now, the Lord hath restrained me from bearing: I pray thee, go in unto my maid; it may be that I may obtain children by her. And Abram hearkened to the voice of Sarai. And Sarai Abram's wife took Hagar her maid the Egyptian, after Abram had dwelt ten years in the land of Canaan, and gave her to her husband Abram to be his wife. And he went in unto Hagar, and she conceived.

The promise to Abraham was, that the Redeemer will come through you. He will come from "thine own bowels". But in Abraham's mind, he thought, How's that possible? My wife is too old to have a child. So how can this Saviour ever be born? How? So he started to worry. He started to think, *Well, this child has to be born because if this Redeemer is not born, I can't be saved.* He felt he had to do something about it. So his wife came to him and said, "We're not going to be saved unless we have a child and I can't bear you a child so go in unto Hagar and let her have your child," and he went in unto Hagar and she had a child.

Abraham thought that he had to do something for his salvation. And we know what the consequences were. We know the situation that the world is in today because of Abraham thinking that he could effect his own salvation.

Can you look at your own life and how you've thought that you've had to do things to save yourself? Can you look at the mess that you've got yourself into trying to work things out yourself? The nail is in the coffin now.

WE CAN NOT. We can do *nothing* to effect our own salvation. And it's a frightful realisation when we meet the law as it really is. We are dead men walking. We can-not. We need to get it very clear in our minds. Because when we get that clear in our minds, when we learn from the experience of Abraham, Jacob and Moses who all tried to effect God's plan for them; when we learn from that, we will give up trying. We will, as the phrase goes, *let go* and we will *let God*. When we will really be honest with ourselves that *I can't do it*, then we will cry unto God. "Oh God, save me in spite of myself, my weak un-Christ like self!" Our prayer will be, " Lord, work in me to will and to do of your own good pleasure." That's why it is that Jesus says, "They that are whole have no need of a physician." If we don't recognize this, we don't need God. I'll save myself thank you. But they that are sick – sinners – He says, "Okay, now I can work with you to change your life to bring harmony out of disharmony."

Let's read *Steps to Christ*, p.31 in closing:

> If you see your sinfulness...

Run from God like Adam did. No?

> If you see your sinfulness, do not wait to make yourself better. How many there are who think they are not good enough to come to Christ.

The question is: are you *bad* enough to come to Christ, because if you don't think that you're too bad, you won't come to Christ.

> If you see your sinfulness, do not wait to make yourself better. How many there are who think they are not good enough to come to Christ. Do you expect to become better through your own efforts? "Can the Ethiopian change his skin, or the leopard his spots? then may ye also do good, that are accustomed to do evil." Jeremiah 13:23.

Romans 7 – Try it. You'll find you can't.

> There is help for us only in God. We must not wait for stronger persuasions, for better opportunities, or for holier tempers. We can do nothing of ourselves. *We must come to Christ just as we are.* [emphasis supplied] [2]

How is that? Sick, wretched, miserable, poor, blind and naked. And that, friends, are the people that God can work with. Do you want God to be able to work with you? Then when He shows you these things, praise the Lord, rejoice in His holiness because He loves you.

I pray that we have gained something from this today and as the pursuance of this subject continues the Lord will increase our understanding of these things in its simplicity that He can work quickly with us, as it says, so He can cut short His work in righteousness (Romans 9:28). May God help us to this end. AMEN.

God's Abounding Grace

Part 2

THE GIFT OF JESUS CHRIST

June 26, 2010

There is therefore now no condemnation to them which are in Christ Jesus, who walk not after the flesh, but after the Spirit. Romans 8:1

"*C*HIEF *of sinners though I be Christ is all in all to me.*" Is Christ all in all to you? "*All my wants to Him are known.*" Are all your wants to Him known? And are all your sorrows His own? Sadness for being persecuted for righteousness sake? Sorrow, crying and sighing for the abominations that are done in the land? Are these your sorrows? Are they His? Sorrow for your sins – are they His sorrows?

We are continuing this morning in the study of God's Abounding Grace and we have found that where sin abounded, grace does much more abound. And that word "abound" means: in a *large quantity* or in a *copious amount* and it is *prevalent*; which describes very well our sinfulness. But also is God's grace. God's grace is to be in a far greater quantity and if the sin abounding was prevalent, then God's grace will be prevalent. Through this series we want to see how God's grace is prevailing; how it can be and will be prevalent in our lives.

Our last study was on 'Waking up to the Reality', and there we went through Romans 7. Slain by the law. Christ came and He said "I call sinners to repentance. He that is sick needs a physician but he that is whole needs no physician." So the law entered to bring to our realisation a recognition of our condition, to help us realise that I am sick; I need a physician; I need repentance! I need a change of mind, a change of heart, a change of life! And as we went through Romans 7 we connected it with the experience of John Bunyan. And I again want to read the description there from *Grace Abounding to the Chief of Sinners*. And there as the law entered into his experience, we remember the Apostle Paul said "it wrought within me all manner of concupiscence." There awoke within him desires and corruptions that he didn't know were there. So John Bunyan writes:

Now I evidently found that lusts and corruptions would strongly put forth themselves within me, in wicked thoughts and desires, which I did not regard before; my desires for heaven and life began to fail. I found also, that whereas my soul was full of longing after God, now my heart began to hanker after every foolish vanity; yea, my heart would not be moved to mind that that was good; it began to be careless, both of my soul and heaven; it would now continually hang back, both to, and in every duty; and was as a clog on the leg of a bird to hinder her from flying.

Nay, thought I, now I grow worse and worse; now am I farther from conversion than ever I was before. Wherefore I began to sink greatly in my soul, and began to entertain such discouragement in my heart as laid me low as hell.

Sometimes I would tell my condition to the people of God, which, when they heard, they would pity me, and would tell me of the promises; but they had as good have told me that I must reach the sun with my finger as have bidden me receive or rely upon the promise; and as soon as I should have done it, all my sense and feeling was against me; and I saw I had a heart that would sin, and that lay under a law that would condemn.

These things have often made me think of that child which the father brought to Christ, who, while he was yet a-coming to him, was thrown down by the devil, and also so rent and torn by him that he lay and wallowed, foaming (Luke 9.42, Mark 9.20).

As he sought to come unto Christ, there came to him a revelation of his inward corruptions. Apostle Paul writes there in Romans 7, "I consent unto the law that it is good." So much so that he desired so much to keep that law. But every attempt that he made to do it, he failed. And there working contrary to that was a working and a doing of the very things he did not want to do. John Bunyan is echoing this experience:

Further, in these days I should find my heart to shut itself up against the Lord, and against His holy Word. I have found my unbelief to set, as it were, the shoulder to the door to keep Him out, and that too even then, when I have with many a bitter sigh cried, Good Lord, break it open; Lord, break these gates of brass, and cut these bars of iron asunder (Ps. 107.16). Yet that word would sometimes create in my heart a peaceable pause, 'I girded thee, though thou hast not known me' (Isa. 45.5).

There is Christ knocking on the heart and Bunyan says, "I want to let him in. I want you to come in Jesus! I want you to help me!" Yet at the same time his shoulder is hard against the door and he's crying: "Come in Jesus, come in! Please come and help me!" But at the same time he's pushing hard against the door not to let Christ come in.

This is the experience of the one who finds the law. They consent that it is good. They want that pure and holy life which brings to them the companionship of that God who is as a consuming fire, but working contrary to that desire is something which always gets in the way and he screams, *Oh wretched man that I am, who shall deliver me from the body of this death?!"*

But my original and inward pollution, that, that was my plague and my affliction; that, I say, at a dreadful rate, always putting forth itself within me; that I had the guilt of, to amazement; by reason of that, I was more loathsome in my own eyes than was a toad; and I thought I was so in God's eyes too; sin and corruption, I said, would as naturally bubble out of my heart, as water would bubble out of a fountain. I *thought* now that everyone had a better heart than I had; I could have changed heart with anybody; I thought none but the devil himself could equalize me for inward wickedness and pollution of mind. I fell, therefore, at the sight of my own vileness, deeply into despair; for I concluded that this condition that I was in could not stand with a state of grace. Sure, thought I, I am forsaken of God; sure I am given up to the devil, and to a reprobate mind.

John Bunyan, *Grace Abounding to the Chief of Sinners*, par. 77-84.

Has this been your experience? Are you able to relate with the testimony of Apostle Paul and John Bunyan? Have you come to a realisation that the very things you want to do, you cannot do? Every time you try to do it, before you even know it, you've done the wrong thing? I have a saying, "Give me a shovel and I will dig a hole." I may not want to dig a hole, but I'll dig a hole anyhow. Sure I could try to just hold it in my hand and not use it, but give it to me and I'll dig myself a hole. This is the human nature that the school master educates us about. And we are left with nothing but the cry: "Oh wretched man that I am, who shall deliver me from the body of this death?!"

Isaiah 57:20 is another way in which we could express it:

But the wicked are like the troubled sea, when it cannot rest, whose waters cast up mire and dirt.

And here in Psalms 55:6 is this plaintive cry:

And I said, Oh that I had wings like a dove! for then would I fly away, and be at rest.

Is that not the longing of your heart? Do you not wish you could just get away from it all? There is this law of sin which is in your members which is constantly working contrary to the law in your mind, and you find yourself constantly tripping over it and giving in to it. Are you not sick of it? Don't you just wish you could fly away and be at rest? Well, God doesn't do things in half measures. He gives us the desire of our hearts but He does not give us the wings of a mournful dove. Isaiah 40:31 is His promise and this morning we want to find how to gain the fulfilment of this promise:

But they that wait upon the Lord shall renew their strength; they shall mount up with wings as eagles; they shall run, and not be weary; and they shall walk, and not faint.

This, friends, needs to be our experience! For many years now, some of us have walked our Christian walk. And we have walked it and walked it, but for many it feels like we've just gone around in circles chasing our tail. *We have not yet broken out from under the law.* We seem to come out from it for a little while and we go well, and then, we fall back under it again. Then out we come, then we fall back under it again. Friends, these experiences are as the clog on the leg of a bird so that it cannot fly.

We need to grow wings like an eagle. This earth is about to be destroyed and if we have not the ability to mount up above it all, above all the condemnation, above all the frustration, and the depression that Satan casts upon us, we will not survive in that day. In our spiritual walk we are reaching experiences where now, we have to run.

We read Romans 8:1 this morning to gain a new appreciation of this promise. In chapter 7 we have had the experience of one who is under the law. And those who are under the law are under condemnation. But here in Romans 8:1:

> There is therefore now no condemnation to them which are in Christ Jesus, who walk not after the flesh, but after the Spirit.

We need to discover the absolute fulfilment of this promise. "There is now therefore no condemnation to them who are in-Christ-Jesus." No con-dem-na-tion. Where? In Christ Jesus.

Do you know what it means to be in-Christ-Jesus? Do you actually *know* what it means? Faith is a hand but that hand doesn't just clasp the air. It lays hold of something that is tangible. To be in-Jesus-Christ, what does it mean? What is the *tangibility* of being in-Jesus-Christ? How do I be in-Jesus-Christ? He says that except we abide in Him we can do nothing. Except we abide in Him, all our right-doings will be as filthy rags.

"In-Christ-Jesus." We are very familiar with the phrase. And in Christ Jesus there is much to be gained. The promises of God are in Christ Jesus. How do we receive the word – "IN"? Does the phrase refer in a sense to Christ being as a container or as a receptacle? And we are to go to that container or receptacle and I am to reach my hand in and take out *from* Christ and then I have that which was *in* Christ. Is that what it means to be "in-Christ"? Am I to take it out of Jesus and say, "Now I have it?" Like I would go to a box and reach my hand in and take something out and say, "I have it?" Is that what it means to have something in – to be *in*-Christ-Jesus? No.

Whatever it is, it is only to be gained *in* Christ Jesus. He is not a receptacle where we can go in and take it out of Him. Only as we are in-Christ-Jesus can we have that which is in Christ Jesus. Do you want what is in Christ Jesus? Then what does it mean to be *in*-Christ-Jesus? I want it, but how do I have it?

I find that there are very few who really know today what it means to be in-Christ-Jesus. Not just in an airy fairy imaginative sense, but in a tangible, practical reality. And this hour, this is what we want to look at. There is the promise: "There is now no more condemnation." And that is the place where we need to stand – where we are no longer under condemnation. We have read that promise so many times, yet we seem to be missing out on it. We know it when we can repeat it over and over again in our heads until we are brainwashed – "There is no condemnation, there is no condemnation."

But if we do that it will only lead us to one place and that is – *presumption*. We will end up in a place where we will think that we are not condemned when the reality is, we are! We say, "Yes, I believe the promise. I know that it is written and I believe it." Then we get upset and annoyed when we make a mistake. It is good to sorrow for our sins – Yes. We are to be disappointed when we fail; and we are to weep bitterly over our failures. But do we get *depressed* when we fail? Do we fall under a sense of not being able to come before God; like Adam and Eve there in the Garden of Eden we want to run and hide ourselves? We don't go to Him in prayer because – I've done it; I've mucked things up and He's not going to have me. And so we get depressed. If this is our experience you may be assured that you are *still under the law*.

We need to get out from under it! There is no condemnation! If we are still being knocked down in our Christian walk by the sense of condemnation, I am not in-Jesus-Christ. Would that be simple Bible reading? That there is "no condemnation," we will deal with in another study. But unless we can understand where the "no condemnation" *is*, then that study will be like all of the other studies we have had on "no condemnation" and we will not gain from it all of the blessing that God has in it for us. So we need to understand what it means to be in-Jesus-Christ. Because only in Jesus Christ is there no condemnation.

I was thinking as I was preparing the study, I was thinking I wonder how long it will take for us to go through this study, to understand it. For there is no use for us to go any further in our studies unless we can understand what it means to be *in*-Christ. And I was thinking how it's sometimes brought to our mind's eye about how people go to the movies and sit there for two and half hours and yet they whinge when you've got to sit in the church pew for an hour or so. It occurred to me that there are those who sit all day long, watching men in white clothes, standing in the middle of a field, waiting for a little ball to come their way. They spend all day just sitting there, waiting for something that might happen! Shame on us if we yawn, if we get tired while the Lord is trying to teach us His salvation. So I'm going to take as long as we need today to find what it means be *in*-Christ-Jesus. Because only then, in-Christ-Jesus, can I have what He offers; only then can I have those wings that will advance me in my Christian walk. So we shall commence where He commenced with us. The law entered. Come to Hosea 6:1-3:

> Come, and let us return unto the Lord: for he hath torn, and he will heal us; he hath smitten, and he will bind us up. After two days will he revive us: in the third day he will raise us up, and we shall live in his sight. Then shall we know, if we follow on to know the Lord: his going forth is prepared as the morning; and he shall come unto us as the rain, as the latter and former rain unto the earth.

This is a precious promise. As we understand this Scripture, the smiting and the healing and the raising up, that appreciation is tied in with the outpouring of the latter rain. This is what we want to study this morning. So listen carefully!

The schoolmaster has flogged us. It is teaching us of our *need* of Christ. It has smitten and bruised and torn. The mighty cleaver of truth has come and chopped its way into our lives. Those who thought they were rich and increased with goods needing nothing – suddenly comes along that two-edged sword which divides asunder and reveals the intents of the heart. And that came with a revelation of their true condition. That they were wretched, miserable, poor, blind and naked but we don't even know it! We are left there like the beaten man in the story of the Good Samaritan, on the side of the road, stripped of our clothing, stripped of anything. "O wretched man that I am. I just have a body of this death!" But the promise is that they shall mount up like an eagle. He will heal us. He will bind us up and on the third day we shall be raised and shall live in His sight.

To live in His sight! To live in the sight of God who is a consuming fire! We who are sinners – wretched, miserable, poor, blind and naked, whose righteousnesses are as filthy rags. And they're filthy because from the sole of the foot to the head, are wounds and putrefying sores. It says, "*We* shall live in His sight." To stand before the sin-consuming God, to live in the sight of those fiery eyes that search the heart through and through, can only be when there is *no condemnation*. But that is not speaking of an experience in the future. It says here: "He will raise us up." Come to Ephesians 2:4. Here it says – He *has*, He *already has*. So this raising up is not in the future. Not in the future of the immortal inheritance, but it is today, it is *now*! Ephesians 2:4-6:

> But God, who is rich in mercy, for his great love wherewith he loved us, Even when we were dead in sins, hath quickened us together with Christ, (by grace ye are saved;) And hath raised us up together, and made us sit together in heavenly places in Christ Jesus.

Have you ever thought, I'm just going through something at the moment, and I know that the Lord, on the third day, will raise me up. And I know it's the third day and sometimes I realise that the third day is figurative and He will raise me up when the time is right. We are reading here that He *has* raised us up! He *has* raised us up together *with Christ*! And when was Christ raised? *On the third day!* We are raised when Christ was raised! So when we feel down and out, and thinking that we have to wait for God to raise me up, friends, let your faith pierce the cloud. *He has raised us up.* He has already lifted you up! So don't go mourning all the day long. He's already done it! Just believe it! But there is that word again, *in*-Christ-Jesus. We have there a clue to understanding its meaning. When Jesus was raised up, *we* were raised up! But why did Jesus need to be raised up? Why did you? Romans 7:24. Why did you have to die?

> O wretched man that I am! Who shall deliver me from the body of this death?

Isn't that why you've died? That is why we have died. And why we need to be raised! Jesus Himself died because of "the body of this death." Now come to Philippians 2:6-8, and here we are going to be picking out Scriptures that we are very familiar with. But we can always become more familiar with God's word. Speaking of Christ:

> Who, being in the form of God, thought it not robbery to be equal with God: But made himself of no reputation, and took upon him the form of a servant, and was made in the likeness of men: And being found in fashion as a man, he humbled himself, and became obedient unto death, even the death of the cross.

Christ died because He became a partaker of the body of this death. It's interesting to note there where He says, "He made himself of no reputation." In the Revised Version it says: "He emptied Himself and was made as a man." And in the French version it actually says that "He *annihilated* Himself and was made as a man."

Now, "He was made in the likeness of men" – what does that word *made,* mean? What word does it come from? It comes from the word *make*. And that word *make* means to what? To *create*. Christ annihilated Himself and He was what? He was *created* in the likeness of men; in the likeness of men who die because of sin. Come over to Hebrew verses 2:9-17 and following this through very carefully. We are looking at God's abounding grace.

> But we see Jesus, who was made a little lower than the angels for the suffering of death, crowned with glory and honour; that he by the grace of God should taste death for every man. For it became him, for whom are all things, and by whom are all things, in bringing many sons unto glory, to make the captain of their salvation perfect through sufferings. For both he that sanctifieth and they who are sanctified are all of one.

Friends, are you created? Have you been made? In fact, where was the first use of the word "make" in the Bible? "Let us make man in our image." He was made as you and I are made. Reading on:

> For which cause he is not ashamed to call them brethren, Saying, I will declare thy name unto my brethren, in the midst of the church will I sing praise unto thee. And again, I will put my trust in him. And again, Behold I and the children which God hath given me. Forasmuch then as the children are partakers of flesh and blood, he also himself likewise took part of the same; that through death he might destroy him that had the power of death, that is, the devil; And deliver them who through fear of death were all their lifetime subject to bondage. For verily he took not on him the nature of angels; but he took on him the seed of Abraham. Wherefore in all things it behoved him to be made like unto his brethren, that he might be a merciful and faithful high priest in things pertaining to God, to make reconciliation for the sins of the people.

Jesus Christ was in all things made like unto you and me. In how many things? In *all* things! He was a partaker of flesh and blood, even as you and I are partakers of flesh and blood. But what kind of flesh do we partake of? Romans 8:3:

> For what the law could not do, in that it was weak through the flesh, God sending his own Son in the likeness of sinful flesh, and for sin, condemned sin in the flesh.

So He was sent in the likeness of sinful flesh. And in Galatians 4:4 it says:

> But when the fulness of the time was come, God sent forth his Son, made of a woman, made under the law.

He was a partaker of the body of this death. He was created. You know the Scripture: "a body hast thou prepared me" (Hebrews 10:5). A body was created for Him – a body of death. He was the *proprietor* of a body of death. Right where you stand, right where I stand, in my flesh, He stood likewise. There was no distinction in the body in which He lived and ours. Now in that body, what *was* your experience? What *is* your experience? Come back to Romans 7:21-24:

> I find then a law, that, when I would do good, evil is present with me. For I delight in the law of God after the inward man: But I see another law in my members, warring against the law of my mind, and bringing me into captivity to the law of sin which is in my members. O wretched man that I am!

Christ dealt with the same present evil that we deal with. Now our issue is that it brings us into captivity. Romans 7:5:

> For when we were in the flesh, the motions of sins, which were by the law, did work in our members to bring forth fruit unto death.

In our experience the sin in the flesh makes a motion; it makes a *proposal* to our mind. Then it works to bring forth fruit unto death. Now this is described in another way in James 1:14-15. What is temptation? Here it says a man is tempted when he is drawn away of his own lust:

> But every man is tempted, when he is drawn away of his own lust, and enticed. Then when lust hath conceived, it bringeth forth sin: and sin, when it is finished, bringeth forth death.

So there the motions of sin work and those lusts within the flesh entice, and when that is cherished, it has conceived and brings forth sin, and then death. But there in verse 13 we read:

> Let no man say when he is tempted, I am tempted of God: for God cannot be tempted with evil, neither tempteth he any man.

And there are those who will take these Scriptures and will combine it as we have seen it. And they will say Christ wasn't tempted. But come back to Hebrews 4:15 again:

> For we have not an high priest which cannot be touched with the feeling of our infirmities; but was in all points tempted like as we are, yet without sin.

Now here is the differentiation. There is a distinction between the flesh and the mind. Ellen White makes it clear that we are not to bring His mind into the corrupted, sinful nature of man. But Christ dwelt in a "*body* of this death" and that is why He died. He was tempted as you and I are tempted. But the *thought* was never cherished, therefore it never became *actual transgression*. Tempted in all points like as we are, yet without sin. If He did, He could not have been a propitiation. But here we "have an high priest which cannot be touched with the feelings of our infirmities." This is a double negative. "We have a high priest which *can* be touched with the feelings of our infirmities." An infirmity is a weakness, a sickness, a frailty. Do you have weaknesses? Jesus feels your weakness. But not only does He feel your weakness but He is touched by your weakness. He is tenderly affected – as He feels what you are feeling in *empathy*, His heart goes out in sympathy and He wants to help us; He is drawn out in tenderness and sympathy. So Christ was made in all points like as we are. And He was tempted in all points like as we, made in all things like unto us. He took part of the same so He could be tempted in all points like as we are.

But have you made a connection between all these verses? In Hebrews 2:11 it said:

> For both he that sanctifieth and they who are sanctified are all of one: for which cause he is not ashamed to call them brethren.

Now connect that with what Jesus said in Matthew 25:40:

> Verily I say unto you, Inasmuch as ye have done it unto one of the least of these my brethren, ye have done it unto me.

Now, the question comes: *If I do it unto them how can I do it unto Him?* How is it that Jesus can be tempted in all points like I am tempted? How? And now here we are coming to an appreciation of what it means to be *in*-Jesus-Christ. He was created in all things like as we are, as you are, as I am. And He feels as I feel. How? How can Jesus be tempted in all points like I am unless He is in *all points* like as I am? For Him to be tempted like I am, He would have to be *like I am*. And how can He feel as I feel unless He is *where I am*, and *as I am*? Only by Him being *my own self all over again* can He be tempted as I am tempted and feel as I feel.

Jesus feels my infirmities. But they were *my* infirmities – they were *His as well*. My feelings – they're His too. Jesus was *made to be me*! If He was not made to be me, He could not feel what I feel or be tempted as I am tempted. He became *you*, He became *me*! And here in Hebrews 7:26 it speaks of that High Priest who was touched with the feelings of our infirmities and was tempted in all points like as we are yet without sin:

> Such an high priest became us, who is holy, harmless, undefiled, separate from sinners, and made higher than the heavens.

Jesus Christ became YOU! Do you believe it? You were where? *In-Christ-Jesus*. Your sinful flesh was His sinful flesh. Your body of death was His body of this death. The life that you live, was *His* life!

As you experience your temptations, He is tempted; as you are afraid, or as you are doubting, or as you are happy, as you are sorrowful, He is feeling afraid, He's feeling doubtful and He's sorrowful. Not a single particle of your experience is not His own experience because He became "*ME*"!* And He was *you* right the way down to the bottom of that pit. That miserable life that you had created for yourself, He was there with you in it. Yes, He did no sin. No guile was found in His mouth, but, you did, you sinned! Guile was found in your mouth! And that is why He says, "My heart faileth me." Psalms 40:12. Not because of what He did, but because of what you've done. And because He has become you, He suffers what you suffer. Your wretchedness – that's His wretchedness. Your misery – He has made to be His own misery. Your poverty – His poverty. Your blindness – His blindness. And your nakedness was His nakedness. As it is written, "They parted His garments" as He hung upon the cross (Matthew 27:35).

Jesus Christ became you! To be *in*-Jesus-Christ is to believe this! Because then as I believe this – as *me*, He lived a perfect life. And in Him I live a perfect life, because He was me. As you can do nothing of your own self, there was nothing that He could do of His own self either. Compassed with infirmities, a partaker of the body of this death; and as you are unable to do the things you want to do, likewise *He. He depended upon God to work in Him to will and to do of His good pleasure.* So as you are tempted, He was tempted. But God *in-Him* overcame the temptation. And this we will enlarge as we continue in our studies. But I'm hoping that we are coming to understand how it is that Christ is my wisdom. "He is made unto us wisdom, righteousness, sanctification and redemption" (1 Corinthians 1:30).

Because He was *given*, He was filled with the fulness of God. And that which was given to Him was given to Him as "WE"! I pray that you are able to understand what it is that we are meditating here. Christ's righteousness is my righteousness because He came as *me*, and as *me* depending upon the Father, He lived a perfect life. He lived a righteous life. But that life that He lived was *my life*! And here is where it is that His righteousness, the righteousness of Christ, is MY righteousness. But it's not mine because He wrought it out. God gave it to Him!

With us, He lives out our miserable life. And friends, there was not a single person in this whole entire world that was not in Christ Jesus. Most won't believe it and most

* *The author is not here saying that we become Christ, neither that Christ loses His personal identity in us. It is a mystery as to how two individuals can inhabit the same life so perfectly that the law may look at one person and see the other, and how they can also share in each other's life experiences; yet this truth is central to the Gospel. This is further clarified by continual reading, also on pages 50, 129, 130, etc. "The unity that exists between Christ and His disciples does not destroy the personality of either. They are one in purpose, in mind, in character, but not in person" (Ministry of Healing p. 483). See also the note on page 258.*

will never avail themselves of it. He was made in "all things like unto His brethren." That is every single soul that has ever been born in this world. He was tempted in all points like they were. He lived the life of every single man upon this world. *But in living their life, He did things right.* So if they will, they can have that life! So with me He lives out my miserable life, right to the point where – "Oh wretched man that I am who shall deliver me from the body of this flesh?" And is that not the same as the anguished cry – "My God, my God why hast Thou forsaken Me?" It's the same cry!

That law kills me! It buries us! It kills us! And there we see Jesus. He's made a little lower than the angels; made to be bone of your bone and flesh of your flesh; made to be in all points like unto you; made of a woman, made under the law. And there because He has become you, He makes *your sins to be His own.* And there, gently pushes us behind His back and He bares His breast to the wrath of God – *as me*! Because the wages of sin is death, friends. And as me, and as He died as me, then so I must also die. You are to die! We are to be planted in the "likeness of His death" (Romans 6:5). And that's only natural, because if He is me and He has been planted, then I am to be planted as well. He is one with me! So then as God raised Him on the third day, so God *raised us up together* and made us sit together in those heavenly places in-Jesus-Christ.

We often have a picture in our mind of Christ standing before the Father as our high priest and advocate. And then there's me standing next to Him and He's there supplicating on my behalf. Friends, there's only one man standing before God! Jesus Christ and we are IN Him! We are *hiding in-Christ*. And there as Jesus lived, now we will live as He lived. We have lived our life as *us*, and He was with us in that life, but now at the bottom of our pit, at the end of the road when there's no way out, when all we see is just a mess of a life, that we have nothing to meet the claims of the law, He comes to us and says, "Here, have a new life." And this new life is whose life? It is *your* life! Because He was you and He lived a perfect life *as you*. He did no sin, neither was guile found in His mouth. It was a life that pleased God. It was that life that satisfied the claims of the law. *But it was your life!* He lived it as you! He was tempted in all points like as you are, yet was without sin. That life of perfect righteousness now is your life! IF, you will believe that you are in-Jesus-Christ. And that perfect life which He has lived as you, will stand for you in the judgment. And that life is the life that the Father sees as Jesus stands before Him! Here it is that we live in His sight because Jesus is "me", and He stands before the Father and as "me" He lived a perfect life! Are you understanding what we are studying here? Can you see how it is that everything else starts to make sense? How it is that *in* Christ there is no condemnation? How it is that *in* Christ is my righteousness! In Christ is my sanctification! In Christ is my redemption! Whatever it is that God has given to us, it is *in* Christ Jesus. Because there, as me, He gave it to His Son and thus He gave it to me. And as I abide in Him, it's mine! It's mine!

2 Corinthians 3:18:

> But we all, with open face beholding as in a glass the glory of the Lord, are changed
> into the same image from glory to glory, even as by the Spirit of the Lord.

Can you now understand why it says "beholding as in a glass"? Beholding as in a *mirror*! Have you ever wondered *why* it said beholding as in a glass? As in a mirror? But don't you look in a mirror and you see you? Friends, when the veil of unbelief is removed from our faces, we see Jesus, we see such an high priest who became *me*. And there looking into the mirror I see not the reflection of myself, but the reflection of the life that Jesus lived as me on my behalf. A pure, holy and righteous life; and as I behold it, and I see Him meeting my temptations, feeling my infirmities – unconsciously – I will be changed from glory to glory so that that same perfect life which He lived in me, as me, will be manifest to the world!

You can only have it as it is *in* Jesus Christ. Those that are of the final remnant are those who keep the commandments of God and what else? "The *faith of Jesus*." How can you be a possessor of something that's not yours unless Jesus became you, and there as you, He exercises His faith and you partake of that? The faith belongs to Jesus and you can only possess it if you are a partaker of Himself. Only if you and Him are one.

Are you grasping what we have studied this hour? I really pray that we are. Because if our faith will lay hold of this, we will mount up like an eagle. There ceases to be any misunderstanding of God's word. Because then we understand how it is that it is in Jesus Christ. Are you *in*-Jesus-Christ? If you are, then there is no condemnation – if you will believe that Jesus lived your life perfectly.

Just one final appreciation here from Matthew 1:23:

> Behold, a virgin shall be with child, and shall bring forth a son, and they shall call
> his name Emmanuel, which being interpreted is, God with us.

Now reading here from *1895 General Conference Bulletins* by Alonzo T. Jones:

> Read two texts: He says of us, "Without me ye can do nothing." Of Himself He says:
> "Of mine own self I can do nothing."

> "These two texts are all we want now. They tell the whole story. To be without
> Christ is to be without God, and there the man can do nothing. He is utterly helpless
> of himself and in himself. That is where the man is who is without God. Jesus Christ
> says: "Of mine own self I can do nothing." Then that shows that the Lord Jesus put
> Himself in this world, in the flesh, in His human nature, precisely where the man is
> in this world who is without God. He put Himself precisely where lost man is. He
> left out His divine self and became we. And there, helpless as we are without God,
> He ran the risk of getting back to where God is and bringing us with him. It was a
> fearful risk, but, glory to God, He won. The thing was accomplished, and in Him
> we are saved.

When He stood where we are, He said, "I will put my trust in Him" and that trust was never disappointed. In response to that trust the Father dwelt in Him and with Him and kept Him from sinning. Who was He? We. And thus the Lord Jesus has brought to every man in this world divine faith. That is the faith of the Lord Jesus. That is saving faith. Faith is not something that comes from ourselves with which we believe upon Him, but it is that something with which He believed–the faith which He exercised, which He brings to us, and which becomes ours and works in us–the gift of God. That is what the word means, "Here are they that keep the commandments of God and the faith of Jesus." They keep the faith of Jesus because it is that divine faith which Jesus exercised Himself.

He being we brought to us that divine faith which saves the soul–that divine faith by which we can say with Him, "I will put my trust in Him." And in so putting our trust in Him, that trust today will never be disappointed anymore than it was then. God responded then to the trust and dwelt with Him. God will respond today to that trust in us and will dwell with us.

God dwelt with Him, and He was ourselves. Therefore His name is Emmanuel, God with us. Not God with Him. God was with Him before the world was; He could have remained there and not come here at all and still God could have remained with Him and His name could have been God with Him. He could have come into this world as He was in heaven and His name could still have been God with Him. But that never could have been God with us. But what we needed was God with us. God with Him does not help us, unless He is we. But that is the blessedness of it. He who was one of God became one of us; He who was God became we, in order that God with Him should be God with us. O, that is His name! That is His name! Rejoice in that name forevermore–God with us! [1]

Friends, I hope we can understand now what it means to be in-Jesus-Christ. And as we gain and cherish that appreciation, when the word of God tells us, this is in Him, that is in Him, friends, *it's ours*! Let's lay hold of it! And only thus can we be like that Son of man, like Jesus. And remember it's written that He sailed like the sun above it all. Do you want to mount up like an eagle? *We have – in Him!* May God help us to believe is my prayer. AMEN.

God's Abounding Grace

Part 3

OUT OF MYSELF AND INTO CHRIST

June 29, 2010

Our study tonight is entitled *Out of Myself and Into Christ*. I pray we all remember what we studied there on the Sabbath day, where we examined into what it means to be "in-Christ". As we have been going through our series and been looking at the abundance of sin, we have found that where that sin abounds, grace is much more abounding.

And we are coming to a realisation that grace abounds even where there is sin, and though we have committed sin, yet there can be no condemnation. But before we continued into studying how it is that there can be no condemnation, we saw fit to study first what it means to be in Christ. So on the Sabbath day we studied into that. And here in *Bible Commentary*, Vol.7, p.926 Ellen White writes:

> If in connection with God the work is carried forward, the human agent, through Christ, will day by day gain victory and honor in the battle. Through the grace given he will overcome, and will be placed on vantage ground.

Now listen to this:

> In his relation to Christ he will be bone of His bone, flesh of His flesh, one with Christ in a peculiar relationship, because Christ took the humanity of man. [1]

"One with Christ in a peculiar relationship." As we studied it there on Sabbath was it not a peculiar relationship – how Christ can be Christ and yet at the same time He can become "me"? And as He is "me", He can still react differently as to how I would react and do things right on my behalf. And this is a peculiar relationship where there is a blending of Christ with me and yet still a distinction of the individual personalities.

"Where sin abounded, grace did much more abound." Romans 5:20. Where I was in my sinfulness, Christ came and dwelt in His righteousness. And here is an interesting revelation of God's abounding grace – it comes from *God's Amazing Grace*, p.10:

> By disobeying the commands of God, man fell under the condemnation of His law.

This fall called for the grace of God to appear in behalf of sinners.

Because man fell, grace had to appear. And it's interesting: where sin abounded, grace did much more abound. The law had to enter to make *what* abound? *Grace* abound. We often read that the law had to enter to make sin abound. But no, the purpose of it was to bring in an abundance of grace.

> We should never have learned the meaning of this word "grace" had we not fallen. God loves the sinless angels, who do His service, and are obedient to all His commands; but He does not give them grace. These heavenly beings know naught of grace; they have never needed it; for they have never sinned. Grace is an attribute of God shown to undeserving human beings. We did not seek after it, but it was sent in search of us. God rejoices to bestow this grace upon every one who hungers for it. To every one He presents terms of mercy, not because we are worthy, but because we are so utterly unworthy. Our need is the qualification which gives us the assurance that we shall receive this gift. [2]

Because we have sinned we now have this precious gift of grace. But shall we sin that grace may abound? God forbid. It would have been better if we had never fallen. But because we have fallen and Christ has taken us right into His divine-ship, then man is exalted even way above the angels; whereas beforehand he was a little bit lower than the angels. But, as we studied on Sabbath, now He has made us sit together in heavenly places in Christ Jesus.

We have been studying how the law brings about an abundance of grace. This abounding grace is described here in Hebrews chapter 2:17-18 as we studied it there on the Sabbath day. We have a comfort as we discover our wretched condition; as we discover our weakness in regard to the promptings of sin and the subsequent consequences. Hebrews 2:17-18 is this abounding grace:

> Wherefore in all things it behoved him to be made like unto his brethren, that he might be a merciful and faithful high priest in things pertaining to God, to make reconciliation for the sins of the people. For in that he himself hath suffered being tempted, he is able to succour them that are tempted.

Because Jesus was made to be me. Because He was made to be me in all things, He therefore was able to be tempted in all things like as I am tempted. And as He goes through that temptation, I am able to have a succour in it, because I have a companion. And as we saw on the Sabbath day, we wake to this reality that I've dug myself this hole, but there, in that hole with me, is Jesus, suffering exactly the same that I am suffering. And we can be comforted because we're not alone in our suffering. And then, as we know, He didn't sin so that victory can become mine.

But focusing on Christ in my pit, Christ in myself – it's interesting as we turn to the experience of the Israelites as they wandered in the wilderness. If we come to Exodus

15:24 we see God's abounding grace towards the Israelites, and it must be confessed that these Israelites of old are no different to us today. Here it says:

> And the people murmured against Moses, saying, What shall we drink?

What did the people do? They murmured. Things weren't how they would like them to be, so they murmured. And over in the next chapter, in that situation they said, "We're thirsty. We want to drink." So God gave them a drink. The waters were bitter. He made it sweet for them. And then just in the next chapter, Exodus 16:2-3:

> And the whole congregation of the children of Israel murmured against Moses and
> Aaron in the wilderness: And the children of Israel said unto them, Would to God we
> had died by the hand of the Lord in the land of Egypt, when we sat by the flesh pots.

Now they were hungry, and they murmured; there was nothing for them to eat so they murmured. What did God do? God gave them manna and their need for food was satisfied. And then over here in Exodus 17:3:

> And the people thirsted there for water; and the people murmured against Moses,
> and said, Wherefore is this that thou hast brought us up out of Egypt, to kill us and
> our children and our cattle with thirst?

These people had a genuine situation. Let's not discount their situation. They were thirsty. Do you get thirsty? We get thirsty. And in their thirst there was water but the water was bitter. You can understand why they would murmur. And then they were hungry but there was no food, so they murmured. These were afflictions which come to us, our own selves every day. And I don't know about you, but I often find myself murmuring because there are things that I *think* I need, and things that I *know* I need, but I can't see them and so I become distrustful. And here again in Numbers 14:2-3:

> And all the children of Israel murmured against Moses and against Aaron: and the
> whole congregation said unto them, Would God that we had died in the land of
> Egypt! or would God we had died in this wilderness!

Then in Numbers 16:41. And this was after Korah, Dathan and Abiram were slain:

> But on the morrow all the congregation of the children of Israel murmured.

The Israelites, as they wandered through the wilderness, met with circumstances that were uncomfortable to them. And because they were uncomfortable to them, they found themselves complaining. And when do we find that we complain? We complain when things aren't going our way. We complain when things aren't comfortable to us, when things are not conducive to what we *think* are conducive to our peace of mind.

And as the Israelites went through their situation they thought, *Poor me, poor, poor, poor me.* That's why we murmur. We murmur when we are caught up in sympathies of our own self. But where that sin abounded, grace did much more abound, and as they went through all of these afflictions, we read here in Isaiah 63:9:

> In all their affliction he [CHRIST] was afflicted, and the angel of his presence saved
> them: in his love and in his pity he redeemed them; and he bare them, and carried
> them all the days of old.

As they went through their trials and their afflictions in the wilderness, Christ went through it with them and He Himself was afflicted with the same afflictions that they were afflicted with. While they were caught up in poor-little-me, and my poor-little-me's suffering, and my poor-little-me's hurts, and my poor-little-me's disappointments, there was Christ suffering the same thing. Exactly the same thing in all their afflictions. In all points tempted like as we are! In all their afflictions He was afflicted.

Now let's bring this to our day: In *1888 Materials*, p.552 it is written here very simply:

> We have felt Him in the humiliation; we have felt Him in the sacrifice; we have felt
> Him in the trials; we have felt Him in the test. [3]

Now *there* is a great comfort for us. When we are afflicted, Jesus is afflicted. He's suffering what I'm suffering and we can have this precious companionship and fellowship in that suffering.

We often speak among ourselves and one may say to another, "Yes I understand what you're going through because,yes, I'm going through the same thing." And we get comfort from that. Even though we're still going through our own experience, and they are going through theirs, we're still comforted because we know that someone understands. So as we go through humiliation, as we have to make sacrifices, and the trials when we're tested, whatever affliction it is, we have a succour. And I love *Desire of Ages,* p.483:

> Through all our trials we have a never-failing Helper. He does not leave us alone
> to struggle with temptation, to battle with evil, and be finally crushed with burdens
> and sorrow. Though now He is hidden from mortal sight, the ear of faith can hear
> His voice saying, Fear not; I am with you. "I am He that liveth, and was dead; and,
> behold, I am alive forevermore." Revelation 1:18. I have endured *your* sorrows,
> experienced *your* struggles, encountered *your* temptations. I know *your* tears;

And that word "know" – Adam *knew* Eve and they had a son. Adam was *intimately* acquainted with his wife. When Christ says, "I know what you are going through," He says it because He is *intimately acquainted* with your experience; because He is bone of your bone and flesh of your flesh.

> I know *your* tears; I also have wept. The griefs that lie too deep to be breathed into
> any human ear, I know. Think not that you are desolate and forsaken. Though your
> pain touch no responsive chord in any heart on earth, look unto Me, and live. "The

mountains shall depart, and the hills be removed; but My kindness shall not depart from thee, neither shall the covenant of My peace be removed, saith the Lord that hath mercy on thee." Isaiah 54:10. [4] [emphasis supplied]

Can you say, "Amen" to these words? Can you say, "Amen" with a real heart feeling? We are afflicted, we are tempted and tried; we go through hard times, and there we get caught up with me and my poor little trials, and Jesus understands what I'm going through. Jesus has sympathy for me. Jesus loves me and when I'm crying He's crying, what I'm feeling, He is feeling. And we have this precious comfort, *for me*, in that time of trial. Jesus has become me! And there He became me and He can be *my* comforter. He can comfort *me*.

But let's change our perspective. We've looked at the comfort that *I* can gain from Jesus being one with me, but we want to come *out of self and into Christ*. Out of self and *in-to* Christ. Come to Psalms 69:9. This is one of those beautiful Psalms of Christ's experience in Gethsemane and upon the cross:

> For the zeal of thine house hath eaten me up; and the reproaches of them that reproached thee are fallen upon me.

Are you being reproached? You don't like it, do you? And Jesus comes to you and says, "I'm being reproached too. Take comfort child." But friends, these reproaches are falling upon *Him!* How do you think *He* feels? How does He feel when these reproaches that are falling upon you have fallen upon Him? How does He feel? Verses 1-2 of the same Psalm:

> Save me, O God; for the waters are come in unto my soul. I sink in deep mire, where there is no standing: I am come into deep waters, where the floods overflow me.

Who is talking here? You? Jesus is talking here! You think that *you're* suffering because of these reproaches? Hey, out of self and into Christ. *Christ* is suffering because of these reproaches. Christ is *drowning* because of these reproaches!

When we are in the situation, where is our mind? Is it on poor-little-old-me and *my* sufferings? Am I seeking to gain comfort from Jesus to comfort *myself* in that suffering? Or am I *out of myself* and looking to Jesus? Looking to Him? We see Jesus who was made a little lower than the angels for what? The suffering of death. Hebrews 2:9 Do we see our situation and poor me in that situation? Or do we see Jesus and what Jesus is going through?

Now Gethsemane is one of the greatest testimonies to the humanity of Christ and His oneness with me. Does your heart long for sympathy in suffering? Does it? It says here in *The Desire of Ages*, p.687:

> The human heart longs for sympathy in suffering.

If your heart doesn't long for sympathy in suffering then you don't have a human heart. But did Jesus have a human heart?

> This longing Christ felt to the very depths of His being.

See? He's touched with the feelings of our infirmities. He feels what we feel. He felt it to the very depths of His being.

> In the supreme agony of His soul He came to His disciples with a yearning desire to hear some words of comfort from those whom He had so often blessed and comforted, and shielded in sorrow and distress.

What did He want? He wanted succour. He wanted comfort. He was there being tempted beyond what we could ever be tempted; but it was our temptations and He wanted succour. He wanted comfort. From who? From those whom He had comforted! Who's that? *US!*

> The One who had always had words of sympathy for them was now suffering superhuman agony, and He longed to know that they were praying for Him and for themselves.

We go into trials and we forget to pray. But when we go into that trial, Jesus is there and He's longing that we're going to pray for Him and ourselves. And when we don't pray and we fail, how is His heart broken?

> How dark seemed the malignity of sin! Terrible was the temptation to let the human race bear the consequences of its own guilt, while He stood innocent before God. If He could only know that His disciples understood and appreciated this, He would be strengthened. [5]

Did you catch that last part? What would strengthen Jesus? That His disciples could understand *His* temptations. How often do we take comfort to ourselves that Jesus understands *my* temptations? Here is Jesus, and He wants us to understand *His* temptations! And what was His temptation? *To let you go.* To say, "No, no, Camron is too much for me, he has really made a mess. It's too dark, it's too black, and no, I could just leave him alone, leave him to his own misery, leave him in that pit of misery that he dug for himself and I could go and sit on my Father's throne and have all the angels worship me and everything can be fine."

Jesus wants us to know that He was tempted to think that. When? At the same time we are tempted! At *exactly the same time* we are going through our temptations, not only is Jesus tempted as I am tempted, but He is tempted to leave it all and go home.

Friends, every single trial that you overcome, every single temptation that you endure, praise the Lord! Because Jesus had to endure *His own* temptations at the same time as enduring your own temptations.

Now if we let that sink into the mind, into the heart, what does it do to that cold stony heart? It obliterates it, doesn't it? Over the page on p.690:

> Again He had felt a longing for companionship, for some words from His disciples which would bring relief, and break the spell of darkness that well-nigh overpowered Him.

When you're feeling lonely, do you manage to distract yourself a little while but then it comes back in a wave? Oh I need companionship, I need to ring this person, I need to see that person. Jesus felt that as well. The waves of need that we have, He experienced it. He experienced it and He needed relief.

> But their eyes were heavy; "neither wist they what to answer Him." His presence aroused them. They saw His face marked with the bloody sweat of agony, and they were filled with fear. His anguish of mind they could not understand. "His visage was so marred more than any man, and His form more than the sons of men." Isaiah 52:14.

> Turning away, Jesus sought again His retreat, and fell prostrate, overcome by the horror of a great darkness. [6]

When we don't countenance Christ in our trials, what is His experience? He is overcome by the horror of a great darkness! We get so caught up with me and my sufferings and my poor-little-old-me, and we forget about Jesus. We forget all about Him. Yes, we gather to our own souls all the comforts and all the promises and everything like that, to comfort *myself*, to keep *myself* happy, but what about *Jesus*? We've heard the phrase, "Who cares about Jesus?" Do I care more about me and my little-old-self, or do I care about Jesus? We need to come out of myself and in-to Jesus.

"But, oh," you might say, "Jesus died on the cross 2,000 years ago. This is all past experience. It doesn't have anything to do with me today. Jesus doesn't go into darkness when I neglect Him. He's in heaven not in Gethsemane any more. Not at Calvary." Don't be so selfish and narrow minded. Listen to this statement from *Manuscript Releases*, Vol.13, p.369:

> The cup of suffering was placed in His hand, as if He were the guilty one, and He drained it to the dregs. He bore the sin of the world to the bitter end. And yet men continue to sin, and Christ continues to feel the consequences of their sin as if He Himself were the guilty one. [7]

He "continues to feel the consequences of [our] sins." Jesus is the " I AM" – time is nothing to Him. Past, present and future are all the same. And He relates with each one of us as though there is not another person on the earth. His Gethsemane experience today is as real as it was 2,000 years ago! But it's just Him, and you. So what happens when I sin? What is His experience when I neglect Him? Yes! He is overcome by the horror of a great darkness!

When I first read *Testimonies*, Vol.2, p.205 it was a real kick in the head with a pair of steel-capped boots. Here it is:

> Again the Saviour turned sadly from His sleeping disciples, and prayed the third time, saying the same words. Then He came to them and said: "Sleep on now, and take your rest: behold, the hour is at hand, and the Son of man is betrayed into the hands of sinners."

We are told to watch and pray lest we enter into temptation. If we enter into temptation, we are putting Jesus in temptation. Let's watch and pray so Jesus doesn't have to go through the temptation. But we are just so Laodicean aren't we? We're sleepy-heads, and we're so prone to sleep, just like the disciples. We seem to be oblivious to the very fact that we're walking on the very precipice of the last seconds of earth's history. And our eyes are closed and the arms are folded and we're sleeping, teetering on the brink of eternity. Now listen to this:

> "Sleep on now, and take your rest: behold, the hour is at hand, and the Son of man is betrayed into the hands of sinners." How *cruel* for the disciples to permit sleep to close their eyes, and slumber to chain their senses, while their divine Lord was enduring such inexpressible mental anguish! [8] *(emphasis supplied)*

Does that hit you? When I get caught up in my own little old me, and I neglect Christ – I am being *cruel*. This is startling. It is really, really startling! And if we are prone to sleepiness, friends, may this be a wakeup call! "How cruel for the disciples to permit sleep to close their eyes, and slumber to chain their senses, while their divine Lord was enduring such inexpressible mental anguish!" Are we getting this? We're not going to know if we've got this or not until our next trial, as to whether we are going to be caught up in poor-little-old-me or we're going to think of Jesus and step out of myself and into Christ.

What was it that He wanted when He was there in Gethsemane? He wanted succour. He wanted sympathy. He wanted them to know *His* temptations. May God really help us to take this on board. And why is He suffering that? Because of me! I made the mess, I sowed the seed, and now I've got to reap the consequences, and He's come to reap the consequences with me. And as I'm reaping the consequences, I'm like: "Oh poor-little-me, I've got to put up with this and, oh, it's too much, it's too hard." And then comes Jesus and He says, "Here, I'm here with you, I understand what you're going through. Your tears, I have also wept; they are *my* tears, in fact I'm weeping them right now." And we have this comfort. *But we put Him there!* He did no sin neither was guile found in His mouth.

What right does He have to be there? Why should He be there? He's there because *He chose to be there*. And friends He wants us to *understand* that. He wants us to understand that He has chosen to be there so that He can come and be with you, and comfort you. But do you know when you get the most comfort? It's when you don't look at yourself. It's when you look at someone else in their suffering – and there is Jesus who has come to comfort you and He is suffering.

When we get caught up in ourselves, we can all testify that we are not comforted. Even though we can take all of these precious rays of Jesus Christ and all His promises to our soul, we're comforted. But it's not the same, because it's *me* that's being comforted. Who's me? Is there any room for *me* in Christ? Christ *emptied* Himself. I am to be emptied of myself as well. So let's snap out of our poor-little-old-me. Let's snap out of it! Do you care about Jesus?

But we can go from another perspective again. And I want to close with this perspective. It is cruel for us to leave and abandon Christ in His sufferings. It is cruel for us to leave and abandon and not consider Christ in *my* sufferings, because that's whose His sufferings are. And it is cruel to cause Him to suffer in the first place.

So when we're tempted to do something and indulge ourselves, have a second thought. What's it going to do to Jesus? Ah! I don't want to do that! Instead of indulging ourselves, let's think of the consequences upon the Son of man, upon Jesus. So if it is cruel to cause Christ to suffer, come to Galatians 3:28, we add now a new dimension. Christ has become one with me – now here it says:

> There is neither Jew nor Greek, there is neither bond nor free, there is neither male
> nor female: for ye are all one in Christ Jesus.

So not only is Christ in me, and I am in Christ, but my brother, my sister, are in Christ and Christ is in them. In-Christ is my brother, my sister, and me, and we are all one. So much so, exactly as we've studied this oneness with Christ. When we suffer, Jesus suffers. In all my afflictions, Jesus is afflicted. Now here 1 Corinthians 12:25-26, this is profound:

> That there should be no schism in the body; but that the members should have the
> same care one for another. And whether one member suffer, all the members suffer
> with it; or one member be honoured, all the members rejoice with it.

Now that adds a new dimension again, doesn't it? When I am afflicted Christ is afflicted because He and I are one. But I in-Christ am one with my brother, one with my sister, and there as I'm afflicted, they are afflicted. As I suffer, as Jesus suffers, they suffer also.

When we cause our brothers and sisters to suffer, we are causing ourselves to suffer and we are causing Jesus to suffer. And there is Jesus and He's suffering with my fellow brother or sister and He's suffering with me. We have a double suffering that we are causing Jesus Christ. Do you like suffering? Does Jesus like suffering? Then how ought we to treat one another? We are familiar with Matthew 25:31-46:

When the Son of man shall come in his glory, and all the holy angels with him, then shall he sit upon the throne of his glory: And before him shall be gathered all nations: and he shall separate them one from another, as a shepherd divideth his sheep from the goats: And he shall set the sheep on his right hand, but the goats on the left. Then shall the King say unto them on his right hand, Come, ye blessed of my Father, inherit the kingdom prepared for you from the foundation of the world: *For I was an hungered, and ye gave me meat: I was thirsty, and ye gave me drink: I was a stranger, and ye took me in: Naked, and ye clothed me: I was sick, and ye visited me: I was in prison, and ye came unto me.* Then shall the righteous answer him, saying, Lord, when saw we thee an hungered, and fed thee? or thirsty, and gave thee drink? When saw we thee a stranger, and took thee in? or naked, and clothed thee? Or when saw we thee sick, or in prison, and came unto thee? *And the King shall answer and say unto them, Verily I say unto you, Inasmuch as ye have done it unto one of the least of these my brethren, ye have done it unto me.* Then shall he say also unto them on the left hand, Depart from me, ye cursed, into everlasting fire, prepared for the devil and his angels: For I was an hungered, and ye gave me no meat: I was thirsty, and ye gave me no drink: I was a stranger, and ye took me not in: naked, and ye clothed me not: sick, and in prison, and ye visited me not. Then shall they also answer him, saying, Lord, when saw we thee an hungered, or athirst, or a stranger, or naked, or sick, or in prison, and did not minister unto thee? Then shall he answer them, saying, Verily I say unto you, *Inasmuch as ye did it not to one of the least of these, ye did it not to me.* And these shall go away into everlasting punishment: but the righteous into life eternal. [emphasis supplied]

Are we getting the picture? It is cruel for us to let Christ suffer. But if we cause our fellow brethren to suffer, we are causing Christ to suffer. I'm sure a thousand different ways that we can cause our brethren to suffer come to our minds, and so they should, because we are to watch and pray lest we enter into temptation. Watch and pray lest I myself perhaps, somehow, am casting a stumbling block before Jesus and causing *Him* to fall? If we cause others to fall, and He is one with them, then He bears that too...

"Inasmuch as ye have done it unto one of the least of these my brethren, ye have done it unto me." How cautious ought we to be in our dealings with one another? How cautious ought we to be in even opening our mouths? Because we don't know what's going to come out half of the time. James describes it there – it's a fire, it's set on hell! (James 3:6). Every single thing we do has consequences. Every single thing we say causes a crop to come up and Jesus reaps that crop.

But if someone causes me to suffer, if someone puts a stumbling block before my path don't worry about getting back at them. Worry about Jesus! He is hurting, just like you're hurting, but you're not hurting because *He* is hurting. Who am I to hurt? Out of myself and into Him. Let's think of Jesus. Let's care about Jesus. And when we do this, then John 17 really comes into our focus now. Let's just read this to close and seal our appreciation.

Now I really, really plead that sometime soon we can have the upper chamber experience – that we can all come into *one accord*. That the Holy Spirit, the latter rain can be poured out upon us. And here is what needs to happen. Jesus says in John 17: 20-23:

> Neither pray I for these alone, but for them also which shall believe on me through their word; That they all may...

Now note that word, "may". If we don't treat each other right, we do not believe that we are in Jesus, or that they are in Jesus. If we don't believe that, then we are not.

> That they all may be one; as thou, Father, art in me, and I in thee, that they also may be one in us: that the world may believe that thou hast sent me. And the glory which thou gavest me I have given them; that they may be one, even as we are one: I in them, and thou in me, that they may be made perfect in one; and that the world may know that thou hast sent me, and hast loved them, as thou hast loved me.

That they may be perfect in one! That the world may know the love of God! Greater love hast no man than to do what? "Lay down his life for his friends." John 15:13. Instead of thinking about them, he cares for the things of the other. He cares for the things of Jesus.

It is my prayer that *I* am listening to these things. That *I* will put these things into practice. That *I* will practice the very things I'm preaching. And that friends, we can all do this. So we can get off from this planet and get out of this flesh of ours. But even then while I suffer it, OK, let's be like Jesus and sail like the sun above it all. We've got no excuse so may the Lord help us to do this. AMEN.

God's Abounding Grace

Part 4
READY WHEN YOU ARE

July 3, 2010

O to grace how great a debtor
Daily I'm constrained to be!

GRACE, grace! Romans 5:20-21 has been the focus of our appreciation these last few studies. Let us turn there again:

> Moreover the law entered, that the offence might abound. But where sin abounded, grace did much more abound: That as sin hath reigned unto death, even so might grace reign through righteousness unto eternal life by Jesus Christ our Lord.

Over the last few weeks we have been in consideration of the law of God and of His grace. We have seen how it is that the law is the schoolmaster that brings us to Jesus Christ. As the law entered, it makes the offence to be evident. Not just evident, but to *abound*. "By the law is the knowledge of sin" (Romans 3:20). So in order to bring grace about, the law needed to enter in order to create in man a *sense of need*, that as that sense of need becomes the experience, then there is a yearning and a desire for something better.

Often we read that the law entered to make sin appear. But if we follow it through, we see that the law entered that *grace* might abound. That is why God gave the law. To show man his sins is a means to an end. That end was grace "that as sin hath reigned unto death, even so might grace reign through righteousness unto eternal life by Jesus Christ our Lord" (Romans 5:21).

This law of God entered into our experience and there in that great moral mirror we have come to understand the law as it really is; how our condition really is before that law. And we have spent some time studying Romans 7. But as we have considered the law, it is interesting to note that as the law has come and has brought to us the knowledge of sin, it's amazing how many there are who seek to gain righteousness by that same law. They think that they can get righteousness out of that law – out of that very thing which comes to us in its purity as it really is. There are those who get something else out of it rather than the conviction and reproof of sin.

They look at that law as it is written and they say, "I've done that, and the law says that is sin so I'm not going to do that any more." They go on in their lives and they use that law as their *guidebook*. It is their standard and they seek to live according to that standard.

They are kind to their parents, they give them respect. They are careful not to lie. They do not commit adultery. They are conscientious objectors. They are kind to their fellow brethren. If something is not theirs, they don't seek after it. They are respected in their neighbourhoods and esteemed by society. They go to church every week. They are there at church every week. They sit through the Sabbath school lesson and they participate in the discussions. They're always at the prayer meeting, always standing up and having something to testify of. Careful with what they eat, what they wear and they're even very careful with what they say.

It all sounds good, doesn't it? It all sounds so *right*. In fact it sounds like *Seventh-day Adventists*. There's so much that they do right. They go to that law and they look at that law and they say, "Yeah, we're pretty good. We've done it all right." The word of God actually says that those who declare that, are Seventh-day Adventists. The testimony to the Church of Laodicea is that they say they are rich and increased with goods and have need of nothing.

What kind of goods is it that they say that they are rich with? They are rich and increased in spiritual *stuff*. Spiritual goods. So much so, they consider they have it all, they have everything and there's no need for anything else. *They have it.* They have it all and, friends, do they not? Do they not have the oracles of God today? They have the writings of the prophet. They have the interpretations of the prophecies. The pioneers' books and pamphlets. They have the health reform. Some have the dress reform. There is so much light that they have and they say, "Look! Look! We have it! We have it! And because we have it Jesus loves me. God loves me because I have all of these rich spiritual blessings. And therefore because God loves me and I have all of this, I am just fine thank you very much."

Seventh-day Adventists today are often referred to as *modern Israel*. What was the experience? What is written of Israel of old? Come to Romans 10:1-3 – those who think that they have it all. And it's interesting how it's worded here:

> Brethren, my heart's desire and prayer to God for Israel is, that they might be saved.
> For I bear them record that they have a zeal of God, but not according to knowledge.
> For they being ignorant of God's righteousness, and going about to establish their own righteousness, have not submitted themselves unto the righteousness of God.

They have a zeal of God, a zeal for God, for His ways, for His law. But what's the problem with it? It is "not according to knowledge." Oh! I know the Ten Commandments.

I memorised them when I was a child and I stood up the front and even recited them before all the people. I did, honestly. Perhaps you did as well. But we are ignorant of *God's* righteousness.

When we went through our previous studies, what was it about the law that drives that final nail into the coffin? What was it? We discovered that the law requires *perfect obedience*. But whose perfect obedience was it? *God's perfect obedience.* God's righteousness is what the law requires. The law is a transcript of His character. That is His standard and those who do not meet the standard of His character are not fulfilling the law.

Let's get this particular point clear in our minds. There is no righteousness for us to take out of that law. There is no righteousness for us to take out of ourselves. It requires perfect right-doing because righteousness is right-doing. But, it wants the perfect right-doing of God. That is what the law wants.

In one of our previous studies we focused on this and we came to realise that there is nothing I have to offer to the law. There's *nothing*. Do I have the perfect right-doing of God? Is all of my good works equal and as good as God's works?

It's true that there are those who say, "Well, if right is right and I've done that which is right, then I've done that which is right. If God has done this right and I have gone and done it in the same way that God has done it, then I must have done it right."

Do you catch the thought there? If God has done it this way and I've gone along and done it just like God would do it, then have I done it right? No, because *I* did it. I might have done it like God did it but who did it? It was me. It has to be *God* that does it. You see, the law demands from us perfect righteousness and by perfect righteousness it means *from the day you are born right through to the very day you die – a life of having done absolutely nothing wrong, but a life that is totally full of God doing it.*

Being the good Seventh-day Adventists that we are, have we been ignorant of the righteousness of God? Have we sought to establish our own righteousness? The word of God says that we have been. The word of God says that we haven't understood these things as we should have understood them. And how many of us have tried and tried and tried and tried? We've changed our style of dress, we've modified our diet, we've done all these different things, but have we done it right? *Have we done it right?*

The law wants perfect right-doing – but not yours, not mine. We can be as right as we want to be, but that's irrelevant to the law. We're still condemned. And again I labour on that point because we *need to get this clear*. There is *nothing* of ourselves. And we looked at Abraham who thought he had to do something; and today, because he thought he had to do something to effect his own salvation, we have trouble in the Middle East – because he thought that he had to do something to save himself; because through that son, his line, was to be born the Saviour, and so he and his wife had to manipulate things in order to have a child.

If we think that we can look at the law of God and say, "I have done that right," we are deceived. Sin is the transgression of the law. What is sin? *Sin is the failure – our failure – to provide the law with the right-doing of God.* That is sin. If it's my right-doing, my own commandment-keeping, it is sin.

The word of God declares that our all righteousness's are as filthy rags. In other words: all our right-doings are as filthy rags. We can say, "I have it, I am rich and increased with goods" but the reality is, I'm naked. And this is the reality that God is wanting to wake us up to, to bring us to that point where, O wretched man that I am! Who shall deliver me from the body of this death?

If this is the case, then how am I to gain eternal life? How can I ever be saved? I'm not God. I can't work the works of God! Well, come to Romans 6:23:

> For the wages of sin is death; but the gift of God is eternal life through Jesus Christ our Lord.

What is eternal life? Eternal life is a "*gift*". If you are given something, was it yours beforehand? Did it come from you? It didn't. A gift is something given to you. You did not produce it yourself.

We have this in an illustration in Zechariah 3:1-5. Here we have Joshua the high priest, and as the high priest he stands there as the representative of the people, the representative of you and me:

> And he showed me Joshua the high priest standing before the angel of the Lord, and Satan standing at his right hand to resist him. And the Lord said unto Satan, The Lord rebuke thee, O Satan; even the Lord that hath chosen Jerusalem rebuke thee: is not this a brand plucked out of the fire? Now Joshua was clothed with filthy garments, and stood before the angel. And he answered and spake unto those that stood before him, saying, Take away the filthy garments from him. And unto him he said, Behold, I have caused thine iniquity to pass from thee, and I will clothe thee with change of raiment. And I said, Let them set a fair mitre upon his head. So they set a fair mitre upon his head, and clothed him with garments. And the angel of the Lord stood by.

Here Joshua the high priest stands as your representative, and therefore here *we* are. And he stands before the angel of the Lord in filthy garments; in the filthy garments of his own righteousness, of his own right-doings. There the Angel says, "I have caused thine iniquity to pass from thee, and I will clothe thee with change of raiment." There now needs to be a change of righteousness, a change of right-doing, a change of character. His was filthy garments. But there was given to him – *given* to him – clean garments.

First He says, "Take away the filthy garments." This is what the law is seeking to do. The law comes to bring that about. It shows us that all our righteousnesses are as filthy rags, that all of our right-doings, things that we thought we've done right – they weren't. Then, we come before Him confessing our sins and there He causes the iniquity to pass from thee. Then He clothes us with a change of raiment, with His righteousness, with His perfect conformity to the law. The law has come to us and said, "I want an entire life of obedience." We don't have that. But *He* does; and that is what He gives us. He gives us a life of total conformity to His law, from birth until death. And don't forget, it's a *gift*.

Now picking up from where we left off last week, we come to Ephesians 2:4-9:

> But God, who is rich in mercy, for his great love wherewith he loved us, Even when we were dead in sins, hath quickened us together with Christ, (by grace ye are saved;) And hath raised up together, and made us sit together in heavenly places in Christ Jesus:

Last week we looked at this raising up, how God had promised that even though we had been smitten and torn and bruised, He would bind up the wounds, He would heal us, and on the third day He would raise us up. And we saw how when Jesus Christ was raised on the third day, He raised us up with Him, because we were in-Jesus-Christ. Reading on:

> That in the ages to come he might show the exceeding riches of his grace [THAT ABUNDANCE OF GRACE] in his kindness toward us through Christ Jesus. For by grace are ye saved through faith; and that not of yourselves: it is the gift of God: Not of works, lest any man should boast.

The grace is a gift. It is unmerited. As we studied last week, Jesus Christ became at one with me. He became "us". "For such an high priest became us" (Hebrews 7:26). We. Ourselves. He died because He was a partaker of the body of this death, the same body of death that I have, with its sinful flesh, with all of its promptings and all of its tempting to sin. And just as we studied it in Romans 7, He became a partaker of our reality within that flesh, this hard struggle to try and not do that which we don't want to do.

We consent unto the law that it is good, but in us is a present evil, so that the things that we would do, we don't do; and the things that we don't want to do, we do them (Romans 7:15,19,21).

We, in our experience, discover that everything that we do, all of what we think is right-doing, is sin. We come to a point where we realize, I can't actually do anything. I'm almost too scared to move, to open my mouth, because before I know it, I've done the things that I don't want to do, and I've said the things that I don't want to say. I just wish I was a statue.

This horrible pit – we've dug it for ourselves and there's no way out. The more we move, the more we squirm, the further down we go. So we saw last week that Christ came right into that very pit which I had dug. He emptied Himself and became us. As He did that, because He became us, we understand how it is that He was able to say these words in John 2:24-25:

> But Jesus did not commit himself unto them, because he knew all men, And needed not that any should testify of man: for he knew what was in man.

We understand now why He could say these words. He knew what was in man because He had become as that man – every single man on this earth that was ever born – He became one with them. He dwelt in their sinful flesh, He lived their life, suffered as they suffer and was tempted in all points like as we are tempted because He was in all points like as we are. He felt what we feel because He was where we are, and just as we are. He was our own selves all over again.

And there He can say, "I know what is in man. I don't need to be told what is in man, I know what is in that man because I am in that man." And knowing what was in man, He says here in John 15:4-5:

> Abide in me, and I in you. As the branch cannot bear fruit of itself, except it abide in the vine; no more can ye, except ye abide in me. I am the vine, ye are the branches: He that abideth in me, and I in him, the same bringeth forth much fruit: for without me ye can do nothing.

He could say this because He knew what was in man. He knew that of His own self, as me, He couldn't have done anything right. He couldn't. He says, "Except I am in you and you are in me, you cannot do anything." It's interesting that He says, "Except you abide in me and I in you, you cannot do anything." But didn't He become as me? So if I'm abiding in Him and He's abiding in me and He is in my situation, where is the hope in that for me? Because He's emptied Himself, and He's become like I am, and He is right where I am, He is going through what I am going through, where is the benefit? How can I do things right if He Himself couldn't do things right? He confesses it here in John 5:30:

> I can of mine own self do nothing.

"Without me you can do nothing," and "I can of mine own self do nothing." He couldn't do anything either so where is my benefit? Why could He do nothing? Because *you* can't. Because *you* cannot do anything, He could not do anything. As man, you cannot do that which is right. But could Christ have used His power, as God, to do things right?

He laid it down. He *emptied* Himself. He came right into your hopeless and helpless situation where He could honestly say, "I can of mine own self do nothing." If He had used His divine power, then that would have put Him beyond our experience. We have no divine power to use. If He had done that, the example would have been useless; none of Him coming to earth would have been of any use whatsoever. *It would have been a waste of time.*

For those who do not consider that Jesus Christ came right down to the very, very bottom of their pit, they might as well not even believe in Jesus Christ, because what good is that for them? It's no use.

I once heard a description of Jesus Christ being like a tow truck that parks on the side where the ground is firm to pull out the other car that is stuck in the bog. There is this picture that there was Jesus on a higher level than man, and He reached from there down to where man was, and pulled man out of the bog without getting muddy and dirty Himself. Friends, that is a waste of time. It's a waste of time. *Don't even think those things.* He came right into the bog. He came right into the muck; and there He wraps His arm around me and lays hold of the rope that God gives Him, and together we go up. That's more of the right picture. There is no distinction whatsoever. As He came and He entered right into my experience, right down to the little jot and tittle, the minutiae of your life, He came and did that so that He could bring to us His right-doing? No. *The right-doing of His Father.* He emptied Himself, He of His own self could do nothing. Where is our benefit? John 14:10:

> Believest thou not that I am in the Father, and the Father in me? the words that I speak unto you I speak not of myself: but the Father that dwelleth in me, *he doeth the works.*

We are to abide in Christ, but God abided in Christ. And there as He emptied Himself and became me, God filled Him, and God worked in Him right-doing. As He met my temptations, God worked in Him the victory. It was God-in-Him that overcame every temptation. It was God-in-Him that worked righteousness. Now what does the law want from us? The right-doing of God. So there, as Christ became us, and as He became us, as us, God worked through Him *God's* works. Can you actually understand how simple this really is? Nothing for us to philosophize about it. Christ became me. As He became me, God in Him in me, fulfilled the law. Because the law wanted *God's* right-doing. So as Christ became me, He performed God's right-doing as me. So what do I have in Christ? God's right-doing. Do you think that the law will be happy with God's right-doing? It wants of me a perfect life, but through the working of God in Him, Jesus lived a perfect life. But whose life was it? It was *our* life.

When the law comes to you, and it says, "I want from you a perfect life." What are we to say? Well, Jesus says, "Here is a perfect life. Here is a life that will satisfy." Christ said that the devil could find nothing in Him. From birth right the way through to His death, He never sinned. All the way along God worked in Him, and He was *we.* So when the law says, "I want a perfect life" we can say, "Here is a perfect life. I have a perfect life in Jesus."

Jesus was in me, and I am in Him, and God was in Jesus. Do we believe this? Do I sound like I'm repeating myself? I hope I do, because we've got to get it clear. We've got to get it simple. Jesus was me, and that life was perfect. But God was in Jesus, and therefore it was the very life of God Himself, because He became as me and was filled with God, and God worked in Him.

It might sound a lot simpler than we thought it has been all these years. If Jesus Christ became me, and His life was righteous, then is not that righteous life my life because He became me? So His righteousness is my righteousness. And if we will believe that in Jesus Christ we have lived a life of perfect obedience, then we can come and we can stand before the law of God with no condemnation – none whatsoever. Because there is no condemnation to them that are in Christ Jesus. If we will really believe that my life was His life.

There cannot be any condemnation there. There literally, *factually*, cannot be any condemnation. It's actually impossible for there to be any condemnation in Christ Jesus, because *God cannot condemn Himself.* He is the law-Giver. He is the One who worked. Is He going to condemn His own workings? No!

Man fell. He came to this position where He could not do anything right. But God wanted to save man. Could He change His law in order to save man? If He was to change His law, He would have to change Himself. He would have to cease being God. So He could not change His law. Instead, God so loved man that He entered into the very man himself and *in* man and *as* man, fulfilled the law.

Behold what manner of love that God would do this! So every individual who will believe this has a life before God that is *completely sinless. Steps to Christ*, p.62:

> Since we are sinful, unholy, we cannot perfectly obey the holy law. We have no righteousness of our own with which to meet the claims of the law of God. But Christ has made a way of escape for us. He lived on earth amid trials and temptations such as we have to meet. He lived a sinless life. He died for us, and now He offers to take our sins and *give us His righteousness*. If you give yourself to Him, and accept Him as your Saviour, then, sinful as your life may have been, for His sake you are accounted righteous. Christ's character stands in place of your character, and you are accepted before God *just as if you had not sinned*. [emphasis supplied] [1]

"Just as if you had not sinned." Because there, standing before Him, He sees Christ's life. But that life which Christ lived was as you. In God's consideration, the life that Christ lived was your life and He lived it perfectly. So God sees the life of Christ; because He became you, He sees it as your life.

Will you consider the life of Christ in that manner as well? Will you? You are accepted before God just as if you had not sinned. Who? You. Have you sinned? We have to confess that we have. But as far as God is concerned, we haven't; *if* we will *believe*. He sees an entire life of perfection from the day you were born, right the way through to the end of your life.

Where sin abounded, grace does much more abound; right in that very same place. Right there, in your sinful flesh, in your sinful life, dwelt the fullness of the Godhead bodily, and it worked a righteous life. Right there when I have failed in a temptation and sinned, Jesus, as me, has overcome in that temptation.

Right there when I'm feeling tempted and I'm wanting to do what's right but it's so hard to do the right, He is *doing* that which is right and He has *already done* that which is right, *as me*. But when I fail, He experiences the failure; and when He is in that situation and we fail, He says, "Father, as I have become them, look not upon this wayward child, but look upon me. Count *Me* as being the wayward one. I will take the penalty in their place."

At the same time that He is a sacrifice for our sins, He is also our high priest. In that very place He says, "Father, as I have become him, look not on this wayward child, but look upon *me* and behold the perfect life which you wrought in me." This is the life that God sees.

We have to get this very clear, *very clear*. If we want to break out from these hellish shadows of condemnation, we need to believe this. We, in Christ, have lived a perfect life before God. Will you by faith lay hold of that life? Will you believe it? Will you believe that when God looks upon you, He does not see your vileness? *The Desire of Ages*, p.667:

> He [God] does not see in them the vileness of the sinner. He recognizes in them the likeness of His Son, in whom they believe. [2]

Will you believe it? *Will you believe it?* Believe it! We *have* a perfect life to present before God. And that life is in His Son. Not in us, it's Jesus. Therefore, there is now no condemnation if you believe that you are in Jesus Christ, if you are by faith abiding in Him, and He in you.

If I do make a mistake, if I err in my Christian walk, and I come before God confessing my guilt, I am not condemned. I'm not. Because that life stands in place of my life. But it's interesting. I want to bring to your experience a little secret. Often we do really believe these things, but sometimes when we fail, we experience a bit of a sense of the disapproval of God, and we sense that, Oh, I've done it now and we're separated from Him. Often we actually get confused with this experience. We think, *Well, God's attitude has changed.* We're tempted to think that. We're tempted to think that God's attitude has changed towards me, or something in me has changed towards Him. We say, "Well, okay, He's going to raise us up in three days" but we learned last study, He *already* has raised us up.

Even though we believe that He does not see my failure, we believe that there is no condemnation, we truly believe it from the heart, and we know that God's attitude towards me is still the same, we know that His thoughts are not of evil but of peace and of that expected end, and that He still only sees in me the likeness of His Son; and even though I'm sorry for my sins, my thoughts towards Him have not changed, I love Him just as much, I still want to do what's right, but still we can have a sense of disapproval and separation. We can actually think that, I thought I was in Christ but I'm not any more.

I'm just letting you in on a little understanding here, that we can get confused. Where your heart can be the same towards God, and you know that God hasn't changed towards you; you know that He is not looking upon you with disapproval, but you will at times have a sense of that. It's a *sense.* When we commit a sin, physically speaking the body is poisoned. The chemical structure of the being becomes unbalanced, and it deranges the human organism. We may have been intemperate with something. Or, we might have eaten something we shouldn't have, or we have indulged our passions, whatever it is, and we come to realize, Oh, I shouldn't have done that. Straight away we have a comfort, God doesn't see in me my sins, He doesn't see my vileness, He's looking only at Jesus. But, *the body has changed.* Don't get confused between your heart toward God and the body, because it's imbalanced. It creates feelings and senses that are not originating from your heart, your pure heart toward God.

It takes time for the body to balance itself out again. I'm just sharing this with you so that you can understand. Don't get confused. If you really believe this, Satan will try to cause you to think you don't. But what does faith have to do with feelings? Let faith go beyond that. If we've failed, we can get back up again. We don't have to give in to those feelings, because that's all they are. It might take a couple of days for the body to balance itself out, but you'll find peace with God again.

We have before God a perfect life, and that perfect life is what He sees. But that perfect life is a gift. Now I want to close with one last consideration. We read there in Romans 5:17 of the gift of righteousness:

> For if by one man's offence death reigned by one; much more they which receive abundance of grace and of the gift of righteousness shall reign in life by one, Jesus Christ.

Our Scripture reading said "their righteousness is of me [God]." Isaiah 54:17. It's not ours. God gives it to us. If it is a gift, it has come from someone.

In the days of Christ He spoke of a marriage feast. He spoke of the guests being invited to the marriage feast. But before they could go into the marriage feast, there needed to be an examination of whether they had on the wedding garment or not.

In those days the master of the feast provided the garment. In order for those people to meet the expectations, a gift was given to them so that they could go in. This is how it is also that we have been invited to the marriage supper of the Lamb. God is examining in this investigative judgment to see whether we are prepared for the marriage supper or not.

What is it that He is examining to see if we have? He is examining to see if we have the gift that He has given us. Often we think that He is examining to make sure we're doing everything right. No, He is looking to see if we have that gift – that wedding garment – that He has provided, that perfect life that Christ wrought as us. Now in *Christ's Object Lessons*, p.311:

> Christ in His humanity wrought out a perfect character, and this character He offers to impart to us. "All our righteousness are as filthy rags." Isaiah 64:6. Everything that we of ourselves can do is defiled by sin. But the Son of God "was manifested to take away our sins; and in Him is no sin." Sin is defined to be "the transgression of the law." 1 John 3:5, 4. But Christ was obedient to every requirement of the law. He said of Himself, "I delight to do Thy will, O My God; yea, Thy law is within My heart." Psalm 40:8. When on earth, He said to His disciples, "I have kept My Father's commandments." John 15:10. By His perfect obedience He has made it possible for every human being to obey God's commandments. When we submit ourselves to Christ, the heart is united with His heart, the will is merged in His will, the mind becomes one with His mind, the thoughts are brought into captivity to Him; *we live His life.* This is what it means to be clothed with the garment of His righteousness. Then as the Lord looks upon us He sees, not the fig-leaf garment, not the nakedness and deformity of sin, but His own robe of righteousness, which is perfect obedience to the law of Jehovah. [emphasis supplied] [3]

And that is a gift. You cannot produce it. It is a gift. Now on that point have you ever looked around you, have you ever looked at the world and the conditions of things and at the church and your fellow members and then looked at yourself and thought, *We're never going to be ready!*? We can't do anything right! We are so close to Christ's coming. There's too short a time for us to be ready, too short a time for us to get it right! Have you ever thought that? Have you ever thought, *How can we ever be ready?*

Well, we can stop worrying, because it is a gift. The Lord's righteousness is a gift and we can have that gift now, *if* we will believe and *receive*. If God Himself is the one that provides the gift, if He is the One that gives that garment, that fits us for the time of judgment, and the time of trouble, then if we will but believe His great love that He has towards us, and take that gift, and make it our *reality*, then He could come tomorrow, couldn't He?

Do we not have in Jesus the perfect life that He is looking for? It's there. It's just waiting for us to lay hold of it, to receive it by faith. Perfect conformity to the law, and the heavenly society. Perfect conformity and obedience to Him. His life was my life. He was me, and He was perfect. He lived a perfect life. So if God came, and said, "Camron, I want a perfect life." I can say, "God, in Jesus Christ I have a perfect life." And I can be ready if I will believe this. I will be ready for Him to come and take me home.

You see, the thing is God is not waiting for us to keep His law. Get this clear. *God is not waiting for us to keep His law.* He would be waiting forever because He knows what's in man. He is waiting for us to believe, for us to stop wallowing in my own poor-little-old-self – to snap out of it.

He comes and He says, "Why do you not believe me? Why? Here is a perfect life." He has it, it's a gift. He says, "Just believe me and I can come and take you home. I've made it for you, here it is. It's yours. Have it. Take it. Live it. Breathe it. Will you not take it?" It's not about what we do, it's about what we believe and *how much* we believe.

Except you become as little children – "Yes, Daddy, I believe you." That's what He is waiting for. That's what He wants. That life God will count as my real life. So we can come boldly before the throne of grace. We can come boldly before the judgment of God! And we can enter boldly into the closing scenes of this world. The hard part – the fear and trepidation part – will be the part to *believe. That* will be the hard part.

We *can* mount up with wings like an eagle, and sail like the sun above it all, because we're not condemned. There needs to be no more clogs on the feet to stop us from flying any more.

If we believe this we can fly, friends! Our spiritual walk can be so much faster, because I have what God wants, and that is what He sees. No time, no use any more, no need for us to wallow around in the muck. Get up. A just man falls seven times. Why does it say seven times? Because He finally falls and his fall is complete. Finally, self is dead, and it stays dead. But he's righteous because he's learned: "I can't do it." But Jesus Christ has *done it*!

In Jesus we have a perfect life, perfect conformity to the law of God, and yes, I will repeat myself, because we need to get it. *We need to get it.* Satan and the whole world can say whatever they want. They can throw at you whatever they want, like Joshua there before the angel and the accuser of the brethren. The world can say whatever they want, but what really matters is what God thinks. And friends, get this clear – He thinks of Jesus.

To some it might sound presumptuous what I have shared today, we have not finished our series yet. But believe it! If it sounds too simple, if it sounds too easy, it's not as simple and as easy as it really is. We've grown up in a world of philosophy, theosophy, theology. Break out of it. It is easier and simpler than we think it is. It really is. The hard part, and it will be the hardest thing that you will ever do in your life, is to believe. But according to your faith, it will be unto you. AMEN.

God's Abounding Grace

Part 5
RIGHTEOUSNESS BY FAITH SIMPLIFIED

July 10, 2010

O give me Samuel's mind,
A sweet unmurm'ring faith,
Obedient and resigned
To Thee in life and death,
That I may read with child like eyes
Truths that are hidden from the wise.

"TRUTHS that are hidden from the wise." Have you found that as we have been proceeding through our studies, that to be "wise" as the world regards wisdom, can very much be a clog on the leg of a bird to stop it from flying? As we have come together each week, we have been examining very simply Righteousness by Faith. And particularly as we came to our last study last week there called *Ready When You Are*, didn't it sound too easy, too simple? In fact, to some it may have even have come to them as, "Well, that sounds *presumptuous*. Surely there is more to it than just believing. Surely there's more." And indeed we might be tempted to say, "That sounds like cheap grace." But in Romans 5 it describes the grace of God as free! Free! it is a free gift! The fact of the matter is, as we have been examining, we don't have anything to buy it with. *We don't.* All our right-doings are as filthy garments. We have nothing with which to purchase what the Lord seeks to give us. It is, as we saw there – a gift! We have been invited to this feast and God has provided the robe.

So as we come to our study today, continuing in these understandings, let's commence with Mark 10:13-15. And we want to get this clear right from the start:

> And they brought young children to him, that he should touch them: and his disciples rebuked those that brought them. But when Jesus saw it, he was much displeased, and said unto them, Suffer the little children to come unto me, and forbid them not: for of such is the kingdom of God. Verily I say unto you, Whosoever shall not receive the kingdom of God as a little child, he shall not enter therein.

Except we receive the things of God as a little child, we will have no part in the kingdom of heaven. So today we need to do that. As we go back over our previous studies again and little questions want to come in and you want to say, "Oh, *but...*!" Remember – except you receive it as a little child, you shall not enter into the kingdom.

So today we want to receive God's word in the same manner in which a child receives the word of the father. A little child – he's weak, he's helpless, he's dependent upon the father. That is the point that we want to be at today. And as we have continued through our studies, have they not brought us to that point? We met the law. We who thought that we were good, so mature, so wise, quite capable thank you very much, discovered that we have been deceived by our own wicked hearts. We came to realise that even though we thought we were rich, increased with goods and don't need anything, the reality is that I am miserable, poor, blind, and naked and I am a wretched man trapped within this body of death.

The very things that we want to do, we can't do it. *We cannot do it!* And the things that we don't want to do, we do that. We have a heart that would sin and that lay under a law that would condemn. And just like Solomon there, all broken before the Lord, feeling distrustful and scared of his own self, we say, "I don't know how to go out and I don't know how to come in, I am but a little child" (1 Kings 3:7). The word of God brought us to that appreciation: we are helpless, we are weak, we are dependent upon God. So this morning it is my prayer that this is where we will be; that as we come to our study this morning, we will be weak, helpless, dependent upon God, sitting at His feet and listening to every word that proceeds out of His mouth. Not taking from it, not adding to it, just simply reading it as Daddy says so.

Our study is entitled this morning, and by God's grace we will have the fulfilment of the title, *Righteousness by Faith Simplified*. And in our study again I will take the time that we need to take. Please, listen carefully. I will lead on softly, as children are able to bear. And children like stories, so I'm going to tell you a story. Come over to Genesis 1:1-3.

> In the beginning God created the heaven and the earth. And the earth was without form, and void; and darkness was upon the face of the deep. And the Spirit of God moved upon the face of the waters. And God said, Let there be light: and there was light.

Now in the beginning God created the heaven and the earth. He came to this earth and He had a thought in mind. Do we think before we speak? Well, we're supposed to. So God "*said*" and that "*said*" was in consequence of a thought. In His mind He had the thought of a world, a beautiful world, with flowing mountains and gentle valleys, happy bubbling, burbling brooks, luscious meadows of beautiful, delightful flowers, forests of tall, magnificent trees reaching up with their limbs as though reaching out in praise to God, and the birds dwelling amongst its boughs and the animals dwelling in the shadows at the ground, the fish jumping and playing joyfully in the sea. So this was the thought that He had in mind. But there was the earth and the earth was without form and void and darkness was upon the face of the deep. But was He discouraged? No, He wasn't, because He had this *thought*. He had in His mind this *vision* of an end product.

So as He came there, and there was just darkness, He thought, and as He thought He *spoke* and He said, "Let there be light" and what? There was light. But in the picture in His mind, there were living creatures; and living creatures need air to be able to breathe to survive. But this earth was void. There was no air there. So was He discouraged? No. He came there and as there was no air, in the picture in His mind there was air, so that thought produced the words in verse 6:

> Let there be a firmament in the midst of the waters.

And there was a firmament.

But in His mind there was land. There was only water there. But He wasn't discouraged. He had a picture in mind. He had a thought. He had an *expected end*. And so there with that expected end in mind, He "said" (verse 9):

> Let the waters under the heaven be gathered together unto one place, and let the dry land appear: and it was so.

But it was pretty ugly though because it was just this vast expanse of water and then there was this vast expanse of land but it was just dirt, ugly brown dirt. It wasn't like what He had in mind. So what did He do? He "said" (verse 11):

> Let the earth bring forth grass, the herb yielding seed, and the fruit tree yielding fruit after his kind, whose seed is in itself, upon the earth: and it was so.

Each day He came to the earth, it was not quite like what He had in mind; but rather than get discouraged, He spake and it was, He commanded and it stood fast. God had expectations. He had an expected end. But to all appearances, it was far from that expected end. But He had a thought in mind and that thought produced the *word* and as that word came forth, "it was". The thought produced the word and *the word itself produced the thing itself.* Psalms 33:6,9 says it exactly here. How were the heavens made:

> By the word of the Lord were the heavens made; and all the host of them by the breath of his mouth... For he spake, and it was done; he commanded, and it stood fast.

The "*word*" did the making. As He said, it was. Isaiah 55:10-11:

> For as the rain cometh down, and the snow from heaven, and returneth not thither, but watereth the earth, and maketh it bring forth and bud, that it may give seed to the

sower, and bread to the eater: So shall my word be that goeth forth out of my mouth: it shall not return unto me void, but it shall accomplish that which I please, and it shall prosper in the thing whereto I sent it.

Thoughts produce words, and God's word produces the thing itself. *The word itself will accomplish that which the thought intended.* So as God came to the earth and it was not according to that expected end, He simply spoke the word and that word made it to be so. Simple isn't it? Is it that simple? *It is that simple.* God's word creates. There's nothing to philosophise about it. There's nothing! It's black and white. In fact, it's all white. It's all light. God's word creates and produces that which is not there; and if we will be like little children, we will believe that. We're not going to ask, "How can that be? I don't know how that is, so I'm not going to believe it." But like a little child – "That's what Daddy says, and that's the way it is". Have we got it? *Have we got it?* Because we have to get this clear. *God said and it was.*

Now I want to ask you a question. What if the earth had said, "No, I don't want you to bring light out of my darkness" and it had resisted God? Do you think that was possible? Well you know that the sun hid its face from Christ as He hung upon the cross on Calvary.

So God came there and He said, "Let there be light." He said, "Let! Do not resist My word from creating that light." And the earth received that word, and the light came. It didn't back up against Him and say, "I don't think so. Look how dark it is. It's so black, so deep, I don't think it's possible." Neither did it say, "I'll do it! I'll bring the light out. I don't need you to do it, I'll do it myself thank you very much." No, it *let*. The earth *let* the light shine out of its darkness.

And that's how it was on each day. God came and said, "Let..." What was that? He *spoke* to His creation: "Let..." And who are *we*? *We are God's creation.* Isn't it the Sabbath day today? And on the Sabbath day we are to remember that we are the creation of God. His word will accomplish the thing but, we must *let it*.

As we have proceeded in our study thus far, we have seen that God had a picture in mind – the thoughts of the creation of this earth. And with that picture in mind, He came to the earth and as He came to the earth, He spoke His thoughts and that word produced the thing that was in His mind. This is how God creates. This is His creation.

So there *we* are, void darkness upon the face of our deep, wretched, miserable, poor, blind and naked, from the sole of the foot unto the head, wounds and bruises and putrefying sores (Revelation 3:17, Isaiah 1:6). And we're just barely clothed in scanty, filthy, dirty rags. It's not quite what God had in mind is it? It's not quite what He had in mind. It's not like what man was in the beginning. But you see, His work was interrupted. Man was to replace the fallen angels. That was what creation was all about. So there, when God made man, God's creation was not actually yet finished because

His complete plan, His complete *thought* was not yet fulfilled – because man was to have a period of probation until he proved that he was fit to take the place of the angels. That was what God's expected end was.

So God had not yet finished His purpose. He was still in the *process of creation*. His expectations were not yet met because Satan came along and he interrupted things. He took man aside and he led him astray. Did God get discouraged? No. God said, "Alright. Now I was working along those particular lines, but I'll just work along this line now to My expected end." But His expected end was exactly the same.

So *redemption* – what is redemption then? Redemption is creation and creation is redemption. Redemption is simply God just working in a slightly different line to the way in which He was originally working. It's all for exactly the same end. And it's the same power because the gospel is the power of God. And how did God create in the beginning? With His power, the power of *His word*. But Adam had fallen, and when he fell he ran and he hid himself. What did God do? He came walking in the garden in the cool of the day, just like He had every other day, *just as though nothing had gone wrong*. Why? Why did God come walking in the garden in the cool of the day and say, "Where are you?" It's because He had in thought the "expected end". That's why.

So here we are today. We are fallen into sin and when He comes to us, generally we go and do the same thing, we go and hide ourselves. But we want to take Jeremiah 29:11 to heart:

> For I know the thoughts that I think toward you, saith the Lord, thoughts of peace, and not of evil, to give you an expected end.

So when He comes to us, He has something else in mind other than what we think He does. Because we think, *That's it, I've done it now, I'm going to cop it.* But no, His thoughts are of peace and of what? The expected end! He sees the end product! And why does He see the end product? Because that thought produces a word and that word cannot help but produce the very thing that it says. So as far as He sees things, the expected end is already met. And that expected end – there it says – is to *give* us an expected end.

He has the thoughts, and thoughts produce words, and He comes to us in our sinful condition with His thoughts all full of this expected end. And so what does He do? Just like He came to the earth and there was darkness upon the face of the deep and He had a picture in His mind of light. And there we are in our sinfulness and God comes to us, but He has a picture in His mind of righteousness, so what does He do? Romans 23:25-26. He does exactly the same thing as He did in creation:

> Whom God hath set forth to be a propitiation through faith in his blood, to *declare* his righteousness for the remission of sins that are past, through the forbearance of God; To declare, I say, at this time his righteousness: that he might be just, and the

justifier of him which believeth in Jesus.

And so God comes to us as He came to the earth and He says, "Righteousness" and there is what? *There is righteousness!* God came to the earth and He said, "Let there be light, and there was light." So when God comes to us and He speaks the word "Righteousness" right there where sin abounded, is righteousness. Do you believe it? Do you believe that it is that simple? Believe it! Please, believe it! He came to the earth and He said, "Let there be light, and there was light." We don't argue with Him about that do we? We don't! But when God comes to me – a sinner – and He says, "Righteousness" we often find ourselves arguing with Him on that one. We say, "Oh no, I don't see how that could be." But friends, God said, and it is so. Believe it! Believe it! Don't argue. The same power of redemption is the same power as in creation. It's that simple! *It is that simple!* But the problem is will you *let* it be so? That is the question. And that with many is the problem! They do not permit God's word to *be*, to *produce*, what it says.

So the question that we want to answer then is: how do I *let* it be? God has declared that where sin was righteousness is, and that word will produce *it* if we will *let it*; and *it* will do that! It will do that both in the sense of Christ's life standing in the place of my life where I have sinned, as we have studied previously, and in the sense of Him living His life through me right now.

So when God declares His righteousness, He is speaking of both the *imputation* and the *impartation* because His word will fulfil itself, and He sees that expected end. He sees the end product before that end product is produced. Therefore you have your justification and you have your sanctification in that one declaration of righteousness, the one working of His word.

So what does it mean then to *let*? Well it's simple – *don't resist it.* Just *allow* it to be so. One definition of the word is actually to '*release as if from confinement*'. God just wants to give us this gift of righteousness and it's there, it's just waiting to come gushing out upon us! Amos 5:24:

> But let judgment run down as waters, and righteousness as a mighty stream.

So it's waiting to come if we will let it, if we will not resist but allow it to be. Then it will come gushing forth into our hearts, it will engulf us and accomplish exactly what it wants to.

But let us ask this question in another way: what does it mean to let? How do I, a sinful human being stand before God as righteous? How do I? And this now is the purpose of our meditation. What is it that God counts as righteousness? What does He consider as being righteousness? And then when I know that, oh, that's how I stand before God because that's what He considers as righteousness.

Do we really know what it is that God counts as righteousness? Do we? We always thought that for us to go and keep the Ten Commandments was righteousness. But haven't we learned that's filthy rags? Filthy garments? We might be surprised. We might be surprised as to what it is that God actually counts as righteousness. But the thing that will surprise you the most is how simple it is. And I want us to see today *by God's grace* how simple it is. And I pray that the Lord will forgive me today if any of my human frailties come into this study and the simplicity of it is lost sight of.

So here we were in sinfulness and God has come and He has spoken the word "Righteousness." And if I will *let* that word have its effect, then I can stand before God just as if I had not sinned. So how do I *let*? What does God count as righteousness? They're both one and the same question. To *let* is to be counted as righteous. What does it mean then to *let?*

We want to spend a bit of time in Romans 4. And here if we will believe that every word of God is pure, don't add to it, don't take away from it, we will be able to read Romans 4 exactly as a little child would, exactly as it reads. Verses 1-2:

> What shall we say then that Abraham our father, as pertaining to the flesh, hath found? For if Abraham were justified by works, he hath whereof to glory; but not before God.

And haven't we found that in our studies? Justification doesn't come through our own working. It comes through the belief in that propitiation, through the working of God in Jesus Christ in me, as me! Verse 3:

> For what saith the scripture? Abraham believed God, and it was counted unto him for righteousness.

Now, friends, in that one verse, if we will come to it with a childlike mind, we have the entirety of the doctrine of righteousness by faith. Abraham believed God, and it was counted unto him for righteousness. Abraham believed God and *what* was counted to him for righteousness? He believed! His belief was counted to him. *It! I.T.!* It – *His believing God* – was counted as *righteousness.* Who counted it as righteousness? God did. God considered his *believing Him* as righteousness. Does that sound too easy? Did God make a mistake? All that Abraham did was believe God! He believed what God had said and God counted that as righteousness. Don't add to it. Don't take away from it. *It's that simple.* What was it that he believed? Come to Genesis 15:4-6 but keep your finger in Romans 4. What did Abraham believe?

> And, behold, the word of the Lord came unto him, saying, This shall not be thine heir; but he that shall come forth out of thine own bowels shall be thine heir. And he brought him forth abroad, and said, Look now toward heaven, and tell the stars, if thou be able to number them: and he said unto him, So shall thy seed be. And he believed in the Lord; and he counted it to him for righteousness.

God said to Abraham, "Look at the stars, tell the number of them and so shall thy seed be." And Abraham believed God. He said, "Amen." And what did God say? He said, "You are right – you are righteous"! Are you willing to believe that is how Abraham became righteous? But does that sound too easy? Come back to Romans 4 and we will follow it through. And in this particular chapter it repeats the same thing a number of times. Reading here verses 4-10:

> Now to him that worketh is the reward not reckoned of grace, but of debt. But to him that worketh not, but believeth on him that justifieth the ungodly, his faith is counted for righteousness. Even as David also describeth the blessedness of the man, unto whom God imputeth righteousness without works, Saying, Blessed are they whose iniquities are forgiven, and whose sins are covered. Blessed is the man to whom the Lord will not impute sin. Cometh this blessedness then upon the circumcision only, or upon the uncircumcision also? for we say that faith was reckoned to Abraham for righteousness. How was it then reckoned? when he was in circumcision, or in uncircumcision? Not in circumcision, but in uncircumcision.

Now note that: when was Abraham's faith counted to him as righteousness? When he was a heathen. *Before* he was circumcised. And we often think, I've got to become a member of the church before I can have righteousness, before I can be considered of God as being righteous. I've got to do this and I've got to do that and all these things I've got to do. But Abraham – he was in *uncircumcision*, he was a heathen and God said, "You are righteous."

How do you feel? Well it doesn't matter how you feel. It doesn't matter whether you feel you're part of the church or not, does it? It doesn't matter whether you are circumcised or not. It was when he was in his uncircumcision that it was then reckoned. And verse 11:

> And he received the sign of circumcision, a seal of the righteousness of the faith which he had yet being uncircumcised: that he might be the father of all them that believe, though they be not circumcised; that righteousness might be imputed unto them also.

It's not of works as it read there. So here in verse 18:

> Who against hope believed in hope, that he might become the father of many nations, according to that which was spoken, So shall thy seed be.

God had said and he believed it. And because he believed it, he hoped for it. He believed – he was convinced – that what God had said would be. Verses 19-22:

> And being not weak in faith, he considered not his own body now dead, when he was about an hundred years old, neither yet the deadness of Sarah's womb: He staggered not at the promise of God through unbelief; but was strong in faith, giving glory to God; And being fully persuaded that, what he had promised, he was able

also to perform. And therefore it was imputed to him for righteousness.

What was? He believed that God would keep His word and that was counted as righteousness. He said, "God what you have said is right" and God said, "You are right." Verses 23-25:

> Now it was not written for his sake alone, that it was imputed to him; But for us also, to whom it shall be imputed, if we believe on him that raised up Jesus our Lord from the dead; Who was delivered for our offences, and was raised again for our justification.

Have we not been studying that in our previous studies? Believing on Him that raised up Jesus our Lord from the dead, this AT-ONE-MENT with God and man? And how if we will believe that then God will count us as righteous? Do you see the simplicity of it? If God says something, if we will but believe what God says, then He will count us as righteous. Because if we believe that His word is true, then God can see the expected end because we then will *let that word* have its place because I believe it. Righteousness comes by believing God. And it doesn't matter what He says, if we will believe Him, then He will count us as righteous. He came to Abraham and He said, "You're going to have seed as numerous as the stars up in the skies." Abraham believed God and that was counted to him for righteousness. Whatever it is, no matter what it is, whatever He says, if we will believe it, God will say, "You are right. *You – are – right.*"

But let's consider this and see if we can simplify this some more. When God says something, is He right? He's right! And if I say that that is so, that what He has said is so, then am I not right as well? If God is right when He says it and I say, "Amen, let it be, so be it" then am I not right? Am I then not as right as He is? Because I am merely assenting to what He has said. And if He is right and I say the same thing that He has said, can He say that I'm wrong? So then when God speaks and we say, "Amen", then we are in a situation where God Himself cannot say that we are wrong. And when we are there, we are in exactly the same place as Abraham was.

God says it, I believe it, I assent to it, and God counts it as righteousness. Can you see how simple it is? It takes a bit of sinking in because it's almost too simple. In Romans 5:1 it says:

> Being justified by faith, we have peace with God through our Lord Jesus Christ.

We have peace with God. Connect that with Amos 3:3:

> Can two walk together, except they be agreed?

If God says a thing and we agree, then we have peace with God. Peace with God is righteousness by faith. And that peace, that righteousness by faith, (there it is again), is through our Lord Jesus Christ as we have been studying. And let's get this clear – our belief is to be the belief of Jesus because we've been learning that I cannot do anything right, I cannot even *believe right*. I must have and keep the *faith of Jesus*, and it is the faith of Jesus that believes God. And we'll examine that in our next and last, final study. But here we are just looking at the simplicity of what God considers as righteousness.

In Romans 4:17 is the key to this understanding:

> (As it is written, I have made thee a father of many nations,) before him whom he believed, even God, who quickeneth the dead, and calleth those things which be not as though they were.

God calls those things that are not as though they are. That's how He considers things. He has an end in mind, and so He relates to it, He calls it as though it is, even though it may not appear. "God counts the things that are not as though they were. He sees the end from the beginning, and beholds the result of His work as though it were now accomplished" (*The Desire of Ages* p.606)

God comes to us and He says such and such. He came to Abraham and He said, "Your seed is going to be as the stars of the sky." But, did it appear that it could be so? He was an hundred years old, and the womb of his wife was dead. It seemed to be not. But God called it as though it was, and Abraham believed God. Abraham believed that God could call those things which be not as though they were; because God would keep His word; because that word was going to produce it. And this is where things start to get quite fascinating.

Do you have sin? Are they like the stars of the sky? Well, if you're able to number them, what does God say? Isaiah 1:18 – He calls that which is not, as though it is:

> Come now, and let us reason together, saith the Lord: though your sins be as scarlet, they shall be as white as snow; though they be red like crimson, they shall be as wool.

That is His word; and what do you say? "Amen!" And the Lord says, "You are righteous." Friends, will you believe this? He can call those things that are not as though they are. So when God comes to us and He says, "There is sin." We say, "It is sin." And then what? They're gone! We believe Him! And He counts us as righteous.

God came to David and He said, "You have sinned and you have done this evil." David said, "I have sinned." Do you know what that is? That is confession. And do you know what confession is? The root idea of confession is to say the same thing – "Amen." So when God says, "That is sin" and for us to confess is for us to say, "Yes it is sin" then what? We are in an agreement. We agree. We believe God and He counts it unto us as righteousness. Sound too simple? 1 John 1:9 spells it out. It couldn't be any more simple:

> If we confess our sins, he is faithful and just to forgive us our sins, and to cleanse us from all unrighteousness.

It's that simple. God says, "There is sin." We say, "Yes Lord. It is sin." We confess that, and He is faithful and just to say, "You are righteous!"

Are we now coming to understand what it means to *let*? If we believe God, then God will count us as righteous. To believe is to *let,* and if we *believe His word,* whatever it is, then we will *let* it work within us. If God says that that is the way it is, even though to all appearances it doesn't appear to be, if we believe Him, if we believe that word that He has spoken; then we will not resist that word. And that word will come gushing in like a flood and that word will do its work, just like it did in the beginning. And do we know how it worked in the beginning? No, we don't know how it worked. How can a word accomplish something? How? I say something, I say, "Piece of paper go over there" and it stays right where it is. I can't understand it, but that's what the word of God says. God *says* and the word accomplishes the thing. So if I receive and believe God's word, then *it will accomplish the thing*; and God counts that which is not as though it is.

So whatever the circumstance is, whatever the promise is, believe it. Believe it! And God will accomplish it, and He will consider it as already done.

So again we see the meaning of the words of Christ – except we become as little children we cannot understand these things, we will not enter into the kingdom of heaven. Just like a little child, Daddy says this is the way it is, and the child says, "Lord, you are right."

Don't argue with it. If you agree with it you're not going to argue with it. So then when we do that, when we are in the place, when we are at that point where, whatever it is that God says to us, we will say, "Lord it is so!" and we will believe it and assent to it; then Jesus can come soon, very soon! Can you see that? Because God says, "Righteousness!" and even though you don't see righteousness, if you believe it, *there is righteousness*. And what's He waiting for? He's waiting for *righteousness*. When He sees His righteous character perfectly reflected in His people, then He will come and take them home.

So He is waiting for us to *believe*, because when we believe, then He can say, "There is righteousness, and I can come and take them home."

Why hasn't Christ come yet? He says, "Behold I come quickly." Revelation 22:12. But what's the problem? Man has said, "My Lord delayeth His coming." God had said, "I come quickly" and man has said, "No, He's not coming quickly." They're telling God that He is a liar, and so they won't let Him come quickly. That's why He hasn't come, because they won't *believe*, because they won't *let* His word. In 1 John 5:10 it says:

> He that believeth not God hath made him a liar.

And If I am going to make God a liar, I make myself to be the real liar. You know what it says – that liars cannot get into heaven. So what we need to be to get into heaven is *believers*. We need to be righteous to get into heaven, but righteousness comes by believing. So if we want to go to heaven, just believe God. Believe what He says, and it will work it, and it will produce it. And that faith will work.

So He says, "Here, in me, is a life that will pass for the judgment." And we say, "Amen!" *And it is so!* He says, "Here, in me, is a faith that will endure the time of trouble." And we say, "Amen!" *And it is so!* He says, "Here, in me, is a character that is fit for eternity." And we say, "Amen!" *And it is so!*

Let all the people say, Amen! And when they do that, we can go home to heaven! May God help us to believe. AMEN.

God's Abounding Grace

Part 6
SANCTIFIED BY FAITH

July 17, 2010

OUR study this morning is titled: *Sanctified by Faith*. To some it may sound a bit of a strange concept. "Sanctified by faith" – it might almost sound a bit paradoxical. We are familiar with the phrase "justified by faith", but *"sanctified* by faith"? A few weeks ago we studied righteousness by faith. How the righteousness of Christ will stand in the place of my unrighteousness. We examined how it was that the second person of the Godhead became we. He became our own selves all over again. And there, as we, He lived our life.

He endured our sorrows, He experienced our struggles, encountered our temptations. He knows our tears, He also has wept. Those griefs that lie too deep to be breathed into any human ear, He knows them because He made them to be His own. And we saw that as He became we, He was tempted in all points like as we are. And as we, He met what we meet: every trial. And as He met those trials He says, "I can of my own self do nothing, but God that dwelleth in me, He does the works." And by God dwelling in Him and working through Him, He lived a perfect life. And that life was our life, because He was we. Therefore, as He was we, God counts that life which He lived as our life, and we stand before God just as if we have not sinned.

How carefully were you listening to those studies that we had? To some it may have sounded that I was preaching the very thing which is echoed from pulpits throughout the Seventh-day Adventist world: that when those plagues are poured out, and hail stones as big as cement bags are raining down from the sky and everyone else is getting a headache, the righteousness of Christ will be like an umbrella, and it will cover for me and I will be singing in the rain and when Jesus comes, He's going to click His fingers and I'm going to be changed in an instant. I ask that God will forgive me if in our studies any one of us got the impression that that is what I am teaching.

There is a time coming when Jesus will step out from between the Father and His people. The Scriptures make it clear that our High Priest will cease His mediation on our behalf. He will cease to intercede for man. He will lay off His priestly robes, He will clothe Himself with the garments of vengeance and will leave the sanctuary. In that fearful time the saints must live in the sight of a holy God without an intercessor, and only those will stand who can stand before that law of God with no condemnation. Those saints themselves must be righteous. They must have reached a point in their experience when, by looking unto Jesus, beholding Him in a mirror, they have been changed into the same image; a point in their life where they have become 'swallowed up' by Jesus. That very life which He lived on their behalf, as themselves and which had stood before God on their behalf – they have grown up into it, it has become merged into their own life. They will have reached that point where they abide so perfectly in Christ and Christ in them, and God works in them to will and to do of His good pleasure and that law is satisfied.

For those who may have been questioning my comments in regard to "believe", I would like this morning to give an answer. In one of our previous studies I stated that God is not waiting for us to keep His Commandments but He is waiting for us to *believe*. I would like to clarify such a phrase as this: "God is waiting for us to believe." If we turn in our Bibles to Luke 18:8, here is a Scripture that puts before our minds such a very thought. And here we read:

> I tell you that he will avenge them speedily. Nevertheless when the Son of man cometh, shall he find faith on the earth?

This Scripture implies that when the Son of man comes He will be looking for something. What will He be looking for? Let's connect this verse with another one. Luke 13:6-9:

> He spake also this parable; A certain man had a fig tree planted in his vineyard; and he came and sought fruit thereon, and found none. Then said he unto the dresser of his vineyard, Behold, these three years I come seeking fruit on this fig tree, and find none: cut it down; why cumbereth it the ground? And he answering said unto him, Lord, let it alone this year also, till I shall dig about it, and dung it: And if it bear fruit, well: and if not, then after that thou shalt cut it down.

We are familiar with this particular parable. And whilst it applies directly to the Jewish nation, we know that as it was with the Jews, so it is with us – that God is seeking *fruit*. He is looking for obedience to His requirements. But in the other Scripture we read that He will be looking for faith.

We have another two Scriptures that we can compare. Deuteronomy 8:3:

> And he humbled thee, and suffered thee to hunger, and fed thee with manna, which thou knewest not, neither did thy fathers know; that he might make thee know that man doth not live by bread only, but by every word that proceedeth out of the mouth of the Lord doth man live.

Man is to live by every word that proceeds out of the mouth of God. But in Hebrews 10:38, how does it say that man to live?

> Now the just shall live by faith: but if any man draw back, my soul shall have no pleasure in him.

We are to live by every word that proceeds out of God's mouth of God, yet we are to live by faith. Are we able to harmonise these appreciations? We are very familiar with these particular Scriptures. Often we have looked at the Scripture that says we are to live by every word of God, and we think that it means I have to go and do this and I have to go and do that. I need to change my diet, I need to change how I dress, I need to try and keep the Ten Commandments and then when I've got all of that right, when I'm doing all of this perfectly, then God will love me and He will take me home to be with Him. Is this how we have read this particular Scripture? And then we find ourselves not quite doing it right! And we think, *Well, sanctification is the work of a lifetime, so I'm not going to get discouraged, I will keep on trying.*

Then we read that we are to live by faith. We believe that God shall supply all my needs whether they be temporal, or financial, or spiritual, whatever they are. And we believe as it says there that God so loved the world that He gave His only begotten Son. And we believe in the atonement of Jesus Christ – that the Word was made flesh and lived a perfect life so I can live one too. And we believe that because Jesus died I have forgiveness of my sins. So if I make a mistake in this program of sanctification I can be forgiven.

Do we have a lifetime in which to be sanctified? Do we have a lifetime to learn to do things right? We often think that we need to go and do this. Are we learning that we *cannot* do it? We think we have to do this, we have to do that, we have to keep the Ten Commandments in order to be saved. Is that what you tell people? Have you told people that they need to be wearing boots to be saved? Or you need to be eating a vegan diet or you won't be saved? There is a day coming, very soon, where there will be those that will cry, "We have prophesied in your name, we cast out devils in your name, in your name we did many wonderful works. And we wore long sleeves and we covered our ankles and we didn't eat meat or drink cows milk, we didn't eat eggs but if we did, they were only from free range chickens." What will Jesus say to them? He will say, "Depart from me you that work iniquity." Has it ever been your thought that you will be saved by keeping the Ten Commandments? That in keeping those Ten Commandments, if you do them strictly and perfectly and all of those reforms, then you will be saved? Have you ever thought that? There comes a simple sentence from the *1895 General Conference Bulletins* by Alonzo T. Jones:

> Man who is trying to seek life in keeping the Ten Commandments and teaching others
> to expect life by keeping the Ten Commandments that is even yet the ministration
> of death. [1]

Before we proceed any further I want to make something very clear. Not in any instance am I doing away with the law of God here. In no instance. If we would go to heaven, we must first have a heaven on earth here. That heavenly society has requirements. There are principles that govern its tranquillity and we must live – be living – in accordance with that society here before we can go there. *Bible Commentary*, Vol.6, p.1073 speaks of God's requirements:

> God requires at this time just what He required of the holy pair in Eden, perfect obedience to His requirements. His law remains the same in all ages. The great standard of righteousness presented in the Old Testament is not lowered in the New. It is not the work of the gospel to weaken the claims of God's holy law, but to bring men up where they can keep its precepts. [2]

That law stands. And if that fruit is not on that tree it will be hewn down. On the point of believing that God will supply all my needs, and that Jesus came and lived a perfect life, and He died for my sins. I would like to ask you if that is *saving faith*? I recently asked some in our midst what they believed faith to be and that was the definition of faith that they gave. I would like to tell you that we do not know what faith is. We do not know what faith is! If you think you know, you know what the Bible says: it says you do not know as you ought to know; there's always more that we can learn. And I'm learning. I don't know it as I ought to know it, but today I want to share with you what it is that I am finding. In the *Review and Herald*, October 18, 1898, the Spirit of Prophecy makes the following statement:

> The knowledge of what the Scripture means when urging upon us the necessity of cultivating faith, is more essential than any other knowledge that can be acquired.

Note there what it says is more essential than any other knowledge.

> We suffer much trouble and grief because of our unbelief, and our ignorance of how to exercise faith. We must break through the clouds of unbelief. We cannot have a healthy Christian experience, we cannot obey the gospel unto salvation, until the science of faith is better understood, and until more faith is exercised. [3]

Would you like to obey the gospel unto salvation? Then we need to understand the *science of faith*. What is the science of faith and how do I exercise faith? But first I would like to tie faith in with salvation. What does faith have to do with salvation? In our aforementioned texts we saw there faith and fruit, faith and works. Let us turn to James 2:20-24:

> But wilt thou know, O vain man, that faith without works is dead? Was not Abraham our father justified by works, when he had offered Isaac his son upon the altar? Seest thou how faith wrought with his works, and by works was faith made perfect? And the scripture was fulfilled which saith, Abraham believed God, and it was imputed unto him for righteousness: and he was called the Friend of God. Ye see then how that by works a man is justified, and not by faith only.

By works a man is justified, not by faith only. Do we understand what these Scriptures are conveying? In order for Abraham to be accounted as being righteous, his faith had to do something: it had to work. And here in verse 18:

> Yea, a man may say, Thou hast faith, and I have works: show me thy faith without thy works, and I will show thee my faith by my works.

The works reveal what kind of faith it is. Abraham's works revealed that he believed God. We are justified by works, not only by faith, because *the works testify to what kind of faith it is.* A good tree will bring forth good fruit and a bad tree bad fruit, and that is not what God is looking for. By the appearance of *genuine fruit*, if there is right works, then God knows that there is *genuine faith.* True faith will work. So when the Son of man cometh what is He looking for? Faith that works! Genuine faith! So you see God is waiting for us to believe and when we believe there will be fruit and by that fruit He will know that we believe. So what then is faith? We know Hebrews 11:1:

> Now faith is the substance of things hoped for, the evidence of things not seen.

Now reading from the *Advent Review and Sabbath Herald*, December 6, 1888, and the comment is made:

> And it is sadly true that, though the Lord has made this perfectly plain in the Scriptures, there are many church-members who do not know what faith is. They may even know what the definition of faith is; but they do not know what the thing is; they do not grasp the idea that is in the definition. [4]

So what then is faith? We know the definition but what is it that it is defining? In the Bible we have an absolutely profound illustration of faith. Matthew 8:5-10. And you will find here one of the most clear definitions of faith:

> And when Jesus was entered into Capernaum, there came unto him a centurion, beseeching him, And saying, Lord, my servant lieth at home sick of the palsy, grievously tormented. And Jesus saith unto him, I will come and heal him. The centurion answered and said, Lord, I am not worthy that thou shouldest come under my roof: but speak the word only, and my servant shall be healed. For I am a man under authority, having soldiers under me: and I say to this man, Go, and he goeth; and to another, Come, and he cometh; and to my servant, Do this, and he doeth it. When Jesus heard it, he marvelled, and said to them that followed, Verily I say unto you, I have not found so great faith, no, not in Israel.

This is what Christ declared to be faith. No. This is what Christ declared to be *great* faith. The centurion was a man under authority. He had at his command troops, soldiers. And under his command he would say, "Do this!" They would do it. The word that he would speak would be accomplished. So he said to Jesus, "Speak the word only." What was it that he believed would heal his servant? "*The word only.*" The Centurion believed that *the word only* would heal his servant. He believed that that word *itself* would accomplish the thing. And that is what Christ called faith! So then what is faith? In the *Adventist Review and Sabbath Herald*, December 27, 1898, Alonzo T. Jones makes a definition of faith here:

> Faith is the expecting the word of God to do what it says, and the depending upon that word to do what it says. [5]

In the beginning the earth was without form and void and darkness was upon the face of the deep. And God came there and He said, "Let there be light" and there was light. And Psalms 33:6,9 says:

> By the word of the Lord were the heavens made; and all the host of them by the breath of his mouth. For he spake, and it was done; he commanded, and it stood fast.

He commanded and it stood fast. The word itself produced the very thing itself. Therefore faith is expecting that the word which God has spoken, *itself* will do the very thing that it says, and the depending upon that word to do exactly what it says. And how does faith come? Faith cometh by hearing and hearing by the Word (Romans 10:17). So the word of God comes to us. Take for example the word of God there in Exodus 20 – the Ten Commandments. And they are probably the best example of them all. These Ten Commandments come to us and normally we think that we have to go and keep them. No. *They will keep themselves.* They themselves will work the fulfilling of themselves within us. It tells us this in Isaiah 55:10-11:

> For as the rain cometh down, and the snow from heaven, and returneth not thither, but watereth the earth, and maketh it bring forth and bud, that it may give seed to the sower, and bread to the eater: So shall my word be that goeth forth out of my mouth: it shall not return unto me void, but it shall accomplish that which I please, and it shall prosper in the thing whereto I sent it.

The word itself will accomplish the thing. If we have genuine faith, then we will expect those Ten Commandments to do exactly as they say. And we will depend upon them to do it. We will come to see the Ten Commandments in a whole new light. We will see them, – instead of commandments: Thou shalt, thou shalt not – as precious promises of the divine nature. We will say, "Lord, though hast said. Amen." And it will be so. Come to Psalms 119:11:

> Thy word have I hid in mine heart, that I might not sin against thee.

Thy word have I hid in my heart that I may keep thy law. So it was that faith wrought with Abraham's works. God had said, "In thy seed shall all nations of the earth shall be blessed" and then he had a son. Then the word of God came to Abraham and said, "Now take thy son, thine only son and offer him for a sacrifice." But God had said from that son would spring a multitude of sons! He had believed that God would give him a son, and at that time he was as good as dead, let alone his wife's womb. Yet

God had given him a son. But that son had not reached the point where he had his own children. And now God says, "Go and sacrifice him!" How could he ever be a father of many nations? But God said that he *would* be a father of many nations, so off Abraham went. He believed that the word of God would accomplish itself no matter what. See how that faith wrought with his works? Genesis 22:5:

> And Abraham said unto his young men, Abide ye here with the ass; and I and the lad will go yonder and worship, and come again to you.

Who would come to them again? He and the lad. Abraham believed that God would raise him up. He believed that God's word was true that he would be a father of many nations and that in Isaac would be the blessing.

Now reading from verses 10-12:

> And Abraham stretched forth his hand, and took the knife to slay his son. And the angel of the Lord called unto him out of heaven, and said, Abraham, Abraham: and he said, Here am I. And he said, Lay not thine hand upon the lad, neither do thou any thing unto him: for now I know that thou fearest God, seeing thou hast not withheld thy son, thine only son from me.

So he was justified by works with faith. Faith wrought with his works and by works his faith was made perfect. So faith is expecting the word of God to do what it says and depending upon it to do what it says. And I depend upon it because I'm coming to realise that I can't do it myself! And in *Christ's Object Lessons*, p.60 we read the following:

> None who receive God's word are exempt from difficulty and trial; but when affliction comes, the true Christian does not become restless, distrustful, or despondent. Though we can not see the definite outcome of affairs, or discern the purpose of God's providences, we are not to cast away our confidence. Remembering the tender mercies of the Lord, we should cast our care upon Him, and with patience wait for His salvation.

> Through conflict the spiritual life is strengthened. Trials well borne will develop steadfastness of character and precious spiritual graces. The perfect fruit of faith, meekness, and love often matures best amid storm clouds and darkness.

> The husbandman waiteth for the precious fruit of the earth, and hath long patience for it, until he receive the early and latter rain." James 5:7. *So the Christian is to wait with patience for the fruition in his life of the word of God.* Often when we pray for the graces of the Spirit, God works to answer our prayers by placing us in circumstances to develop these fruits; but we do not understand His purpose, and wonder, and are dismayed. Yet none can develop these graces except through the process of growth and fruit bearing. *Our part is to receive God's word and to hold it fast, yielding ourselves fully to its control, and its purpose in us will be*

accomplished. [emphasis supplied] [6]

Are we getting some idea of what faith is? Faith that works!

Now we want to go in the remainder of our time into one final thought. Ephesians 4:5:

> One Lord, one faith, one baptism.

There is only one faith. Do you know what faith it is? Reveation 14:12:

> Here is the patience of the saints: here are they that keep the commandments of God, and the faith of Jesus.

The only genuine faith is the faith of Jesus. The faith that is of Jesus, which is in Jesus. If we turn to Acts 26:13, what is it that that faith will accomplish? Here the Apostle is recounting meeting Christ and his experience there:

> At midday, O king, I saw in the way a light from heaven, above the brightness of the sun, shining round about me and them which journeyed with me. And when we were all fallen to the earth, I heard a voice speaking unto me, and saying in the Hebrew tongue, Saul, Saul, why persecutest thou me? it is hard for thee to kick against the pricks. And I said, Who art thou, Lord? And he said, I am Jesus whom thou persecutest. But rise, and stand upon thy feet: for I have appeared unto thee for this purpose, to make thee a minister and a witness both of these things which thou hast seen, and of those things in the which I will appear unto thee; Delivering thee from the people, and from the Gentiles, unto whom now I send thee, To open their eyes, and to turn them from darkness to light, and from the power of Satan unto God, that they may receive forgiveness of sins, and inheritance among them *which are sanctified by faith that is in me.*

That faith which is in Christ – if it is in Him, then it is His. It is the faith of Jesus. Do we want an inheritance among the saints? Then we must be sanctified by the faith of Jesus. And in our last moments, we want to take what we have come to understand of faith and see how Jesus exercised such a faith. Faith that believes that God's word will accomplish the thing itself. Now if we turn to Matthew 4:2-6, here is Christ in the wilderness:

> And when he had fasted forty days and forty nights, he was afterward an hungered. And when the tempter came to him, he said, If thou be the Son of God, command that these stones be made bread. But he answered and said, *It is written*, Man shall not live by bread alone, but by every word that proceedeth out of the mouth of God. Then the devil taketh him up into the holy city, and setteth him on a pinnacle of the temple, And saith unto him, If thou be the Son of God, cast thyself down: for it is written, He shall give his angels charge concerning thee: and in their hands they shall bear thee up, lest at any time thou dash thy foot against a stone.

Was that what was written? No. The Scripture says "to keep thee in all thy ways." Psalm 91:11-12. Reading on in Matthew 4:7-10:

> Jesus said unto him, *It is written again,* Thou shalt not tempt the Lord thy God. Again, the devil taketh him up into an exceeding high mountain, and showeth him all the kingdoms of the world, and the glory of them; And saith unto him, All these things will I give thee, if thou wilt fall down and worship me. Then saith Jesus unto him, Get thee hence, Satan: for it is written, Thou shalt worship the Lord thy God, and him only shalt thou serve.

Christ came and said in Psalm 40:8:

> I delight to do thy will, O my God: yea, thy law is within my heart.

And then in Psalm 119:11:

> Thy word have I hid in mine heart, that I might not sin against thee.

The Desire of Ages, p.120:

> Jesus met Satan with the words of Scripture. "It is written," He said. In every temptation the weapon of His warfare was the word of God. Satan demanded of Christ a miracle as a sign of His divinity. But that which is greater than all miracles, a firm reliance upon a "Thus saith the Lord," was a sign that could not be controverted. So long as Christ held to this position, the tempter could gain no advantage. [7]

God will be seeking to know that we have become partakers of His divine nature. What is the greatest sign that we have done that? By "a firm reliance upon a 'thus saith the Lord.'" "So long as Christ held to this position, the tempter could gain no advantage."

Christ depended upon the *word* to fulfil itself. He trusted that what God had said, He would do it. We want to seal this appreciation. John 1:1-3,14:

> In the beginning was the Word, and the Word was with God, and the Word was God. The same was in the beginning with God. All things were made by him; and without him was not any thing made that was made... And the Word was made flesh, and dwelt among us, (and we beheld his glory, the glory as of the only begotten of the Father,) full of grace and truth.

Christ was the Word. In *The Desire of Ages*, p.20:

> He [CHRIST] was the Word of God, – God's thought made audible. [8]

That Word was made flesh. He was made flesh for the suffering of death. "He was made to be sin for us who knew no sin that we might be made the righteousness of God in Him." 2 Corinthians 5:21. And now as man he bore what we are to bear.

Now I want to read to you from *The Desire of Ages*, p.753 to demonstrate His faith:

Upon Christ as our substitute and surety was laid the iniquity of us all. He was counted a transgressor, that He might redeem us from the condemnation of the law. The guilt of every descendant of Adam was pressing upon His heart. The wrath of God against sin, the terrible manifestation of His displeasure because of iniquity, filled the soul of His Son with consternation. All His life Christ had been publishing to a fallen world the good news of the Father's mercy and pardoning love. Salvation for the chief of sinners was His theme. But now with the terrible weight of guilt He bears, He cannot see the Father's reconciling face. The withdrawal of the divine countenance from the Saviour in this hour of supreme anguish pierced His heart with a sorrow that can never be fully understood by man. So great was this agony that His physical pain was hardly felt.

Satan with his fierce temptations wrung the heart of Jesus. The Saviour could not see through the portals of the tomb. Hope did not present to Him His coming forth from the grave a conqueror, or tell Him of the Father's acceptance of the sacrifice. He feared that sin was so offensive to God that Their separation was to be eternal. Christ felt the anguish which the sinner will feel when mercy shall no longer plead for the guilty race. It was the sense of sin, bringing the Father's wrath upon Him as man's substitute, that made the cup He drank so bitter, and broke the heart of the Son of God. [9]

It was so black, it was so dark, it says there "He could not see through the portals of the tomb." To all appearances, that was it – finished. *The Desire of Ages*, p.756:

Suddenly the gloom lifted from the cross, and in clear, trumpet like tones, that seemed to resound throughout creation, Jesus cried, "It is finished." "Father, into Thy hands I commend My spirit." A light encircled the cross, and the face of the Saviour shone with a glory like the sun. He then bowed His head upon His breast, and died. [10]

What was it that enabled him to come forth with such trust? Psalms 16:8-10:

I have set the Lord always before me: because he is at my right hand, I shall not be moved.Therefore my heart is glad, and my glory rejoiceth: my flesh also shall rest in hope. For thou wilt not leave my soul in hell; neither wilt thou suffer thine Holy One to see corruption.

If you don't get anything else out of this study, I want you to listen carefully and get this. Take it home with you and do not forget it. How was it that Christ was able to give himself up into the hands of the Father? How was it that no matter how dark the malignity of sin was, how terrible the weight of guilt, how impossible it seemed that there was any way out, how did He conquer? *He believed that God would keep His Word.* By faith Christ was victorious! "And this is the victory that overcometh the world, even our faith." 1 John 5:4. Is your faith the faith of Jesus?

Do you meet experiences in your life where the malignity of sin is so black, so dark? Where it seems impossible that you can ever be accepted by God? That the weight of guilt is crushing you into the ground? And it seems as if, No! Not a chance of eternal life. God's forgiveness is not for me. Do you meet those experiences? Remember Jesus upon the cross. Remember the Word Himself who believed that God would keep His Word!

If you have the faith of Jesus you will not be idle; you will not wait to feel that you are made whole. You will believe His word. You will put your will on the side of Christ. You *will* to serve him and in acting upon His word you will receive strength. Of Christ it is written in *The Desire of Ages*, p.73 that:

> He expected much; therefore He attempted much. [11]

God says He will cut short His work in righteousness (Romans 9:28). Did you know that that is His word? Will you believe it, and receive it, and let that word do it? Yes, God is looking for fruit. There are many standards that we need to live up to. We have a lot more reading to do. Right down to the very minutiae of our lives. But friends, if we never hear it, if we don't know what it says, it will never work, and we will never do it.

Then when we start to exercise this faith and that fruit comes forth, when someone comes to you and says why do you do this? And why do you do that? What will your answer be? It won't be just "That is what the word says," but, *"That is what the word does!"* And what an opportunity you will have to preach the gospel.

When we reach the point where our faith and trust in God is so full that it doesn't matter what He says, no matter how impossible it seems, therein will be the righteousness of God revealed. And Christ – He will see His image reflected because we will be living up to every word that proceeds out of His mouth, by and through every word that proceeds out of His mouth. And then He will come, and we can go home. So may the Lord help us to understand the science of faith. AMEN.

<u>Why the Sanctuary Service was Given</u>
<u>to the Israelites</u>

PART 1

December 11, 2010

When shall I reach that happy place and be forever blessed?
When shall I see my Father's face and in His kingdom rest?
When will I sing that song of Moses and of the Lamb?

WE want to spend our hour this morning looking at *when*. When will we? When can we?

I would like to return to history and see what we can glean for our admonition – for our learning – up on whom the ends of the world are come. Now if we turn in our Bibles to Genesis 12 we want to study the experience of Abraham. And this particular subject is one that really thrills me because out of it I get encouragement and at the same time I get warning and real strong admonition. Genesis 12:1-5:

> Now the Lord had said unto Abram, Get thee out of thy country, and from thy kindred, and from thy father's house, unto a land that I will show thee: And I will make of thee a great nation, and I will bless thee, and make thy name great; and thou shalt be a blessing: And I will bless them that bless thee, and curse him that curseth thee: and in thee shall all families of the earth be blessed. So Abram departed, as the Lord had spoken unto him; and Lot went with him: and Abram was seventy and five years old when he departed out of Haran. And Abram took Sarai his wife, and Lot his brother's son, and all their substance that they had gathered, and the souls that they had gotten in Haran; and they went forth to go into the land of Canaan; and into the land of Canaan they came.

And then verse 10:

> And there was a famine in the land: and Abram went down into Egypt to sojourn there; for the famine was grievous in the land.

And then Genesis 13:1-15:

> And Abram went up out of Egypt, he, and his wife, and all that he had, and Lot

with him, into the south. And Abram was very rich in cattle, in silver, and in gold. And he went on his journeys from the south even to Bethel, unto the place where his tent had been at the beginning, between Bethel and Hai; Unto the place of the altar, which he had made there at the first: and there Abram called on the name of the Lord. And Lot also, which went with Abram, had flocks, and herds, and tents. And the land was not able to bear them, that they might dwell together: for their substance was great, so that they could not dwell together. And there was a strife between the herdmen of Abram's cattle and the herdmen of Lot's cattle: and the Canaanite and the Perizzite dwelled then in the land. And Abram said unto Lot, Let there be no strife, I pray thee, between me and thee, and between my herdmen and thy herdmen; for we be brethren. Is not the whole land before thee? separate thyself, I pray thee, from me: if thou wilt take the left hand, then I will go to the right; or if thou depart to the right hand, then I will go to the left. And Lot lifted up his eyes, and beheld all the plain of Jordan, that it was well watered every where, before the Lord destroyed Sodom and Gomorrah, even as the garden of the Lord, like the land of Egypt, as thou comest unto Zoar. Then Lot chose him all the plain of Jordan; and Lot journeyed east: and they separated themselves the one from the other. Abram dwelled in the land of Canaan, and Lot dwelled in the cities of the plain, and pitched his tent toward Sodom. But the men of Sodom were wicked and sinners before the Lord exceedingly. And the Lord said unto Abram, after that Lot was separated from him, Lift up now thine eyes, and look from the place where thou art northward, and southward, and eastward, and westward: For all the land which thou seest, to thee will I give it, and to thy seed for ever.

There is an interesting observation here. God had said, "Get thee out from thy kindred and I will show you a place that will be your inheritance." Abraham left with Lot his kindred. He journeyed down to Canaan and then down into Egypt and back to Canaan with his kindred. And God had said that when he should leave his kindred, He would show him his inheritance. And so here, *after* Lot was separated, God said, "Lift up thine eyes and look from the place out and northward and southward and eastward and westward and all that the land you see I will give it to you and your seed." Verses 16-18:

And I will make thy seed as the dust of the earth: so that if a man can number the dust of the earth, then shall thy seed also be numbered. Arise, walk through the land in the length of it and in the breadth of it; for I will give it unto thee. Then Abram removed his tent, and came and dwelt in the plain of Mamre, which is in Hebron, and built there an altar unto the Lord.

God had promised Abraham an inheritance. He had promised him land. And this is so beautiful here because he was standing upon this inheritance and he had said to Lot, you go that way or that way, I am not worried. If you go that way I will go *that* way, but if you go *that* way I will go that way. Then God came to him and He said, Look to the north, look to the south, look to the west and look to the very direction Lot has gone, I will give it all to you. That will all be your inheritance. Northward, southward, eastward, westward. Walk through the land in the length of it and in the breadth of it for I will give it unto you. As far as the east is – how far does the east go? How far does the west go? This promise of land made to Abraham was the promise of more than just the land of Canaan – it was the length and breadth of the whole entire earth. And we want to follow this through. "The land which thou seest, to thee will I give it *and* to thy seed."

We can pick up this story from Stephen, the martyr. Come to Acts 7:2-5 and here he gives the same story in a condensed version:

> And he said, Men, brethren, and fathers, hearken; The God of glory appeared unto our father Abraham, when he was in Mesopotamia, before he dwelt in Charran, And said unto him, Get thee out of thy country, and from thy kindred, and come into the land which I shall show thee. Then came he out of the land of the Chaldaeans, and dwelt in Charran: and from thence, when his father was dead, he removed him into this land, wherein ye now dwell. And he gave him none inheritance in it, no, not so much as to set his foot on: yet he promised that he would give it to him for a possession, and to his seed after him, when as yet he had no child.

Abraham journeyed into this land and God had promised him this land and *yet* he didn't get to set his foot on his inheritance. It was not a land that Israel is fighting for today. That land of Palestine was not the Promised Land as so much of Christianity thinks today. This can be very clearly collaborated from the Scriptures, but I am just giving you a brief overview here. It would be a land given to him and to his *seed*.

Now come to Galatians 3:16 – his *seed* would receive this land:

> Now to Abraham and his seed were the promises made. He saith not, And to seeds, as of many; but as of one, And to thy seed, which is Christ.

The promise to Abraham was the promise also given to Jesus Christ Himself that this possession would be possessed by Jesus Christ.

We know that Abraham looked for a city whose builder and maker is God. When David was king of an empire which was more wealthy and powerful than any other in the world at that time, he prayed before the Lord and he said, "We are strangers and sojourners as were all our fathers" (1 Chronicles 29:15). Those who were of the faith of Abraham did not look to the land of Palestine as their inheritance, they looked to the inheritance of Jesus Christ. Hebrews 2:5-9 speaks of the inheritance of Jesus Christ:

> For unto the angels hath he not put in subjection the world to come, whereof we speak. But one in a certain place testified, saying, What is man, that thou art mindful of him? or the son of man, that thou visitest him? Thou madest him a little lower than the angels; thou crownedst him with glory and honour, and didst set him over the works of thy hands: Thou hast put all things in subjection under his feet. For in that he put all in subjection under him, he left nothing that is not put under him. But

now we see not yet all things put under him. But we see Jesus, who was made a little lower than the angels for the suffering of death, crowned with glory and honour; that he by the grace of God should taste death for every man.

This inheritance that was given to Christ was the world to come, and this world was given to man and who is *the* man? The man is Jesus Christ. The inheritance of Abraham was the inheritance of a world made new; of the recreation, the reorder, of nature and the resurrection of the dead.

Return back to Galatians 3:29. It would be given to him and his *seed*:

And if ye be Christ's, then are ye Abraham's seed, and heirs according to the promise.

Come again to Acts 7:6-7. Stephen understood what it is that we are studying:

And God spake on this wise, That his seed should sojourn in a strange land; and that they should bring them into bondage, and entreat them evil four hundred years. And the nation to whom they shall be in bondage will I judge, said God: and after that shall they come forth, and serve me in this place.

And then verses 17-20:

But when the time of the promise drew nigh, which God had sworn to Abraham, the people grew and multiplied in Egypt, Till another king arose, which knew not Joseph. The same dealt subtly with our kindred, and evil entreated our fathers, so that they cast out their young children, to the end they might not live. In which time Moses was born, and was exceeding fair, and nourished up in his father's house three months.

The time of the promise drew nigh. The time of the promise made to Abraham that God would renew the earth – that there would be an everlasting inheritance received by people that would live and have an everlasting life. At the end of that 400 years God would retrieve the Israelites from Egypt. And it was His purpose that they would march into *the* Promised Land.

Exodus 15:13-18 – the Song of Moses. When we examine the song of Moses we find that what we are concluding here was very much God's intention.

Here is part of the song that they sang when they had passed through the Red Sea:

Thou in thy mercy hast led forth the people which thou hast redeemed: thou hast guided them in thy strength unto thy holy habitation. The people shall hear, and be afraid: sorrow shall take hold on the inhabitants of Palestina. Then the dukes of Edom shall be amazed; the mighty men of Moab, trembling shall take hold upon them; all the inhabitants of Canaan shall melt away. Fear and dread shall fall upon them; by the greatness of thine arm they shall be as still as a stone; till thy people pass over, O Lord, till the people pass over, which thou hast purchased. *Thou shalt bring them in, and plant them in the mountain of thine inheritance, in the place, O*

Lord, which thou hast made for thee to dwell in, in the Sanctuary, O Lord, which thy hands have established.

Who? The people who passed over the Red Sea. God would bring them in and plant them in the mountain of His inheritance. Of whose inheritance? Of *God's* inheritance – the inheritance of Jesus Christ.

And in which sanctuary? In the earthly made with the hands of mankind? No. In the sanctuary which the Lord pitched and not man. This was the promise that God made to Abraham: that in the fourth generation they would come from their captivity and Abraham would be resurrected from the dead with Isaac, Jacob, Joseph and his brethren and the earth would be made new.

Come to Revelation 15:2-3. We are seeking to understand the relevance for us today. The Israelites had before them a precious opportunity and there is in Revelation 15 a people who will actually sing the same song:

> And I saw as it were a sea of glass mingled with fire: and them that had gotten the victory over the beast, and over his image, and over his mark, and over the number of his name, stand on the sea of glass, having the harps of God. And they sing the song of Moses the servant of God, and the song of the Lamb, saying, Great and marvellous are thy works, Lord God Almighty; just and true are thy ways, thou King of saints.

This is a people who march into an inheritance. This is a people who receive an eternal possession and an eternal possession can only be possessed by a people who have *eternal life*. They sing the same song that Moses sang on the banks of the Red Sea. The parallels are exactly the same.

Why did the Israelites never receive that inheritance? This is for our consideration today. Because if they did not receive it back then, what could stop us from receiving it today? Come to 1 Corinthians 10:11. This is very much the advice we are given:

> Now all these things happened unto them for ensamples: and they are written for our admonition, upon whom the ends of the world are come.

We have often considered that the ends of the world are come upon us and so we are limited as to what we can gain from them. But in God's original plan, the ends of the world *had* come upon them. What admonition is there for us to receive from them? Indeed, verse 12:

> Wherefore let him that thinketh he standeth take heed lest he fall.

Why did they not enter in? Why? What admonition is there for us upon whom the ends of the world have come again? In Hebrews 3:16-19 we find the answer:

> For some, when they had heard, did provoke: howbeit not all that came out of Egypt

by Moses. But with whom was he grieved forty years? was it not with them that had sinned, whose carcases fell in the wilderness? And to whom sware he that they should not enter into his rest, but to them that believed not? So we see that they could not enter in because of unbelief.

This is our admonition today. If they could not enter in because of unbelief then we cannot enter in if we do not believe. Was their experience any different to ours whatsoever? They were baptized. They went through the Red Sea – they were baptized in the sea. They ate of the bread from heaven – Jesus says, "I am that bread that came down from heaven." They drank of that spiritual rock which was Christ – He had said, "I will stand upon the rock and you will smite it."

They drank from that life giving water that flowed from the side of Jesus Christ. That smitten rock of ages that was given for the life of the world. They were baptized and they partook of the ordinances of God. They showed the Lord's death until He comes; and it was going to be a very short time until He would have come. They were – to draw a parallel with our day to day – they were the generation that would not pass till all those things would be fulfilled. But – and that is often called a "big-little" word – *but* they could not enter in because of unbelief.

In Exodus 16 we find something very interesting. Indeed another parallel to our day and perhaps you haven't considered it before. They could not enter in because of a failure and this particular failure was lack of belief. Here in Exodus 16:3-5 we have an identification of what it is that they failed to believe:

> And the children of Israel said unto them, Would to God we had died by the hand of the Lord in the land of Egypt, when we sat by the flesh pots, and when we did eat bread to the full; for ye have brought us forth into this wilderness, to kill this whole assembly with hunger. Then said the Lord unto Moses, Behold, I will rain bread from heaven for you; and the people shall go out and gather a certain rate every day, that I may prove them, whether they will walk in my law, or no. And it shall come to pass, that on the sixth day they shall prepare that which they bring in; and it shall be twice as much as they gather daily.

What is this? This is a *test*. What is it a test of? It is a test of the Sabbath day. Before they could receive their inheritance, they needed to be tested on the Sabbath, because if they could keep the Sabbath, God would know whether they would walk in His laws or not. It is a striking parallel for us today. *The Sabbath was God's test to see if they would believe or not.* And there in Hebrews 3, we read that their hearts were not right toward Him. There were those who went out on the Sabbath and tried to gather manna, but there was none there. Those who disobeyed and did not gather twice as much on the sixth day, went hungry.

So this promise of an inheritance, according to Hebrews 3 and 4, was the promise of rest – of God's rest. We want to look at what kind of rest it is; what kind of rest this inheritance is.

Do you have rest. Do you have peace? Isaiah 57:20, 21:

> But the wicked are like the troubled sea, when it cannot rest, whose waters cast up mire and dirt. There is no peace, saith my God, to the wicked.

So if you want to enter into the rest of God, what must you be without? *Wickedness.* Because there is no peace to the wicked. The promise of God was the promise of *peace.* And peace cometh by what? What are the effects of righteousness? Peace, rest, quietude (Isaiah 32:17). The promise of God was the promise of *righteousness.* That land in Abraham's day could not be possessed because the Amorites had not yet filled their cup of iniquity. It was a land that in his time that still had iniquitous people, so the earth had to fill up their cup of iniquity; their probation had to close and *then* it could be made new. An eternal inheritance can only be possessed by those who have eternal life. And only the righteous will have eternal life. So this promise of rest by believing was a promise of *righteousness by faith.*

And Hebrews 11:7, speaking of Noah, of this inheritance that God had promised to those that were of the faith of Abraham, to those that were of the seed of Jesus Christ:

> By faith Noah, being warned of God of things not seen as yet, moved with fear, prepared an ark to the saving of his house; by the which he condemned the world, and became heir [OF AN INHERITANCE] of the righteousness which is by faith.

This is the promise of God's rest, the promise of righteousness.

Romans 3:22 says:

> Even the righteousness of God which is by faith of Jesus Christ unto all and upon all them that believe.

The Sabbath was a test to see whether they could receive this righteousness or not; to see whether they could have this rest.

Now come to Hebrews 4:1-11, and we want to look at this rest and what the Sabbath has to do with the promised rest, the promised inheritance:

> Let us therefore fear, lest, a promise being left us of entering into his rest, any of you should seem to come short of it. For unto us was the gospel preached, as well as unto them: but the word preached did not profit them, not being mixed with faith in them that heard it. For we which have believed do enter into rest, as he said, As I have sworn in my wrath, if they shall enter into my rest: although the works were finished from the foundation of the world. For he spake in a certain place of the seventh day on this wise, And God did rest the seventh day from all his works. And in this place again, If they shall enter into my rest. Seeing therefore it remaineth that some

must enter therein, and they to whom it was first preached entered not in because of unbelief: Again, he limiteth a certain day, saying in David, To day, after so long a time; as it is said, To day if ye will hear his voice, harden not your hearts. For if Jesus had given them rest, then would he not afterward have spoken of another day. There remaineth therefore a rest to the people of God. For he that is entered into his rest, he also hath ceased from his own works, as God did from his. Let us labour therefore to enter into that rest, lest any man fall after the same example of unbelief.

The Sabbath day and righteousness by faith – how interconnected are they? Many Christians today are very confused and very slack in regard to the Sabbath. And the very reason for it is because of a false understanding of righteousness by faith. They say, "Oh, righteousness comes by faith. It's like an umbrella and I can get away with whatever I want." That is what is being taught in the churches today. They say, "I have nothing to do, all I have to do, my only part is to just believe and then that righteousness will be mine." And so they go on in their own lives thinking they have this insurance, this cover, and it doesn't matter what they do.

It is interesting to perceive they are very careful *not* to live up to the Christian standards and they're very careful *not* to not take up the principles of a reformed life. They are very careful *not* do this and *not* to do that that because they say, "That is works and we have nothing to do with works - we are saved by faith not by works lest any man should boast." But righteousness by faith is *right-doing* by faith. Genuine faith will *work*. It will produce a harvest that is pleasing to God, a harvest of fruit. Yes, the faith of Jesus, by believing in His blood which cleanses us from sin will justify us, but the *life* is in the blood. It is the life of Christ that saves us as the Scriptures say (Romans 5:10), not just His death as that only reconciles us to God. But the life, the sanctifying influence of Jesus' life, is righteousness by faith. The two are one. You cannot say, "I am justified," without being a partaker of the process of sanctification. And you cannot be sanctified unless you have been justified. So for these people to say that they have an umbrella – OK, but what happens when Christ steps out from the sanctuary? Your umbrella is not going to hold the weight of a seventy pound chunk of ice. In fact, there is no longer any umbrella, because Christ has ceased His intercession on your behalf. But as much as this faith of Christ will work in us the right-doing of God, there is a work we have to do, and this is where many people get confused. People think, *I have the Ten Commandments – I have to go and do it*. You do, you have to, it is His standard. But you cannot do it in your own strength, that is the problem. People take the Ten Commandments and the principles of a reformed life and say, "Look! I've done that and that and I'm fine," and they become Pharisees. We fail to understand what our labour is. We have a work of labour and yes we are to even do that work on the Sabbath day. What is it? Hebrews 4:10-11:

For he that is entered into his rest, he also hath ceased from his own works, as God did from his. Let us labour therefore to enter into that rest, lest any man fall after the same example of unbelief.

What is our labour? Our labour is to cease from our *own* works. We are to labour to stop doing our own thing.

Isaiah 58:13-14, let's turn there. God ceased from doing His labour on the Sabbath so it is we are to enter into *that* rest:

> If thou turn away thy foot from the Sabbath, from doing thy pleasure on my holy day; and call the Sabbath a delight, the holy of the Lord, honourable; and shalt honour him, not doing *thine own* ways, nor finding *thine own* pleasure, nor speaking *thine own* words: Then shalt thou delight thyself in the Lord; and I will cause thee to ride upon the high places of the earth, and feed thee with the heritage of Jacob thy father: for the mouth of the Lord hath spoken it.

"The heritage of Jacob thy father": what is that? That is the inheritance of *righteousness*. Our labour, our work, is to cease from our own pleasure, to cease from doing our own ways or speaking our own words.

I am going to ask you a very simple question: Have you ever found it very laborious to keep your mouth shut when you know you shouldn't speak? That is labour. It is laborious for us to not do our own thing – extremely laborious! In fact it is one of the hardest things you will do. Ellen White writes that the "I" is a hard personality to kill, nevertheless, die it must (*Manuscript Releases*, Vol.21, p.368). Then she says that we can put it under but given the least opportunity up it pops again. This is our labour and our rest is found in not doing our own works, not seeking to do our own thing.

The Israelites failed to understand this principle. They were tested on the Sabbath and it was found that they couldn't keep the Sabbath. They should have entered in their generation into the earth made new. And it is interesting to note that the Adventist pioneers of 1888 should have entered in as well. Within a few years they should have been in the kingdom of God if they received the message of righteousness by faith. But they did not enter in. Why not? Because of unbelief. Have you entered in yet? We haven't. Why not? Because of unbelief. It is interesting that they came up to the borders of the Promised Land and they wouldn't believe so God led them the long way around. Have you ever been led the long way around in your life because of unbelief? It was Moses that led them but it was according to their lack of belief. God had to meet them where they were at. We are now 120 years plus since 1888. We have wandered through the wilderness of sin three times longer than the ancient Israelites. In our own life are we like a troubled sea? Are we gaining this inheritance of peace and rest?

Come to Galatians 3:19. What is it that destroys your peace much of the time? And I pray that you are able to follow me here and through what we are studying:

> Wherefore then serveth the law? It was *added because of transgressions*, till the

seed should come to whom the promise was made; and it was ordained by angels in the hand of a mediator.

The Israelite came to Mount Sinai and there from the mount thundered the condemnatory tones of the law. Why? Well, the law was *"added."* God had no initial intention to speak that law to them. It was added because of transgressions. What was the transgression? Let's read this here in Exodus 19:3-9:

> And Moses went up unto God, and the Lord called unto him out of the mountain, saying, Thus shalt thou say to the house of Jacob, and tell the children of Israel; Ye have seen what I did unto the Egyptians, and how I bare you on eagles' wings, and brought you unto myself. Now therefore, if ye will obey my voice indeed, and keep my covenant, then ye shall be a peculiar treasure unto me above all people: for all the earth is mine: And ye shall be unto me a kingdom of priests, and an holy nation. These are the words which thou shalt speak unto the children of Israel. And Moses came and called for the elders of the people, and laid before their faces all these words which the Lord commanded him. And all the people answered together, and said, *All that the Lord hath spoken we will do.* And Moses returned the words of the people unto the Lord. And the Lord said unto Moses, Lo, I come unto thee in a thick cloud, that the people may hear when I speak with thee, and believe thee for ever. And Moses told the words of the people unto the Lord.

God had made a covenant with the fathers of Israel, a covenant with Abraham that he would receive righteousness; that by faith if, he would believe God, then God would give him righteousness. And here at the foot of Mount Sinai God was seeking to ratify the same covenant. Look at verses 5 and 6 again:

> If ye will obey my voice indeed, and keep my covenant, then ye shall be a peculiar treasure unto me above all people: for all the earth is mine: And ye shall be unto me a kingdom of priests, and an holy nation.

But the law entered. Why? Because of transgression. What was their transgression? Verse 8:

> And all the people answered together, and said, All that the Lord hath spoken we will do.

Big mistake! That was not what they were supposed to say. The rest that God wanted to give them was His rest – that rest from their own works. But instead they said, "I will do it! We will do it!" and so God had to give them a law, a school master, a task master to show them – No, you need to rest from *your* works. Then He gave them a sanctuary – a type of the original, a shadow. And you remember that Moses would have to put a veil over his face when he came to speak with the people. When he spoke to God it was face to face, but the people couldn't handle the glory of God that shone from Moses' face. Over their hearts was a veil of unbelief and because of that unbelief God gave them the sanctuary system, the Levitical system. Through that, He was seeking to teach them that *He* would make sacrifices for them. But instead they got all uppity and thought that *they* could make sacrifices for Him.

God would work in them to will and to do of His good pleasure. He would fulfil His promise of right-doing. They couldn't do it. He was calling them to cease from *their* work.

They made the same mistake that we make today. Why do we not have peace? Why do we not have rest? Because the law was added because of *our* transgressions. We say, "I will do it! I will do it!" Big mistake. But God is wise enough to work with that, and when you make your mistake – Oh, OK, I will try again. And I will read you a quote in a moment.

We in our day take up the principles of a reformed life, we endeavour to live up to the Christian standard, and these are things that we should do. But we are not to depend upon *ourselves* for the performance of these things. We are not to prop ourselves up and think, I'm alright because I'm doing this and I'm doing that and therefore I'm fine. Yes we have to labour, but our labour is to labour to cease from *my own* works; to labour to let God work His will within us and in our lives.

The Israelites did not enter in because of unbelief. God came to them and said, "You can't do it." He taught them that. He brought them into this deadlock situation by the Red Sea where the whole enemies of their past were chasing them down. They couldn't do a thing. *He* delivered them. Do the sins of your life pursue you as the armies of Egypt? They cried unto God and He delivered them. Have you ever tried to untangle yourself from a situation and found all you ever do is make things worse? Then labour not to try and sort it out yourself. Pharaoh and his hosts were washed away in the sea.

They came to the bitter waters of Marah. Is there bitterness in your life? Do you find that right here, at the very brink of eternity, roots of bitterness are springing up in your heart, catching you off guard, destroying your peace? God made the bitter sweet.

The Israelites despaired for their lives as they had no food; they could not provide for themselves. Does your soul crave for something better than this world has to offer? Have you been able to satisfy yourself? They cried unto God and He gave them bread from heaven.

They were perishing for want of the water that is necessary for life. Do you hunger and thirst after righteousness or have you been drinking from the broken cistern of your own righteousness? Jesus stands and He says, "If any man thirst let him come unto Me and drink."

The Israelites passed through all of those educational experiences but they wouldn't believe. They wouldn't believe that *they could not*, and they wouldn't believe that *God could*. And after all that they still perished, then let us fear that we should also come short.

Our prayer needs to be:

"Oh Lord, thou great God and Creator of the Universe, the Mighty One who ruleth over all, I exceedingly tremble and quake before my own heart. Yeah oh Lord, how love I thy law, it is my meditation all the day, but I am so scared that I shall be found seeking to perform Thy will in my own strength. Yeah, Lord, though my imitation may be perfect, my copy exact, yet if it be not thee that buildeth the house, then I know that in that day it shall be burnt as stubble. And I am so afraid that this deceptive heart of mine shall cause me to glory in that which You do in me, that I will take and ascribe the honour of obedience to myself, and that my heart shall become uplifted in vanity. Truly, Lord, it must needs be that I be saved from myself. Yet I glory in Thy wisdom, I glory in Thy perfection and I aspire unto Thy likeness, and Thou has called me to be as Thyself – holy, harmless, undefiled, yet I cannot, except as Thou wilt, and I believe that thou wilt. I believe oh Lord that Thou can, yea and will, work in me to will and to do of Your good pleasure, that I may have the testimony of Enoch, that I may have the inheritance of Abraham, and that I may have the righteousness of Jesus Christ. I believe that the blood of Jesus Christ cleanses me from all sin – that that life which is in the blood will purify my heart and perfect my character – and that that blood, that life, shall become as my very own, that I may receive an inheritance among them which are sanctified by the faith that is in Jesus."

This is to be the prayer of our heart. This is the prayer of one who labours to enter into rest. And such a prayer God will never ever turn away.

In *Selected Messages*, Vol.1 p.337 we have this here:

> We shall often have to bow down to weep at the feet of Jesus, because of our shortcomings and mistakes; but we are not to be discouraged...

Yes. You will find many times self trying to do the works, self trying to glorify in the works, but, and yes, we shall often have to bow down and weep, but we are not to be discouraged.

> ...we are to pray more fervently, believe more fully, and try again with more steadfastness to grow into the likeness of our Lord. As we distrust our own power, we shall trust the power of our Redeemer, and render praise to God, who is the health of our countenance, and our God. [1]

Righteousness by faith – we have a part, but our part is to labour to cease from our works and to try again to believe more fully.

May the Lord help us to see His beautiful doctrine that falls as the dew as more than just words on a page, as not just a theory as is taught by so many of the churches today but it will become and be to us a practical reality. May the Lord bless us to this end. AMEN.

<u>Why the Sanctuary Service was Given to the Israelites</u>

PART 2

December 18, 2010

O<small>UR</small> study this morning is a continuation of what we studied last week. In Hebrews 4:1-2 we find a very brief summary of what we studied:

> Let us therefore fear, lest, a promise being left us of entering into his rest, any of you should seem to come short of it. For unto us was the gospel preached, as well as unto them: but the word preached did not profit them, *not being mixed with faith in them that heard it.*

Here was the song of Moses as the Israelites had just crossed the Red Sea. We saw last week that by connecting Scripture with Scripture there was a very precious privilege offered to the Israelites at that time. Exodus 15:13-18:

> Thou in thy mercy hast led forth the people which thou hast redeemed: thou hast guided them in thy strength unto thy holy habitation. The people shall hear, and be afraid: sorrow shall take hold on the inhabitants of Palestina. Then the dukes of Edom shall be amazed; the mighty men of Moab, trembling shall take hold upon them; all the inhabitants of Canaan shall melt away. Fear and dread shall fall upon them; by the greatness of thine arm they shall be as still as a stone; till thy people pass over, O Lord, till the people pass over, which thou hast purchased. Thou shalt bring them in, and plant them in the mountain of thine inheritance, in the place, O Lord, which thou hast made for thee to dwell in, in the Sanctuary, O Lord, which thy hands have established. The Lord shall reign for ever and ever.

Verse 17 denotes for us very powerfully the privilege and opportunity of Israel. God's promise to Abraham was that in the fourth generation His word, His promise, to Abraham was that he would inherit forever a habitation. God said He would fulfil it in that fourth generation. And through the works that God did in Egypt, His name was proclaimed around the whole earth. And as the Israelites proceeded out from Egypt, it was God's intention to fulfil this song – that the very people that passed over the Red Sea would be planted in the mountain of God's inheritance. And as we saw last week, the promise to Abraham was the promise to his seed, and his seed was Jesus Christ. The inheritance of Jesus Christ was an earth made new. When the Israelites came out of Egypt, they were to walk through the Red Sea into the world made new. "Which thou has made for thee to dwell in, in the Sanctuary, O Lord, which Thy hands have established."

We saw last week the parallels of them in their experience and us in our experience today; that the Israelites were even tested on the Sabbath question and if they were able to keep the Sabbath then God knew they would be fit for a holy and eternal habitation. But, as we saw, they could not enter in because of unbelief. They came to mount Sinai and there God sought to ratify the Abrahamic covenant that He would work and walk in him, that God would supply His righteousness; but instead they said, "All that the Lord has said, we will do it." Big mistake. "*We* will do it," was what they said.

Come to Matthew 7:22-23. Where was their error? These things are written for our admonition and we want to be admonished today:

> Many will say to me in that day, Lord, Lord, have we not prophesied in thy name? and in thy name have cast out devils? and in thy name done many wonderful works And then will I profess unto them, I never knew you: depart from me, ye that work iniquity.

But they worked wonderful works! In His name they did this and in His name they did that! These wonderful works! Yet He says, "Depart from me, ye that work iniquity." What was the problem? The problem was *we*. We have done it. We will do it. *That* was the problem.

God had been trying to teach the Israelites the same thing He taught Abraham. He came to Him and He said, "You are going to have a son." But how could they have a son – his wife was barren? And they were getting very old. How could he ever have a son? How could God's word ever be fulfilled? *We have to do something*, were their thoughts and Abraham's wife gave him the maidservant. She gave birth to a son and it did not bring joy to the home. Instead it brought bitterness and jealousy. And it is interesting as you follow it through there. God came to Abraham and He said, "You are going to have a son;" but Abraham was like – "I've just had a son!" That was not what God regarded as Abraham's son. When Abraham was asked to take Isaac and slay him, God said, "Take now thy son, thine *only* son." This son that was produced by his own working was discountenanced by God. Abraham thought that he had to do something. He thought his works were needed in order to effect the promise of God. But God would have done it if he had let Him.

So it was with the Israelites. And those at Christ's second coming say, "We have done this and that, and all these wonderful works. *We* have done them."

But at Mount Sinai, as soon as they made that commitment, the law entered. It was added because of their transgression in saying that they would make themselves holy. They failed. And last week we saw what our labour is and that our labour is to labour to cease from our own works. Israel had missed the point. He had taken them through varied experiences in their wanderings to show them their incapability to deliver themselves from sin. He led them into the narrow confine of the Red Sea and shut them up in a dead end. Have you ever been shut up in a dead end? Behind them were the enemies – Pharaoh and his troops. Before them – the Red Sea. They couldn't do a thing to save themselves. Nothing! God delivered them. He opened the Red Sea and they marched through. Then they came to the waters of Meribah and they were really, really thirsty but the water was bitter – God made it sweet. They journeyed on. They ran out of food – God rained bread for them from heaven. They needed water and from a dry, flinty rock in the middle of the desert God poured out the water of life. They could not do a thing to provide themselves with the necessities of life. God was seeking to teach them that they could not provide themselves with the necessities for *eternal life*. He wanted to put them in the mountain of His inheritance, in the place of His sanctuary, but He is as a consuming fire. In order to dwell in that place they needed to have a fitness – a righteousness – in order to dwell in a righteous habitation.

They needed to be a glorious church not having spot or wrinkle or any such thing but that they should be holy and without blemish (Ephesians 5:27). Could they provide that for themselves? Well, they thought they could. "Yes! All that you have said – we will do it!" Time and time again they missed the point. God had tried to show them the futility of trying to trust in themselves but like Abraham they thought they had to do something to save themselves.

The promise to Abraham was that through his line would come Jesus the Saviour of the world. "In thee," God said, "all the nations of the earth shall be blessed." But he didn't have a child and unless he has that child to produce more children – "How can I be saved? How can this Deliverer and Redeemer of my sins ever be born if I don't have a child? I have to do something to save myself." And so he manipulated the circumstances and today, what do we have today? We have in the Middle East – because of Abraham thinking he could effect his own salvation – we have the very thing between the Jews and the Arabs that is precipitating a third world war. Abraham, though, he learned the lesson and Isaac was born; but the Israelites never got it.

They never got Isaiah 64:6. Do we get it today? Much of Christianity today does not get it and much that does get it deals with it in the wrong way:

> But we are all as an unclean thing, and all our righteousnesses [RIGHT-DOINGS] are as filthy rags; and we all do fade as a leaf; and our iniquities, like the wind, have taken us away.

Because that is the fact, Isaiah 54:17 is God's promise. Because our righteousness is as a filthy rag, He says here:

> No weapon that is formed against thee shall prosper; and every tongue that shall rise against thee in judgment thou shalt condemn. This is the heritage of the servants of the Lord, and *their righteousness is of me*, saith the Lord.

Return to Hebrews 3:17-19:

> But with whom was he [GOD] grieved forty years? was it not with them that had sinned, whose carcases fell in the wilderness? And to whom sware he that they should not enter into his rest, but to them that believed not? So we see that they could not enter in because of unbelief.

They could not enter in because of unbelief. They wouldn't believe that they *couldn't*, and they wouldn't believe that God *could*.

Chapter 4:9-11, as they missed out:

> For he that is entered into his rest, he also hath ceased from his own works, as God did from his. Let us labour therefore to enter into that rest, lest any man fall after the same example of unbelief.

Because they didn't enter in back then we have the opportunity today.

We saw last week that this is our work. Our work is not to do our works because self wants to continuously rise up and say, "I'll do it! Pick me! I can do it!" And the old little red caboose story was always drilled into me: I can do it! I can do it! – WRONG! I *can* do all things *in Christ* who strengthens me, but in my own strength – *forget it*! You will only fall flat on your face. To cease from our own works is where true rest is found. Hebrews 4:1-2:

> Let us therefore fear, lest, a promise being left us of entering into his rest, any of you should seem to come short of it. For unto us was the gospel preached, *as well as unto them:* but the word preached did not profit them, not being mixed with faith in them that heard it.

This is our admonishment for today. The gospel was preached to them. Do you believe that? Oh no – weren't they under a different dispensation? That's what much of Christianity thinks today. The Scriptures say the gospel was preached to them.

What is the gospel? Romans 1:16 tells us what the gospel is and this gospel was preached unto them:

> For I am not ashamed of the gospel of Christ: for it is the power of God unto salvation to every one that believeth; to the Jew first, and also to the Greek.

What is the gospel? It is the gospel of Christ, the power of God unto a fitness for that heavenly Canaan, unto *"salvation."* This gospel was preached to the Israelites.

They received bread from heaven, the heavenly manna. And in John 6:32-35 you read there where Christ says:

> Then Jesus said unto them, Verily, verily, I say unto you, Moses gave you not that bread from heaven; but my Father giveth you the true bread from heaven. For the bread of God is he which cometh down from heaven, and giveth life unto the world. Then said they unto him, Lord, evermore give us this bread. And Jesus said unto them, *I am the bread of life:* he that cometh to me shall never hunger; and he that believeth on me shall never thirst.

The Bread from heaven. There in their desperate need of the sustenance of life, Jesus was given.

Then they needed water as they were thirsty. And come to Exodus 17:1-7:

Start at verse 7:

> And he called the name of the place Massah, and Meribah, because of the chiding of the children of Israel, and because they tempted the Lord, saying, Is the Lord among us, or not?

This was their question. We're dying of thirst here – "Is the Lord among us or not?" Now verses 1-6:

> And all the congregation of the children of Israel journeyed from the wilderness of Sin, after their journeys, according to the commandment of the Lord, and pitched in Rephidim: and there was no water for the people to drink. Wherefore the people did chide with Moses, and said, Give us water that we may drink. And Moses said unto them, Why chide ye with me? wherefore do ye tempt the Lord? And the people thirsted there for water; and the people murmured against Moses, and said, Wherefore is this that thou hast brought us up out of Egypt, to kill us and our children and our cattle with thirst? And Moses cried unto the Lord, saying, What shall I do unto this people? they be almost ready to stone me. And the Lord said unto Moses, Go on before the people, and take with thee of the elders of Israel; and thy rod, wherewith thou smotest the river, take in thine hand, and go. Behold, *I will stand before thee there upon the rock in Horeb;* and thou shalt smite the rock, and there shall come water out of it, that the people may drink. And Moses did so in the sight of the elders of Israel.

What happened there? Jesus was smitten. He says, "I will stand upon the rock and thou shalt smite it." There flowed out from the side of Jesus Christ on the cross water and blood. Here was Jesus Christ smitten for the needs of the people – the sustenance of eternal life, of righteousness. They had said, "Is the Lord among us or not?" A flinty rock in the middle of the desert pouring out enough water to feed millions of people and all their cattle and sheep – the Lord was among them. But what kind of a Lord was among them?

We want to come to the writings of Apostle Paul to find something very interesting. We want to see how this gospel of Christ was preached to them. Come to Galatians 1:6-9:

> I marvel that ye are so soon removed from him that called you into the grace of Christ unto another gospel: Which is not another; but there be some that trouble you, and would pervert the gospel of Christ. But though we, or an angel from heaven, preach any other gospel unto you than that which we have preached unto you, let him be accursed. As we said before, so say I now again, If any man preach any other gospel unto you than that ye have received, let him be accursed.

Apostle Paul preached the gospel; but where did he preach the gospel from? From the Bible? From the *Old Testament*. From the writings of the Old Testament he preached the gospel. Do you know what the Berean's did when he preached amongst them? They went home and they searched the Scriptures daily whether those things were so.

What was the gospel of Christ which he preached from the Old Testament? Galatians 3:1-11:

> O foolish Galatians, who hath bewitched you, that ye should not obey the truth, before whose eyes *Jesus Christ hath been evidently set forth, crucified among you?* This only would I learn of you, Received ye the Spirit by the works of the law, or by the hearing of faith? Are ye so foolish? having begun in the Spirit, are ye now made perfect by the flesh? Have ye suffered so many things in vain? if it be yet in vain. He therefore that ministereth to you the Spirit, and worketh miracles among you, doeth he it by the works of the law, or by the hearing of faith? Even as Abraham believed God, and it was accounted to him for righteousness. Know ye therefore that they which are of faith, the same are the children of Abraham. And the scripture, foreseeing that God would justify the heathen through faith, *preached before the gospel unto Abraham*, saying, In thee shall all nations be blessed. So then they which be of faith are blessed with faithful Abraham. For as many as are of the works of the law are under the curse: for it is written, Cursed is every one that continueth not in all things which are written in the book of the law to do them. But that no man is justified by the law in the sight of God, it is evident: for, *The just shall live by faith.*

The apostle got this gospel from the Old Testament, because this gospel was preached to the Israelites in the wilderness. Christ was "evidently set forth, crucified among" them to teach that by the works of the law they couldn't be justified. Only through faith could those who are justified live. The Israelites had it all played out before them but they did not enter in because of unbelief. They were lacking in faith so God threw them out and forgot them. Did He? No, He didn't. He didn't just cast them aside like that. He thought now, OK, I'm going to put you in a school; I'm going to give you an *institution* that you can learn from. So He gave them the earthly sanctuary which was a shadow of that which was in the heavens.

In Exodus 34:29-35 we see this lack of faith very clearly:

> And it came to pass, when Moses came down from mount Sinai with the two tables
> of testimony in Moses' hand, when he came down from the mount, that Moses wist
> not that the skin of his face shone while he talked with him. And when Aaron and all
> the children of Israel saw Moses, behold, the skin of his face shone; and they were
> afraid to come nigh him. And Moses called unto them; and Aaron and all the rulers
> of the congregation returned unto him: and Moses talked with them. And afterward
> all the children of Israel came nigh: and he gave them in commandment all that the
> Lord had spoken with him in mount Sinai. And till Moses had done speaking with
> them, he put a veil on his face. But when Moses went in before the Lord to speak
> with him, he took the veil off, until he came out. And he came out, and spake unto
> the children of Israel that which he was commanded. And the children of Israel saw
> the face of Moses, that the skin of Moses' face shone: and Moses put the veil upon
> his face again, until he went in to speak with him.

Moses talked with God face to face as with a friend, but the people did not have
the faith. There was a veil upon their hearts. The veil that Moses had to put on his face
was for their sake because if he did not put a veil on his face each and every single
one of them would have had to put a veil on their face. Their hearts were veiled by
unbelief. The plain, simple things of God that He tried to teach them all along were not
comprehended; so God had to give them something that they could see in the hope that
they would see the things that were not seen. But did they see them?

Do we see them today in the educations that the Lord grants us? 2 Corinthians
3:13-15:

> And not as Moses, which put a veil over his face, that the children of Israel could not
> stedfastly look to the end of that which is abolished: But their minds were blinded:
> for until this day remaineth the same veil untaken away in the reading of the old
> testament; which veil is done away in Christ. But even unto this day, when Moses is
> read, the veil is upon their heart.

Even though God gave them a sanctuary system, they never got the point. Through
that system they still had the same opportunity of entering into rest, but they didn't.
They were blinded. There was a veil over their minds. They couldn't see the end of that
which was before them. They couldn't grasp the reality of the type. The bread from
heaven was just something they could eat and they took it for granted it was going to
be there every day. The water from the rock was pretty exciting at first, it satiated their
thirst, but then, ah, so what, it just flowed and flowed and became normal.

The sanctuary system was given as a shadow because of the shadow upon their
own hearts. But a shadow is cast in the form of the shape of the reality. He hadn't given

up on them. He gave them not just the sanctuary system but He actually gave them a whole entire economy. Their whole entire lives were regulated to provide them with constant visual, practical, demonstrations of the unseen.

The sin offering which was slain was to be a constant teacher to them that the wages of sin is death. The blood of the innocent victim poured on the altar was to constantly teach them of the blood of Christ that was shed for the sins of the world. The flesh of some of those sacrifices was eaten like the bread from heaven was eaten. The flesh of Christ was given for the life of the world – like the *impartation* of the righteousness of Christ, our sanctification; as the blood flowed out from the victim – the *imputation* of righteousness, the justification. There was the laver of brass for the washing, the washing away of the past life of our own works and doings – the baptism into the death and resurrection of Jesus. Then there was the table of shewbread in the holy place. There was the seven candlesticks which represented the seven Spirits of God, the completeness of the Holy Spirit who as it says there according to John 16:15 takes of the things of Jesus and shows them unto us. There was the dress of the priests, there was total and complete covering from the neck right to the very feet, a representation of the righteousness of Jesus Christ to cover the shame of our nakedness – our wretched miserable poor blind and naked souls.

Every ordinance of the sanctuary and their whole entire economy was to teach them of these realities which would have been a reality *if* by faith they had laid hold of it. Every single aspect of their life was regulated. Right down to the very minutiae they were constantly surrounded with representations of what God had done and would do for them if they looked *beyond the veil*. God was trying to teach them that He was making sacrifices for *them*; but instead they said, "Yes, *we* can do it." And day by day, year by year they slew their sacrifices thinking *they* were making sacrifices for Him – that He would be happy with them because of their wonderful works. They missed out. Are we missing out today? The reality is that we are no different to them. It is natural for us to say, "All that the Lord has said I will do." It is a normal reaction which God catered for and today He caters for that as well. As proud self-important humans just like you see in little innocent children – "Mummy, Mummy, I'll do it! I'll do it!" We do that with God too. Abraham did it.

God does give us works. There are reformations that need to take place in our lives – changes in our whole entire life need to be made – but those works are to be mingled *with* faith. Faith is to be wrought with our works. Everything that we do is to be bound up in the things of God. The seen is to be indissolubly involved in the unseen.

And in a sermon that I recently heard, this was described in such a practical manner that I want to share it with you this morning;

"God designed that everything around us would send messages to us of himself so where ever we looked would speak of him. Is that not what it is equated to? Someone waking up out of sleep? If we would wake up and say Lord, may I be part of the resurrection? Then you might look out of your window and you would see the sun rising and your mind would think: "But the path of the just is as the shining light, that shineth more and more unto the perfect day" (Proverbs 4:18). As you saw that, you would say Lord, may you please cause me to shine in your character as I live? You might consider you are in your house and it hasn't fallen down and that the wise man built his house on the rock and it didn't fall. Then you might think Lord help me to build my house upon the rock. Then you would hop out of bed and would get dressed and say Lord please cloth me your righteousness, please give me the garment of salvation that I might go out and no one would see my shame. As you dress yourself with these thoughts you would open the door and you would think Lord, help me to open my door when you knock at my heart because you do stand at the door and knock. Then as you open that door you would say Lord I'm opening my heart to you this morning, please come in and you would venture out of your room to have some breakfast and you would take the bread and you would say give me your bread, the bread of life this morning. Give me the sustenance that I may live by every word that proceeds out of your mouth. As you put your bread down, you might put oil on your bread and you would say Lord, give me the oil of your holy spirit. Then you would take the salt to put it on your bread and you would say Lord, let me be the salt of the earth this morning. If we would understand what God is trying to speak to us, we would have the most amazing devotional time in the morning. Our minds would be constantly looking at the physical and thinking of the invisible. That is what the Scripture says, the visible things explain the invisible." Paul Godfrey, Sermon: *The Marriage Supper of the Lamb.*

This is such a practical description of what our lives ought to be that as we go about our daily duties, the requirements of God, we are to see the unseen. Are we doing that? Are we living a reformed life to make God happy with me or am I living it so we can be happy with God? What is our motive? Because I have to? Because I think that if I do this then God will love me and in that day I can say, "Look! Look! I did this and I did that!?" Friends, do it because God loves you. He so loved the world that He gave His only begotten son. Do what God requires of you *because* your faith is so weak that you need to be surrounded with reminders of God's love toward you. All these little things He gives us today, His little requirements, His ordinances of life, are for exactly the same purpose as of old, where we might have constant visual reminders of His salvation. Do it because you are so slow of heart to believe. Do it because you *don't* believe, so do it so that when you experience that His commandments are not grievous, that this is the love of God, you will be encouraged, you will be motivated. Do it because you believe.

When we believe, you will rejoice in every light that comes your way. Every standard of God's kingdom will be appreciated and welcomed, but not because of the thing itself, but because of the unseen in the reality of it. Because of what it represents. God gave the Israelites a beautiful economy and nations around them ever since then have always been picking bits and pieces out of them. The Roman Empire itself was so successful in battle because in the formations of its armies and camps in warfare, it imitated the Israelites in the wilderness.

But if you find it hard to believe, hard for your faith to pierce beyond what you see – and I will tell you that it is *the* hardest thing you will ever do, that you will at times need to make sacrifices as though the very life blood is being taken out – even in that, let your faith grasp the reality.

I want to close with one really powerful thought. Philippians 3:8-11. Here Apostle Paul says:

> Yea doubtless, and I count all things but loss for the excellency of the knowledge of Christ Jesus my Lord: for whom I have suffered the loss of all things, and do count them but dung, that I may win Christ, And be found in him, not having mine own righteousness, which is of the law, but that which is through the faith of Christ, the righteousness which is of God by faith: That I may know him, and the power of his resurrection, and the fellowship of his sufferings, being made conformable unto his death; If by any means I might attain unto the resurrection of the dead.

He counted everything that he saw as dung. But his prayer was that he would know Christ and the power of His resurrection and His sufferings. The fellowship of whose sufferings? The sufferings of Jesus. Do you ever feel that when God requires something of you, do you find it hard, is there a bit of a hurt there? Does it hurt to have to give up your own way? Let faith grasp the unseen. Whose sufferings are they? They are not your sufferings. What you are feeling is the shadow of the feelings of Jesus. Your experiences are the experiences of Jesus Christ. Will you get all caught up in your own little self or will you let your faith lay hold of this reality? Do you ever feel condemnation for sin? The guilt and the woe of a guilty heart? Jesus made our sins to be His sins. So when you are feeling so unworthy and you feel that you cannot come before the throne of God and ask His forgiveness, remember the reality.

The reality was that Christ hung upon the cross, and in the Psalms He says, "I am a worm and no man" (Psalm 22:6). "My sins are more than the hairs of my head" (Psalm 40:12). "My God, my God why has thou forsaken me?" (Psalm 22:1). But then He cried out, "Father into Thy hand do I commend My spirit" (Luke 23:46). How could He say such a thing? How could He say, "Into Thy hands I commend My spirit," when He is feeling so deplorable? In fact, how dare He say a thing? He was naked. He was *naked!* God wouldn't accept Him naked would He?

Let's come to Psalm 69:1-3. I love this Scripture here. When there is mental affliction and you feel like you are drowning in your own sorrows:

> Save me, O God; for the waters are come in unto my soul. I sink in deep mire, where
> there is no standing: I am come into deep waters, where the floods overflow me. I
> am weary of my crying: my throat is dried: mine eyes fail while I wait for my God.

Who is speaking here? Read verse 21:

> They gave me also gall for my meat; and in my thirst they gave me vinegar to drink.

And verse 20:

> Reproach hath broken my heart; and I am full of heaviness: and I looked for some to
> take pity, but there was none; and for comforters, but I found none.

So who is it that is crying out, "Save me O God for the waters are come in unto my
soul?" This is Jesus Christ. Verses 4-5:

> They that hate me without a cause are more than the hairs of mine head: they that
> would destroy me, being mine enemies wrongfully, are mighty: then I restored that
> which I took not away. O God, thou knowest my foolishness; and my sins are not
> hid from thee.

Who is speaking? This is Jesus. There – naked, feeling deplorable, totally sinful.
He says in verse 13:

> But as for me, my prayer is unto thee, O Lord, in an acceptable time: O God, in the
> multitude of thy mercy hear me, in the truth of thy salvation.

When? In an "acceptable time." When He was there at rock bottom and He could
do nothing. That was the "acceptable time." Have you ever met experiences in your life
where you see your past and you see you haven't done anything right and you realise
you can't do anything right unless He helps you – and you really want to? That is where
the promised rest is. Right there. God was trying to teach the Israelites through the
ceremonial system that they couldn't – they couldn't deliver themselves. Everything
had to demonstrate to them that it was only by believing and acting on a belief in Jesus
Christ. Enoch "was not" because God took him. He had the testimony that he pleased
God (Hebrews 11:5). Why did he please God? Psalm 51:16-17:

> For thou desirest not sacrifice; else would I give it: thou delightest not in burnt
> offering. The sacrifices of God are a broken spirit: a broken and a contrite heart, O
> God, thou wilt not despise.

God will not despise a broken and contrite heart. When you wake up as to how
you have missed the point, how you in your own life have done the same thing as the
Israelites, and you have missed the point, you missed the blessing, and you fall all
broken at the foot of the cross, be comforted – God will not despise you. God finds no
joy in the *forms* of service, in the *form* of covering yourself, in the *form* of eating right.
Even in the *form* of keeping His law! That is not where He finds His delight. What He

delights in is the sacrifice of a broken spirit. But whose sacrifice is it that He delights in? Did you note there in verse 17: "the sacrifices of *God* are a broken spirit." The *sacrifices of God* is that which is acceptable. And the Word Jesus Christ which was from the beginning, the Word which was with God and was God, was made in the likeness of your and my sinful flesh. He took our experiences upon Himself and He had to sacrifice to be obedient. This is the sacrifice of God which is acceptable. When you are called to make sacrifice in your life, what is your faith to lay hold of? Your sacrifice? The sacrifice of Christ! Because He was in your experience, He was making the sacrifice. So when you are called to make a sacrifice, don't get caught up in the difficulties of you having to make the sacrifice – it is *His* sacrifice. We know His prayer. He had to pray three times, "Not My will, but Thine be done."

And here in Hebrews 5:7-9. We have read it often, but do we miss it?

> Who in the days of his flesh, when he had offered up prayers and supplications with strong crying and tears unto him that was able to save him from death, and was heard in that he feared; Though he were a Son, yet learned he obedience by the things which he suffered; And being made perfect, he became the author of eternal salvation unto all them that obey him.

He was the what? He was the *Author*. Friends, we are only reading the book; we are only in our experiences looking at the Type; we are only partaking of what He suffered. Will you believe that? Will you believe that even in your self-denial, in your painful sacrifices, that it is a shadow of Jesus' own sufferings? What you are going through, what you must pass through, is like *just reading a book*. It is a shadow of His sufferings. And when you enter into your sufferings, what a joy! because I am not looking at the seen but I am looking at the unseen. Not only am I looking at the unseen but I am *feeling* the unseen. Jesus Christ was a high priest who is touched with the feeling of our infirmities. And when the word of God cuts across your path, praise the Lord for the pain! What a joy it will be when that word cuts across your path. What a joy when the requirements of God lift the standard higher, and they call me to a higher and holier life. More self denial. More life blood to be sucked out. It is not mine, it is His!

I love the quote from *The Desire of Ages*, p.224:

> And of all the gifts that Heaven can bestow upon men, fellowship with Christ in His sufferings is the most weighty trust and the highest honor. [1]

What rest is there by believing? The rest from ceasing from our own works; from ceasing to try and please God by our own efforts. As they say, "Let go and let God." If you are called to make a sacrifice, it is not your sacrifice; it is the sacrifice of Jesus. And just think – if you will let go and let God, you will let Him work in you to will and to do; then there is nothing for you to worry about, absolutely nothing. When you cease from your own works, and it is God that works in you to will and to do, you can honestly say, "I didn't do it." And if you didn't do it then you don't have to worry about what people might think, what they might say or whatever they do in consequence – God will take care of that. Besides, it will be just another opportunity to partake in the fellowship with Christ in the persecution for His right-doings sake. Sounds good doesn't it? Stop dreaming. Wake up to the reality. Let your faith lay hold of something practical. May God help us to do this is my prayer. AMEN.

ANNIHILATING THE CONFUSION OF THE GOSPEL

March 26, 2011

FROM *God's Amazing Grace*, p.259 comes the following:

> When temptations assail you, as they surely will, when care and perplexity surround you, when, distressed and discouraged, you are almost ready to yield to despair, look, O look, to where with the eye of faith you last saw the light; and the darkness that encompasseth you will be dispelled by the bright shining of His glory. [1]

Are we in a world assailed by temptation? Do cares and perplexities surround you? Do you battle with discouragement and distress? And do you sometimes reach the point where you're almost ready to give up? Then look, oh look, to where you last saw the light! In Jeremiah 15:16 he speaks of the discovery of light, precious light, and there as he found this light he declares:

> Thy words were found, and I did eat them; and thy word was unto me the joy and rejoicing of mine heart: for I am called by thy name, O Lord God of hosts.

The words of God come to us in our darkness and those words are light, joy and rejoicing! They give us a comfort, a solace. We find our answers in the word. In Revelation 10:9-10 we read of one who sought the word of God and who found in that word great joy, great delight:

> And I went unto the angel, and said unto him, Give me the little book. And he said unto me, Take it, and eat it up; and it shall make thy belly bitter, but it shall be in thy mouth sweet as honey. And I took the little book out of the angel's hand, and ate it up; and it was in my mouth sweet as honey: and as soon as I had eaten it, my belly was bitter.

We know that this particular Scripture here is a prophecy of the great disappointment of 1844. Yet it is declared that those who will go forth in the last great scene of earth's history will think, "Oh, that I had held my peace!" The word was so precious to them, yet, when it was proclaimed they met with a bitter experience. But as Jeremiah says in chapter 20 verse 9:

> Then I said, I will not make mention of him, nor speak any more in his name...

I love this truth, but oh, it brings so much pain. So many challenges arise from this truth that I wish I could just close my mouth and say nothing. I will not make mention of Him, nor speak any more in His name.

> But his word was in mine heart as a burning fire shut up in my bones, and I was weary with forbearing, and I could not stay.

I couldn't keep my mouth closed. This precious truth, which although it brought so many consequences, is so meaningful to me. It has done so much for me. And If I don't proclaim this truth I will wander for a while, and I need to come back to where I last saw the light. We are so prone to be like stony ground hearers when we receive the word of God. It is meaningful to us but, because of persecution and misunderstandings we let it, and its meaning to us, fizzle away. And in the time of temptation the sun shines and we shrivel up and we die.

This morning I would like to return to where I last saw the light. And perhaps this same point where I last saw the light was likewise where you last saw the light. It is the light of the fourth angel of Revelation and we know that this fourth angel is the message of righteousness by faith.

Yet it is written that those who will go forth and proclaim that message will meet with very distressing experiences. They will be misunderstood. They will be counteracted. And it will be also experienced – I believe – a bit of confusion amongst God's people; where one ministry comes at one truth from one angle and another ministry comes at it from another angel, and even though they're saying the same thing, yet we can still think, Hang on, there's a bit of a contradiction here.

We want Samuel's ear; we want Samuel's heart; we want Samuel's mind which will be open to the word of God no matter which angle it comes from. If it's truth, grab it, make it your own!

This message of righteousness by faith has been to Adventists and Christians a great source of confusion! We are very prone to separate righteousness by faith into two completely different sub-headings. And that is the one sub-heading of *justification* and the other sub-heading of *sanctification*. And because this simple message is divided up into two sections, it leaves the mind with even greater opportunities to become confused. We know that in the world today, Christianity says, "You're justified!" And sanctification is something that God will do when He comes in the clouds of heaven.

Many Seventh-day Adventist's believe this today, that the righteousness which comes by faith is an *umbrella*. And you can live your life however you want to live your life. And then when Christ comes He will click His fingers and He will change you in an instant, in the twinkling of an eye; and heaven, which you once hated you will now love; and the music of heaven which you once hated, suddenly you're going to love that.

But friends, God does not force the will. There is, as others teach the process, that sanctification is the work of a lifetime; a process of learning to love the things of heaven and hate the things of this earth.

When the message of 1888 was given, it was given as *meat in due season* (Matthew 24:45). And I want to read to you now from the *1893 General Conference Bulletins* a little testimony that Alonzo T. Jones shared in 1893. It is in reference to the 1888 Messages. And he says here to the ministers sitting in the audience:

> A sister told me not long ago that before that time four years ago she had just been lamenting her estate and wondering how in the world the time was ever going to come for the Lord to come if He had to wait for His people to get ready to meet him.

Have you ever found yourself in this situation where you look at yourself, and you look at the church, and you think, we're never going to be ready! If sanctification is the work of a lifetime and Jesus is coming in a few short years, what hope have we got?

> For she said the way she had been at it–and she had worked as hard as anybody in this world, she thought–she saw that she was not making progress fast enough to bring the Lord in any kind of reasonable time at all, and she could not make out how the Lord was going to come.

Oh, he's going to come alright! But I'm going to burn because I'm not ready! Aren't these the conclusions that we are forced to come to as we focus on ourselves and not on the word of God? She was really bothered about it. And this is a testimony friends, that I want us to listen to very, very carefully.

> She was bothered about it, but she said when the folks came home from Minneapolis and they said, "Why the Lord's righteousness is a gift; we can have the righteousness of Christ as a gift, and we can have it now." "Oh," said she, "That made me glad; that brought light, for then I could see how the Lord could come pretty soon. When He Himself gives us the garment, the clothing, the character, that fits us for the judgment and for the time of trouble, I could then see how he could come just as soon as He wanted to." "And," said she, "it made me glad, and I have been glad ever since." Brethren, I am glad of it too, all the time. [2]

Light, precious light! But what was that which was gained from that precious message of righteousness by faith? "He himself gives us the garment, the clothing, the character, that fits us for the judgment and for the time of trouble! I could then see how He could come just as soon as He wanted to." This message contained the beautiful parable of Jesus where the king held a marriage feast. And in the ancient days of the Jews, the master of the feast would provide garments for the guests at the feast.

And so it is that we have today an invitation to the marriage supper of the Lamb and God Himself provides the garment. Many people have become confused over the messages of 1888. Many will sway either in one direction or into the other. They will look at it and say, "Well, He gives this garment so then I just have to believe in Jesus and He's going to cover me through all of these experiences."

And then there are others that say, "We have to put the garment on, we have a part to play." And you have this constant *warfare* almost, between those that lift up the doctrine of justification and those who see the doctrine of sanctification to be so important.

People get confused and ask themselves, "Do I have to do something or not?" That is the question. And if I have to do something, what do I have to do? Do I have to make changes in the way that I dress? Or do I need to change the way that I eat? Do I have to eat a vegetarian diet, or not? Others say, "No, you don't need to do any of that!"

Come to this Scripture here in Acts 16:29-31. The Apostle Paul was thrown in prison. There was an earthquake, and the doors of the prison were opened. The jailor was about to kill himself because he thought they would have got away:

> Then he called for a light, and sprang in, and came trembling, and fell down before
> Paul and Silas, And brought them out, and said, Sirs, what must I do to be saved?

And this is the question since September 11, 2001. For the last two weeks since the tsunami in Japan, this has been the question: "What must I do to be saved?" And the Apostle replied:

> Believe on the Lord Jesus Christ, and thou shalt be saved, and thy house.

So Modern Christianity says, "Believe on the Lord Jesus Christ and you will be saved! All you need to do is believe and you will be saved!" To them it's so simple; but for God's people it should be even simpler. And I pray that by God's grace we will find some simplicity in this.

Was the Apostle Paul a minister of God? Were his words true? Then, *what must I do to be saved?* I must believe on the Lord Jesus Christ!

Others kind of say, "Ah hmmm! No. No. We've got to do something as well – there's this work we have to do." And so the problem continues on. They say, "You can't just believe, you have to do something!"

This hope that we have is written in Galatians as being a hope of righteousness – righteousness by faith. What is righteousness? Do you know what righteousness is? Righteousness in the dictionary means: *morally upright, without guilt or sin.* So righteousness simply means: *right-doing.*

So when we speak of righteousness by faith what in reality are we speaking of? *Right-doing* by faith. It's amazing how many Christians today will not stop to actually think about these three little words. I once heard one man say, "If righteousness by faith is so important and it's the central truth, then why do all these people keep talking about food and the way they dress and everything like that?" Well, it's *right-doing by faith*. But I do not blame him for his confusion. Most Christians who make works to be a big thing generally put faith to the side.

This morning I hope and pray that we can come to an understanding of sanctification and justification. There is balanced harmony between these two seemingly confusing subjects. Righteousness by faith is right-doing by faith! What is *doing*? Doing is a *work*, and I'm just taking that word according to the English language. Speaking of justification let's come to Romans 5:15-19:

> But not as the offence, so also is the free gift...

Sound familiar doesn't it to another Scripture that we often use?: "We are saved by grace not of works lest any man should boast, it is the gift God" (Ephesians 2:8).

> For if through the offence of one many be dead, much more the grace of God, and the gift by grace, which is by one man, Jesus Christ, hath abounded unto many. And not as it was by one that sinned, so is the gift: for the judgment was by one to condemnation, but the free gift is of many offences unto justification. For if by one man's offence death reigned by one; much more they which receive abundance of grace and of the gift of righteousness shall reign in life by one, Jesus Christ. Therefore as by the offence of one judgment came upon all men to condemnation; even so by the righteousness of one the free gift came upon all men unto justification of life. For as by one man's disobedience many were made sinners, so by the obedience of one shall many be made righteous.

Justification, the *gift* of justification, *to be made righteous*, is what justification means. And here as we read, this gift of justification is exactly that: it is a gift! *"One man's obedience,"* what did it say there? *"came upon all men,"* so that all those who would be justified have in their stead the obedience of Jesus Christ.

Steps to Christ, p.62 says it here very beautifully. And this is a great source of hope for us, because we look at ourselves, and we try to be obedient, but we fall flat on our face. And even if I can do everything right from today hence forward, what about yesterday? What about the day before?

That law of God doesn't want a partial life of perfection. It demands a whole entire life from the womb right the way through to the end of that life, of perfect conformity to its commandments. And as we look at ourselves, look at our past, what hope do we have? What hope do we have? – we have the hope of justification!

Steps to Christ, p.62:

> Since we are sinful, unholy, we cannot perfectly obey the holy law.

Is that the truth? Have you tried?

> We have no righteousness of our own with which to meet the claims of the law of

God. But Christ has made a way of escape for us. He lived on earth amid trials and temptations such as we have to meet. He lived a sinless life. He died for us, and now He offers to take our sins and give us His righteousness.

The free gift of righteousness, this is justification!

> If you give yourself to Him, and accept Him as your Saviour, then, sinful as your life may have been, for His sake you are accounted righteous. Christ's character stands in place of your character, and you are accepted before God just as if you had not sinned. [3]

Amen, friends. Amen! Because as I look at my past life I am *not* encouraged. And I am told to come boldly before the throne of grace to find help. But how can I come boldly before the throne of God when I'm so decrepit? I stink, as David says in the Psalms, because of my foolishness; I stink and people don't want to come anywhere near me (Psalm 38).

What would the holy God want to do? Would He want to come near me? Well, He did! He sent His only begotten Son to come so close to me that He could meet my experiences and be obedient. So today I can stand before God in total perfection because this exchange has taken place, where Christ has taken upon Himself my sinfulness and He has given me – *given me* – His righteousness.

And much of Christianity today wants to stop right there! And why not? Isn't it beautiful? I've tried and I've tried and I've tried and I've just fallen flat on my face. And so I can come to Jesus and I can stand before God as though I've never sinned. Really, it's so beautiful isn't it? I commit a transgression and I just want to bury my head in the sand, and then the words come: "Look unto Jesus, He has died for your sins."

Oh! Amen! Halleluiah! Praise the Lord! Jesus has died for my sins! And then what happens next? Well I go and I sin again. And I hang my head and then these precious words come to me: "Jesus died for you!" Oh relief, comfort! Then I go and I fall flat on my face again. And again and again this constant hope comes to me: Jesus covers you. His life, His obedience will stand in the place of your short comings.

But friends, if you really appreciate this sacrifice, you will reach the point where when you fall on your face and this word of God comes to you saying, "Look unto Jesus, He has died for your sins," you almost think, *Oh no, not again. I keep putting Him through this pain, this suffering. This innocent Victim! I don't want to keep sinning!*

And this, friends, is where a change of life needs to come in; if you are really not appreciating justification then be most assured that you will never be sanctified. Justification and sanctification will go hand in hand. Those who want to stop at the cross will never make it. *They will never make it!* And it's not true justification if in consequence you do not partake of a change of life.

We sin. Jesus stands in our stead before death. He dies. He suffers the pain of an eternal death, friends. That is the wages of sin. Not just a few minutes of agony and then passing into the grave, but the sense of an eternal damnation.

You hear stories of hell. Well, Jesus has been to hell. And every time we sin we send Him there! We need Jesus! And who is Jesus? What does 'Jesus' mean: "for He shall save His people *in* their sins?" Is that not what the angel said to Mary? But that's what they tell you isn't it? No, no. Read the Bible, it says, *"for He shall save His people FROM their sins!"* If our life is not reforming, we do not know Jesus because Jesus will save me *from* my sins.

We want a justification which is *effective*. We need an *effective* justification. What does that mean? That means we need a justification that is going to take an *effect*, that is actually going to create a *heart reaction*. And will have the effect of leading you to perfect sanctification.

If all I am doing is just running to Jesus for a little band-aid on my scrape, I'm not justified. I do not stand before God as though I have not sinned. I must be engaging *in* sanctification. I need to be engaging in a reformation of my life.

As I have already related, God does not change the character when He comes as much as we might like to think that He does. I grew up thinking that He does, and I was very proud of being a Seventh-day Adventist because my name was written in the church book, and because my name was in the book, I thought my name was in the books of heaven and that I'm going to be there.

Then one day a friend said to me, "Camron, there are no fast cars in heaven. Camron, there's no rock-n-roll in heaven. God doesn't change you in an instant. God does not force the will." And from that day forward my life changed. I went home and I said, "Lord, what must I do to be saved?" And as He said to the rich young ruler, "Sell all that you have, take up your cross and follow me."

I looked at my new television set and DVD player, looked at my Playstation. I put the Bible aside and flicked the switch, turned the television on. But I couldn't silence my conviction.

What we need today is an intelligent religion. Not an emotional religion. Not a band-aid religion. We need a solution! I don't want to keep sinning. I don't want to constantly have to deal with this conviction of sin and this bad conscience. And God doesn't want us to either! So He provided the process of sanctification, a way where we can cease from sinning. In Philippians 2:12 it describes our work:

> Wherefore, my beloved, as ye have always obeyed, not as in my presence only, but now much more in my absence, work out your own salvation with fear and trembling.

Friends, we actually have something to do! We actually have a salvation to work out! And yes, it is with *fear and trembling*, especially now, because this earth does not have long and we do not have a lifetime.

We look at ourselves and say, "I'm so condemned!" As I look at the law of God what hope have I got! And then I look to Jesus and see Him hanging upon the cross dying in my place, in my stead. But friends, when we look there we often don't see that which we need to see. We do not see that which will actually have an *effect* as it needs to have an effect.

The law of God demands perfect righteousness. If I fall short of that, that law says, "That life is mine. You must die!" Who does it demand must die? It demands that I, *the sinner,* must die! And there upon the cross is my Substitute and my Surety dying in my stead.

But have we really made a connection here? That law demands *my* life. What's He (Jesus) doing over there? How can Jesus Christ meet the demands of the law that demands *my* life? That law is perfect, it is righteousness, it is the truth and I am the one that has sinned, and that law demands the life of the *very individual* that has sinned!

A brother once told me why it is that so many Muslims today do not accept the *modern* Christian gospel. It is because they do not see how it makes sense that someone who is completely unrelated to the experience can die in the place of another. That it's like, somebody else can pay the price from their own bank account although it was the original person who had to pay the bill. So many Muslims today reject the atonement as modern Christianity teaches.

There is Jesus dying on my behalf. What's effective about that? Let's read the first part of Hebrews 7:26:

> For such an high priest became us.

Which High Priest is this speaking of here? It is speaking of Jesus Christ. And that High Priest – Jesus Christ – in the simple reading of the word of God says that *He* became *we*.

In Romans 8:5-11 we have an addition. Speaking of this High Priest:

> But God commendeth his love toward us, in that, while we were yet sinners, Christ died for us. Much more then, being now justified by his blood, we shall be saved from wrath through him. For if, when we were enemies, we were reconciled to God by the death of his Son, much more, being reconciled, we shall be saved by his life.

Now stop there for a moment. Reconciliation was the work that was done at the cross. But according to what we have just read, is that which will save us? "If when we were enemies, we were reconciled to God by the death of His son, much more being reconciled we shall be *saved by His LIFE.*"

Now that has the potential to throw spanners in the works of many Christians today. They say, "Oh. No. We're saved by His death!" No, the Bible says that *we are saved by His life* and unfortunately their doctrines don't fit into that picture. Reading on:

> And not only so, but we also joy in God through our Lord Jesus Christ, by whom we have now received the atonement.

His atonement!

AT-ONE-MENT

We can break it up into three sections.

1.   AT – means: *in the position of.*

2.   ONE – means: *perfectly united.*

3.   MENT – means: *in a state of.*

So you put these words together and you have *atonement:* You have man and God in the position of perfect unity at that point, at that time, in a state of total oneness. And therefore we have such an High Priest who became *WE!* One! And therefore as that law of God comes to me and it says, "I demand that life," Jesus Christ can stand in my stead. Why? Because He is "I".

We know that in Jeremiah 3:14 God says:

> Turn, O backsliding children, saith the Lord; for I am married unto you.

What is a marriage? A marriage is an imperfect representation of this union. In *Patriarchs and Prophets*, p.46 it speaks of Adam being given Eve:

> A part of man, bone of his bone, and flesh of his flesh, she was his second self. [4]

"She was his second self," and this is an imperfect representation. The law comes and it says "I demand the life of this sinner." But because Jesus has become as *we*, and that law demands *our* life, He says, "Here I am!"

And isn't that why He says there in Psalms 69: "My sins are not hid from thee?" Why does He say, "My sins are more than the hairs of my head?" Because, friends, He made an atonement. He entered right into our very experience.

No, He did not sin. No guile was found in His mouth. But *we did* sin! Therefore as He became us, as we must die, likewise He must die! But as He died, and as He became we, and therefore we died with Him, what took place next? He rose again. And because He rose again, we rise again! To walk in what do the Scriptures say? "To walk in newness of life" (Romans 6:4). So here now is a new life. But whose life is it? Come to Galatians 2:20 as we read in our Scripture reading:

I am crucified with Christ:

I have to be! If I'm going to believe these truths, I have to be crucified with Christ. There are no "but"s about it!

nevertheless I live; yet not I,

Do you see this beautiful seeming paradox here? I live, but I don't live. So here is a life and that life is my life. But whose life is it? It's Christ's life!

but Christ liveth in me: and the life which I now live in the flesh I live by the faith of the Son of God, who loved me, and gave himself for me.

So now as He has become at one with me; as He partook of my experience, so I will partake of His. Yet the *individualities* are not lost. Jesus Christ is still God and I am still me. And I still have my life and He has His life. But His life is *my* life. Just like previously my life of sin was *His* life and He took it to the grave.

Christ paid the price of sin for us from His account. But what name was on his account? It was my name because it was my account. He made His account to be the very same account. There was no transfer of funds as such. He came right into our very own lives. He became as our own selves, and as we, He paid the price of sin.

Many Christians today have an issue. And I have to confess that for many years I had this issue, where I saw Jesus two thousand years ago, over there, He was way over there! And He was over there resisting sin; He was over there rebuking the devil; He was over there doing everything right. And then I look at me and my life and think, Well, He's overcoming and the Scriptures say He came in sinful flesh but I'm not overcoming!

The problem is that He's too far away! Two thousand years ago is too far away! Over there is too far away! I can't get by with just considering His death on my behalf, as just something I can hail back to every time I need a band-aid for my bump, or a balm for my bruise. It's not enough for me, it's not enough!

Even where we see Jesus as an example – He *is* a perfect example and we *should* follow in His steps – but the Lord needs to "cut short His work in righteousness" (Romans 9:28). We need to learn very quickly! Friends, here is an effective justification! Jesus Christ became we! And there He took upon Him the failings of my life, so that as I stand before God Himself, He sees the perfect obedience of His Son, not my vile acts.

But here is a Jesus that few people are willing to believe in. Here is Jesus who, as *we,* rose again – "I am crucified with Christ nevertheless I live, yet not I." So there am I living a life. But it's *not me* living that life.

Even though in Jesus I am dead, I am buried, I'm still breathing, my heart is still pumping, I still have a life to live! But if I died with Jesus because He took upon Him my sinful life, and in that stead there is a perfect life that stands before God, then I have a perfect life! *I have a perfect life!*

And if that law is met and satisfied, that life has to be not just up until I got baptized, but a perfect life which is my life from the day I was born to the end. And by God's grace there never will be any end.

Jesus Christ became *we*. What we see in the Scriptures two thousand years ago is your life, it's my life. Let's turn and read Hebrews 5:7-9:

> Who in the days of his flesh,

Whose flesh? My flesh, because He became we.

> Who in the days of his flesh, when he had offered up prayers and supplications with strong crying and tears unto him that was able to save him from death, and was heard in that he feared; Though he were a Son, yet learned he obedience by the things which he suffered; And being made perfect, he became the author of eternal salvation unto all them that obey him.

What was His experience? Do you think that after baptism, life's going to be easy because now He "liveth in me?" No! He had to offer up "prayers and supplications with strong crying and tears" unto who? "Unto Him that was able to save Him from death." Now is that not a Saviour in *my* experience? He could not even save Himself. He had to rely upon the Father to save Him.

Are you ever tempted to think that God doesn't hear your prayers? Well, He heard the prayers of Jesus and Jesus is *we*. "Though He were a son yet learned he obedience by the things which He suffered." What is that? Sanctification – being made perfect!

This life of Jesus Christ was a life of sanctification and that life was our life. So if I have accepted this sacrifice of Jesus for my sins that are past, likewise *this* experience will be mine. We've read these Scriptures before. Hebrews 5:1-2:

> For every high priest taken from among men is ordained for men in things pertaining to God, that he may offer both gifts and sacrifices for sins: Who can have compassion on the ignorant, and on them that are out of the way; for that he himself also is compassed with infirmity.

This is our High Priest. He's encompassed with infirmity. Are you encompassed with infirmity? And chapter 4:15:

> For we have not an high priest which cannot be touched with the feeling of our infirmities; but was in all points tempted like as we are, yet without sin.

He is touched with the feelings of our infirmities. And how can He be touched with the feelings of our infirmities? How can He be touched except He's in the same position, in the same experience? And how can He feel the infirmities except He is as I am? Where I am? Verse 16:

> Let us therefore come boldly unto the throne of grace, that we may obtain mercy,
> and find grace to help in time of need.

Have you sinned? This price has been paid. Believe it! But when laying hold of the reality that Jesus stands in your stead, there's a greater reality. Are you tempted? Then Jesus is praying with strong crying and tears unto Him that can save *we* from death.

Friends, we know *Desire of Ages* where Jesus says, "I know your tears, I also have wept" (p.483). He's wept, and He knows your tears! Can you make a connection there? He wept *your* tears! Strong crying and tears unto God and He is heard! And He overcometh! And Satan has nothing in Him! And He was *we*!

Are you reviled? Jesus reviled not again. Do you suffer? Jesus threatened not. And He was *we*. Jesus' life was our life. Your life, my life! When I am tempted to feel that I cannot, in Jesus I *can* and I already *have*.

Will you believe this? Will you believe that when you see the sinfulness of your life that there is for you a perfect life? From this day henceforth you can slot straight into that life and live it? *You can*. But sanctification involves very much a process of learning to believe that. And to believe that means, to *let* it be your life.

Do you ever get provoked? And as that provocation's there you feel your blood start to boil and your flesh wants to rise up and you just want to lash out? Well plead with God that He will give you the Holy Spirit to take of Jesus and show Him to you. To show you Jesus standing before Caiaphas and the Sanhedrin, standing before Pilot and Herod. *The Desire of Ages,* p.710 says:

> Never was criminal treated in so inhuman a manner as was the Son of God. [5]

We've heard stories of what the prisoners of war in the world wars suffered, and even more recent stories that have come through from Iraq and Afghanistan. Never was anyone treated as inhuman as was Jesus. He copped it worse than anybody ever has. And when He was reviled He reviled not. He was as a sheep to the slaughter and He was *we*.

Are you are tempted to get worked up? Let your mind focus on Jesus and when you see Jesus standing firm, meekly bearing it all, friends, believe that He did it as *you!* And that it is a manifestation of what He has already done for you in your life. Take it, if you will, as a prophecy of your own life, that if you follow on to know your Lord you will stand there unmoved. Whatever it is that we read of Jesus Christ in His word, what we see two thousand years ago friends, is a life of Him who became we. We need to see that life. We need the Holy Spirit to take of Jesus and show Him unto us. *The Desire of Ages* p.805 says:

> The impartation of the Spirit is the impartation of the life of Christ. [6]

We are so prone to read "life" as being the life forces, as the electrical currents, not the *living, practical reality*. But the Holy Spirit imparts to us the *living, practical life* of Jesus Christ. We want the outpouring of the latter rain don't we? Then we want His life. And if His life was my life then *The Desire of Ages,* p.668 really starts to make sense:

> If we consent, He will so identify Himself with our thoughts and aims, so blend our hearts and minds into conformity to His will, that when obeying Him we shall be but carrying out our own impulses. [7]

It will be *natural*. It has to be natural, because I have sunk my life in the life of Jesus Christ. And as His heart responded to the will of God, likewise mine will, because His heart was our heart.

"What must I do to be saved?" was the question.

Yes! "Believe on the Lord Jesus Christ and thou shalt be saved." Believe in this precious *AT-ONE-MENT*. We don't need to get confused as so many people do over this word, just *"believe"*. Only *"believe!"* Friends, only believe the *right thing* and it will work righteousness. It is *right-doing by faith*. Believe that the life which Jesus lived was my life. Only as we believe that can we understand that testimony of Minneapolis.

It is a *gift* and God can come as soon as He pleases. We will be ready if we will just *let* Him live out His life within us. We must let His life be our life. Day by day we are to grow up into Jesus; day by day believe more fully that Christ is at-one with me and that I have a perfect life.

There comes a crossroad, a fork in the way, Jesus has already gone that way. "Lord work in me to will and to do of your good pleasure, the right way. Give me, Lord, that perfect life that Jesus has lived on my behalf." It is my life, it is your life. Do you want that life? Do you want to be saved?

The words of John Bunyan in *The Work of Jesus Christ as an Advocate*:

> *He that undertakes to believe sets upon the hardest task that ever was proposed to man;* not because the things imposed upon us are unreasonable or unaccountable, but because the heart of man, the more true anything is, the more it sticks and stumbles thereat; and, says Christ, "Because I tell you the truth, ye believe me not" (John 8:45). Hence *believing is called labouring,* (Hebrews 4:11); and it is the sorest labour at times that any man can take in hand, because assaulted with the greatest oppositions; but believe thou must, be the labour never so hard. [emphasis supplied]

Friends, there was a man who came to Jesus. He wanted his servant to be healed. And he said, "Just speak the word and I'll just take you at that word!" And Jesus said, "According to your faith, may it be unto you."

May it also be unto us is my prayer. AMEN.

FEELING AFTER GOD

November 12, 2011

Never a weakness that He doth not feel,
Never a sickness that He cannot heal;
Moment by moment, in woe or in weal,
Jesus my Savior, abides with me still.

BUT do we abide with him? I would like to commence our study by reading from Exodus 17:1-8. It pays for us to regularly go over the experience of the Israelites because today we are modern Israel and there is no new thing under the sun. The experiences that Israel made are identical to the experiences that God's people in the last days will make. So here in Exodus 17:1-8 we read of a portion of their experience:

> And all the congregation of the children of Israel journeyed from the wilderness of Sin, after their journeys, according to the commandment of the Lord, and pitched in Rephidim: and there was no water for the people to drink. Wherefore the people did chide with Moses, and said, Give us water that we may drink. And Moses said unto them, Why chide ye with me? wherefore do ye tempt the Lord? And the people thirsted there for water; and the people murmured against Moses, and said, Wherefore is this that thou hast brought us up out of Egypt, to kill us and our children and our cattle with thirst? And Moses cried unto the Lord, saying, What shall I do unto this people? they be almost ready to stone me. And the Lord said unto Moses, Go on before the people, and take with thee of the elders of Israel; and thy rod, wherewith thou smotest the river, take in thine hand, and go. Behold, I will stand before thee there upon the rock in Horeb; and thou shalt smite the rock, and there shall come water out of it, that the people may drink. And Moses did so in the sight of the elders of Israel. And he called the name of the place Massah, and Meribah, because of the chiding of the children of Israel, and because they tempted the Lord, saying, Is the Lord among us, or not? Then came Amalek, and fought with Israel in Rephidim.

The Israelites were on a journey and the journey took them to this place called Rephidim and here there was no water and they complained and said, "Is the Lord with us or not?" He had just parted the Red Sea for them. He had just slain some of their enemies for them. He delivered them from Egypt, wiped out Pharaoh, and as soon as something went wrong in their experience, they questioned if God was with them or not. So He solved the problem. Then came Amalek and fought with Israel in Rephidim.

So their experience was going to continue. Although God had provided at that particular point, their experience would continue.

Signs of the Times, September 10, 1896, the Spirit of Prophecy writes here:

> Many today think that when they begin their Christian life they will find freedom from all want and difficulty. But every one who takes up his cross to follow Christ comes to a Rephidim in his experience. Life is not all made up of green pastures and cooling streams. Disappointment overtakes us; privations come; circumstances occur which bring us into difficult places. As we follow in the narrow way, doing our best, as we think, we find that grievous trials come to us. We think that we must have walked by our own wisdom far away from God. Conscience-stricken, we reason, if we had walked with God, we would never have suffered so.

> Perhaps doubt and despondency crowd into our souls, and we say, The Lord has failed us, and we are ill-used. He knows about the strait places through which we are passing. Why does he permit us to suffer thus? He can not love us; if he did he would remove the difficulties from our path. "Is the Lord with us, or not?" [1]

Are you able to relate with this experience? Have you in your experience come to a point where you questioned the same? "Is God with me or not? Does He still love me or not? Is Jesus with me or has He left me?" In John 14:17 we find the problem that humanity has and this problem causes us to constantly run into strait places. And here it is identified:

> Even the Spirit of truth; whom the world cannot receive, because it seeth him not, neither knoweth him: but ye know him; for he dwelleth with you, and shall be in you.

There is the problem that humanity has. Unless it can see with its own eyes, it won't believe. "Is God with us?" Often we may be tempted to ask the question. And in order to find the answer, we might imagine something visual to find this comfort that, "Yes, God is still with me." And perhaps sometimes all we can find is darkness in our experience, and like Jesus on the cross we are tempted to say, "My God, My God why have you forsaken me? Where are you?" But the promise of Jesus is, "Lo, I am with you always even unto the end of the world" (Matthew 28:20). "*I am* with you," He says. "I am with you *always*." Yet despite this precious promise we often find ourselves dealing with powerful senses of loneliness, depression, desolation; feeling that we have been forsaken.

And there in those frames of mind, with this atmosphere of despondency, we meet life's perplexities. And we meet them seemingly alone and therefore we meet them in our own strength. When you go to the shops and buy food you need to eat and you swipe your card and you enter in your pin, and it comes up "Transaction declined: Insufficient funds", how lonely do you feel? Perhaps when you are away from your loved ones, your husband or your wife or your children, for whatever reason – be it employment, sickness, relationship issues, or any other reason – and you speak with them on the phone you say, "Goodbye," and you hang up, how lonely do you feel? When you come home at the end of a hard day's work and there are no children to come running out to welcome you home with their loving arms, how do you feel? When there is no wife or husband to press their lips against your cheeks, to welcome you home with their embrace, how lonely do you feel? And have you ever found yourself crying because of your sense of loneliness? There are many who do. This world is a very, very, lonely place. And then as you meet all the various other challenges that we have in life, and you feel so alone, is it easy to meet those challenges? It is not. It is not easy. We are very, very, *very* quick to forget the promise of Jesus: "I am with you."

Jesus had said to His disciples that on the third day He would be raised and yet they came to the tomb and they believed not. Mary came to the tomb and she spoke with Jesus Himself yet did she believe Him. Did she recognise Him? *The Desire of Ages*, p.794:

> In the garden, Mary had stood weeping, [WHY WAS SHE WEEPING? BECAUSE SHE HAD LOST JESUS AND YET HE WAS RIGHT BESIDE HER] when Jesus was close beside her. Her eyes were so blinded by tears that she did not discern Him. And the hearts of the disciples were so full of grief that they did not believe the angels' message or the words of Christ Himself.

> How many are still doing what these disciples did! How many echo Mary's despairing cry, "They have taken away the Lord, . . . and we know not where they have laid Him"! To how many might the Saviour's words be spoken, "Why weepest thou? whom seekest thou?" He is close beside them, but their tear-blinded eyes do not discern Him. He speaks to them, but they do not understand.

> Oh that the bowed head might be lifted, that the eyes might be opened to behold Him, that the ears might listen to His voice! [2]

– that voice that says, "Lo, I am with you always, even unto that terrible end of the world." And that terrible end of the world is rapidly approaching and today, friends, I want to encourage us for this week that is ahead of us.

We have the other precious promise found there in John 3:16-17:

> For God so loved the world, that he gave his only begotten Son, that whosoever believeth in him should not perish, but have everlasting life. For God sent not his Son into the world to condemn the world; but that the world through him might be saved.

God so loved you that He gave His Son. And here in Romans 8:31-32, if this is the fact, if He so loved us that He gave His Son, then how should we react to life's experiences?

What shall we then say to these things? If God be for us, who can be against us? He that spared not his own Son, but delivered him up for us all, how shall he not with him also freely give us all things?

How many things? "All things." All the money you need to pay your bills. All the energy you need to be able to work to pay your bills. All the companionship you need to keep you company. (All things according to God's will.)

If God be for us so much so that He would give us His Son, then is the Lord with us or not? It answers itself doesn't it? But we need to find in our experience an *assurance*. We need to find in ourselves that true belief that will take God at His word.

Coming before us is an experience. Not just before us, but *presently* we are all making experiences of which we need to endure. We understand the word "endure". It means that there is a painstaking effort required to hang in there and not let go. Painstaking – it is, it is painful. Sometimes it is like you are clinging on so tight to the Lord your hands are frozen stiff and your knuckles are pale white. Things aren't easy and they are not going to get any easier. We need to believe that He is with us always.

Moses believed. Moses made some horrible experiences and here in Hebrews 11:24-25 we read of his endurance and what it was that enabled him to endure:

> By faith Moses, when he was come to years, refused to be called the son of Pharaoh's daughter; Choosing rather to suffer affliction with the people of God, than to enjoy the pleasures of sin for a season.

His experience was the same as ours wasn't it? The world presents itself and it looks so easy, so pleasurable, or we can suffer. Wow! What a choice. Have you ever really sat down and thought about that? We can go and have fun or we can suffer. Isn't that how we think? Is it any wonder that people choose the fun side as humanity only believes what it sees? We can thank the Lord that He has touched our eyes with eye-salve and we can see beyond the suffering – that heaven will be cheap enough. But Moses made the same experience and he would have become the ruler of the greatest empire at the time if he had chosen the world; but he chose rather to suffer affliction with the people of God than to enjoy the pleasures of sin for a season. Verse 26:

> Esteeming the reproach of Christ greater riches than the treasures in Egypt: for he had respect unto the recompense of the reward.

And that's why we are here today because we have respect unto the recompense of reward. We esteem the reproach of Christ as greater riches than all the world can give. Verse 27:

> By faith he forsook Egypt, not fearing the wrath of the king: for he endured, as seeing him who is invisible.

Do you want to endure? Then here is our answer. We must *see*. What does it mean to see? It means to *see* Him who He is invisible.

In *Testimonies*, Vol.5, p.651 the Spirit of Prophecy enlarges Moses experience profoundly. And I want you to listen to it very, very carefully because here is instruction for us:

> Moses had a deep sense of the personal presence of God.

Deep sense. What is a sense? We have five senses don't we? He had a sense of the personal presence of God. So this wasn't just something in his imagination. He sensed it in his being, in his body.

> He was not only looking down through the ages for Christ to be made manifest in the flesh, but he saw Christ in a special manner accompanying the children of Israel in all their travels.

He didn't see Jesus just like Christianity does today, 2000 years ago, dying upon the cross. He saw Christ in a special manner right there with the Israelites in the wilderness.

> God was real to him, ever present in his thoughts. When misunderstood, when called upon to face danger and to bear insult for Christ's sake, he endured without retaliation. Moses believed in God as one whom he needed and who would help him because of his need.

Do you have needs? Well, that's your qualifications. When you come into a strait place and you need help, that is the greatest assurance God will give you the help you need.

> God was to him a present help.

> Much of the faith which we see is merely nominal; the real, trusting, persevering faith is rare. Moses realized in his own experience the promise that God will be a rewarder of those who diligently seek Him. He had respect unto the recompense of the reward. Here is another point in regard to faith which we wish to study: God will reward the man of faith and obedience. If this faith is brought into the life experience, it will enable everyone who fears and loves God to endure trials. Moses was full of confidence in God because he had appropriating faith. [3]

Do you know what appropriating faith is? It means it was a faith that took God's word and applied it to himself. What God provided, what God had promised, Moses didn't see it as for everyone else, he didn't just see it as a blanket blessing, but he took it into his own personal experience.

> He needed help, and he prayed for it, grasped it by faith, and wove into his experience the belief that God cared for him.

Mark those words: "He wove into his experience the belief that God cared for him." We want to build on that this morning.

He believed that God ruled his life in particular. He saw and acknowledged God in every detail of his life and felt that he was under the eye of the All-seeing One, who weighs motives, who tries the heart. He looked to God and trusted in Him for strength to carry him uncorrupted through every form of temptation. He knew that a special work had been assigned to him, and he desired as far as possible to make that work thoroughly successful. But he knew that he could not do this without divine aid, for he had a perverse people to deal with. The presence of God was sufficient to carry him through the most trying situations in which a man could be placed.

The presence of God was sufficient to carry him through. What do we need? We need to know that God is with us always.

Moses did not merely think of God; he saw Him. God was the constant vision before him; he never lost sight of His face. He saw Jesus as his Saviour, and he believed that the Saviour's merits would be imputed to him. This faith was to Moses no guesswork; *it was a reality.* This is the kind of faith we need, faith that will endure the test. [emphasis supplied] [3]

Do you want that experience? Do you want that faith that will enable you to endure the test? Well, how can I have that experience? How can I know that I do have the presence of God? How can I know that God *is* with me? Human beings are very slow to take God at His word. But we are running out of time aren't we? We need to be able to read it as it reads.

The Faith I Live By, p.123 tells us where our evidence is. Because that's what we want, don't we? Something we can lay our eyes upon perhaps?

Our Saviour wants you to keep in close relation to Himself, ...

That's what you want. That's what He wants. Why does He want it?

...that He may make you happy. ...

That's what you want too isn't it? You want to be happy.

...When Christ lets His blessing rest upon us, we should offer thanksgiving and praise to His dear name. But, you say, if I could only know that He is my Saviour! Well, what kind of evidence do you want? Do you want a special feeling or emotion to prove that Christ is yours? Is this more reliable than pure faith in God's promises? Would it not be better to take the blessed promises of God and apply them to yourself, bearing your whole weight upon them? This is faith. [4]

Do you want the evidence? The evidence is right there. You can read it. You can listen to it being read to you. *There* is the evidence that we need, the evidence that we need to take as evidence. I love how the Spirit of Prophecy declares there: "Well, what kind of evidence do you want? Do you want a special feeling or emotion to prove that Christ is yours?" How many people today base their religion on feelings and emotions?

Churches are built on this kind of evidence, but is it more reliable than the word of God? No.

The disciple Thomas is a good illustration. Thomas had the word delivered to him from Christ Himself that He would be raised, and from his friends and fellow disciples that He was! Yet he said, "Unless I can touch and see, unless I can feel and know, then I will never believe. I have to see it with my own eyes and I have to feel it with my own hands." What did Christ say? Who did He pronounce the blessing upon? He said, "Blessed are they that have not seen and yet have believed." The evidence is in the word itself. Is it not? If we want to believe that Jesus is with me always even unto the end of the world, take Him at His word. He came to the earth and He said, "Let there be light." He then said, "Let there be stars in the firmament." Were there stars? Absolutely! And then He says, "I will be with you always." He says, "My word will not return unto Me void but will accomplish the thing whereunto I sent it" (Isaiah 55:11). But there is just one problem and that problem is whether we will believe it or not.

Hebrews gives us a definition of faith as being the substance of things hoped for. You need help – well, what does that help consist of? Faith itself. Faith is the substance of the very thing that we are wanting, that we are needing. God can make all the promises He wants but unless we have that faith that will take Him at His word, then can it fulfil itself? It can't. Because faith, *our* faith, is it's *substance*.

We need to believe, to take Him at His word. We do have a problem though, and that is we often fall into the trap of thinking that I can have this assurance that He is with me if I go and eat that kind of food or if I go and dress like that or I don't go to those kinds of places. Then because I'm doing all of these things, I know He is going to be with me, because that is what He likes; so that is going to guarantee me His companionship. If I do all of these amazing works, then I am going to have this assurance that God is with me. Can you relate with that?

And then what happens when you fail? Suddenly its like, "Oh-oh. Woe. Woe. Woe is me, I failed and now He is gone because I'm not an obedient person any more. I'm so unholy now that the Lord cannot dwell with me any more." But were you any more holy beforehand? You weren't. As human beings, as Christians, we are so prone to base our belief that God is with us, and that God is for us *by our works*; and that when things don't go as well as we had hoped, we are about ready to cast in the lot and say, "Forget it. He's gone. Woe, woe, is me."

Do you know what the Bible declares us to be? Fools. We cannot base our belief in God's presence with us upon our works – we can't. A righteous man is going to fall seven times. So does that mean when he's fallen one of those times that that's it – God has left him? No. Who helps him up? Who extends to him His hand to lift him out of the pit? It is Jesus. Jesus says, "I am with you always even unto the end of the earth."

But oh, no, not me – I'm too bad. Self-pity. Do you know what self-pity is? Self-pity is self-idolatry. And that is what causes us to think that I am too wicked for God to come anywhere near me.

Did you know that those who have grieved the Spirit of God and have driven Him away so He can no longer be with them – they don't feel bad. Do you realise that? Their conscience is seared as with a hot iron. They don't feel so bad that God is not with them. In fact, they couldn't even care less about God! They might care about the circumstances and the consequences, but like Pharaoh, they say, "Who is the Lord that I should obey His voice?" The very fact we feel a sense of sin and that we feel so bad for failing God, is proof that He is with us and hasn't abandoned us. And if we are willing to believe that perhaps He is still here with me, well then we can believe that the only way He can still be with me is because He has provided an atonement and Jesus *has* died for my sins. So we don't need to become easily discouraged. We don't need to become depressed. And do we need to be lonely? Well, the only reason we do is because either we don't believe or, interestingly enough, we try too hard to believe. Yes! – we try *too hard* to believe!

Manuscript Releases, Vol.8, p.221, the angel speaks here:

> The angel said, "Some tried too hard to believe. Faith is so simple. Ye look above it." [5]

True? Faith is so simple we often miss the point and we look above it. So how simple is faith? How simple is that promise and the fulfilment of that promise that the Lord will be with us? Is the Lord with us or not? Well the answer is up to you isn't it?

In Heavenly Places, p.104, speaking of faith:

> Faith is not the ground of our salvation, but it is the great blessing – the eye that sees, the ear that hears, the feet that run, the hand that grasps. It is the means, not the end. [6]

And *Upward Look*, p.72. This faith is the ear that hears, the eye that sees? Here we have an expansion:

> "Faith is the substance of things hoped for, the evidence of things not seen" (Hebrews 11:1). Have we not proved this in the past as we have moved out in faith to produce the things now seen?

Have a think about those words – take them home with you. Every now and then you get a little glimmer of Christ-likeness in your life and you get hope from it. Well that was produced by faith and we can look back on those times and think, Hey, my faith actually has produced something! And if it has, it will continue.

> Faith is not only to look forward to things unseen; it is to be confirmed by looking at past experience, at tangible results, the verification of God's word. . . . Pray, "Lord,

increase my faith." Faith quickens the senses to work diligently to produce results. Faith elevates and ennobles the powers of the soul, enabling it to lay hold upon the unseen. [7]

What are the senses? Eyes, ears, hands, mouth, nose. Faith quickens them – it gives them life. Without faith you are not feeling, you may as well be a dead man walking. Faith gives you *living* senses.

Have a think about these words. That means that faith will actually make things *tangible*. So not only are you having to run on faith in your mind taking God at His word, but that word will react upon your senses. Your perceptions will be quickened. In what manner?

For example, *Child Guidance*, p.52:

> Let the children learn to see in nature an expression of the love and the wisdom of God; let the thought of Him be linked with bird and flower and tree; let all things seen become to them the interpreters of the unseen, and all the events of life be a means of divine teaching. [8]

So when they look at that which is seen, what are they really seeing? They are really seeing the unseen but they are seeing it with their own eyes.

Child Guidance, p.46:

> In the natural world God has placed in the hands of the children of men the key to unlock the treasure house of His word. The unseen is illustrated by the seen; divine wisdom, eternal truth, infinite grace, are understood by the things that God has made.

If you are wondering why you are so slow to catch on to some of God's teachings, it's because you haven't looked in the world around you. The things that we see visually with our eyes will interpret and teach us of the unseen.

It goes on to say:

> Children should be encouraged to search out in nature the objects that illustrate Bible teachings, and to trace in the Bible the similitudes drawn from nature. They should search out, both in nature and in Holy Writ, every object representing Christ, and those also that He employed in illustrating truth. Thus may they learn to see Him in tree and vine, in lily and rose, in sun and star.

Wherever they look, they can see God. Didn't Moses have Him constantly before his face?

> They may learn to hear His voice in the song of birds, in the sighing of the trees, in the rolling thunder, and in the music of the sea. And every object in nature will repeat to them His precious lessons.

Now listen to this:

To those who thus acquaint themselves with Christ, the earth will nevermore be a
lonely and desolate place. It will be their Father's house, filled with the presence of
Him who once dwelt among men. [9]

AMEN! Let this sink in. If we will have that faith which will discern God in the
leaves, in the sun, in the sky, in the things that surround us, and ears that will hear Him
speaking to us, how can we ever be alone? How can we ever fall under this sense of
desolation and loneliness? Things will become tangible. Do you want evidence? Just
look outside! *The Faith I Live By*, p.652 again:

> Moses wove into his experience the belief that God cared for him. He believed that
> God ruled his life in particular. He saw and acknowledged God in every detail of his
> life and felt that he was under the eye of the all-seeing one. [3]

And then, He endured because he saw God, he heard God. In prayer we are often
prone to get on our knees and tell God all our problems and we get up and walk away.
Prayer is the breath of the soul; it doesn't finish when we get up from our knees, that
is the time where I have spoken to God, now I need to get up and go out in nature, go
about my duties, read His word, and now He will talk back to me to tell me the solutions
to all my problems. This faith will colour our every experience. We will believe that
Jesus is with me. We will hear Him, we will see Him and we will never be alone.

Jesus is a *soul mate*. That means He is closer than any earthly companion. He
knows how you feel. He knows where the shoe pinches because He has worn the shoe.
He knows how to comfort you and solve your problems because He has had to meet
them.

In your Bible, seek the Lord. In nature, seek the Lord. The sun in the heavens is
like the Son of Righteousness and rises with healing in His wings. Are you feeling sick,
feeling like you have a tummy bug or something? Look up at the sun. And then that
sun sails through the deep blue sky. And what does blue represent in the sanctuary?
The righteousness of God. And so when you are there feeling self-condemned, look
up! The righteousness of God is covering you! And when things are dark, and you are
sorely tempted and the sun has faded from your life, look up, see the stars – remember
the New Covenant, which is really the old, old covenant that God made with Abraham,
that He Himself will perform the works. When you are out in nature and you hear the
sighing of the trees – I never forget what the margin reading is in reference to Elijah
when he fled to Horeb. There was the mighty earthquake. There was the fire and the
tempest. And there was a still small voice, and in the margin it says: "*As of the wind
in the leaves of the tree.*" Wow! The voice of God is like the wind in the leaves of the
tree. How can you stand under a tree and not hear God's voice talking to you? Have
you ever heard that voice? Have you ever seen Him? We see a lot and we hear a lot but
we haven't always recognised it as God, have we? We need to open our eyes in reality.

Now just in closing I want to end with one final meditation. And we return here to our Scripture reading in Acts 17:26-27. We have seen how faith quickens the senses, now there is a sense that we want to have quickened:

> And God hath made of one blood all nations of men for to dwell on all the face of the earth, and hath determined the times before appointed, and the bounds of their habitation; That they should seek the Lord, if haply they might feel after him, and find him, though he be not far from every one of us.

That they might what? "Haply." Do you know what "haply" means? It doesn't mean cheerfully and joyfully – happily. It means if they *perchance* will. Maybe... Will they? It means perhaps it may be that they will and perhaps it may be that *we* will seek the Lord, feel after Him and find Him. Now this word,and feeling are like the east and the west. But what happens if you put the two together? By faith we can see Him. By faith we can hear Him. Can I feel Him by faith? Well, it says they *will* find Him. How have they sought Him? By feeling after Him. So they will feel Him and find Him. So how – where – can I feel God? To see is one thing, to hear is another, but to touch, handle and sense it in our inner most being, that will be our greatest evidence – that will be that which will help us to endure through to the end.

And here is one of the most beautiful truths and one of the best kept secrets – that we can feel God. But without faith, it is nothing.

So how can I feel God? Let's just read two Scriptures. Hebrews 4:15, and here it speaks of feelings:

> For we have not an high priest which cannot be touched with the feeling of our infirmities; but was in all points tempted like as we are, yet without sin.

We have a High Priest which is touched with the feeling of our infirmities.

And then Hebrews 7:26, first part:

> For such an high priest became us.

Have a think about these two verses and read them exactly as they read. Jesus is touched with the feeling of our infirmities and was tempted in all points like as we are, yet without sin. In order for Jesus to be tempted like I am, He would need to be exactly where I am. Is that not correct? Because if I am tempted, I am tempted right here, right now with whatever the temptation is. In order for Him to be tempted in all points as I am, then He had to be right *here*, right *now*. And in order for Him to actually have within His body a drawing to seek out that temptation, then He had to be *as* I am. So He had to become our own selves and be our own selves in order to be touched with our feelings and tempted as we are.

Touched with our feelings... Now have a think about that. When you are feeling,

He is what? He is touched with the same feelings – so He is feeling what you are feeling. The Scriptures declare that in all our afflictions He is afflicted (Isaiah 63:9) but not only does He feel what we feel – do not the the Scriptures declare that we are only partaking of *His* sufferings? So what we are feeling He has made to be *His* own, so when we are feeling, we are feeling Jesus and all of us which He has taken upon himself, because He "became us".

Sermons and Talks, Vol.1, p.132:

> We have felt Him in the humiliation; we have felt Him in the sacrifice; we have felt Him in the trials; we have felt Him in the test. [10]

Will you read the word of God as it reads? When you are feeling all alone, what does Jesus say? He says, "I have trodden the wine-press alone" (Isaiah 63:3). So when you are feeling all alone, Jesus is feeling alone. And the beautiful reality is that when someone discovers someone else is going through the same thing, WOW! what happens to that feeling of loneliness? We aren't lonely any more as there is someone going through the same thing, and understands exactly what you are feeling. You are not alone – *you can't be alone* – if your faith will believe that. When you feel you have made a mess of things and you don't deserve the companionship of God and and that you are just useless and good for nothing, well, what does Jesus say in the Psalms? "I am a worm and no man" (Psalm 22:6). He is feeling what you are feeling. When your family falls apart and you are separated from the ones you love, Jesus says in Lamentations 1:16:

> For these things I weep; mine eye, mine eye runneth down with water, because the comforter that should relieve my soul is far from me: my children are desolate, because the enemy prevailed.

Isn't that how you feel? When your whole world falls down around you and you just cry and cry and cry until you can cry no more.

In Psalms 69:3 He says:

> I am weary of my crying: my throat is dried: mine eyes fail while I wait for my God.

Do you believe it? Do you believe that whatever you are going through and yes! even if you are being tempted with the negative, whatever those violent feelings may be that you are having to fight off, and you feel the kettle is about to boil and the whistle is about to start blowing, if you will believe this, you will believe that Jesus is feeling the same way? If you will feel after God in the very thing that you are feeling and actually realise that Jesus feels like His kettle wants to start whistling too, then wow! the pressure is gone because even though He was tempted like as we are, He did no sin. Then when we do fail and we take on board and cherish those negative things, let us not forget that He was counted among the transgressors – that our transgressions were laid upon Him. He felt as though He did that exact same thing.

God has given us, by faith, a *tangible reality*. We can walk through this world as we have read there: as though it was heaven, the very home of God Himself. Wherever we look we can see God; whatever we hear we can hear Him speaking to us. And when you are lonely you can seek after God and feel Him and that sense of loneliness will vanish.

When we will do that in all the vicissitudes of life, when our faith will lay hold of the reality that Jesus has become at one with me, then the result will be – what will your feeling be? – Peace. And you know that when we have peace we have no problems whatsoever believing that God is with me then because Jesus says, "Peace I leave with you, My peace I give unto you, not as the world giveth give I unto you. Let not your heart be troubled, neither let it be afraid" (John 14:27).

God means what He says when He says, "I am with you." He is. We don't have to look far. As it said there: that they will seek after Him and find Him though He be not very far. How far away is "right here"? You can't measure it can you? But we need to believe it and let our belief produce something tangible. No matter what our experience may be, no matter where we are, we can have God with us. It is a beautiful thought and may God help it to be our reality. AMEN.

ARE MY SINS FORGIVEN?

February 16, 2013

In the blood from the cross,
I have been washed from sin.

MUCH of Christianity today leaves it at that – that day of rejoicing when Jesus took my sins away. O happy day! But to be free from dross, still I would enter in deeper yet.

The Lord is trying to prepare a people who will reflect His character to the world and it is written that when He sees His image perfectly reproduced in His people, then He will come to claim them as His own (*Christ's Object Lessons*, p.69). And the very fact that He has not come yet is because His image is not yet perfectly reproduced. And the reason His image is not perfectly reproduced yet is because His image needs to be restored from such a decrepit state. Man in the beginning was created in the image of God, but through the transgression of Adam and Eve, man was, in a sense, recreated in the image of Satan. And the possibilities that man had to develop a perfect character – it was rendered practically impossible except through the mercy of God.

There is in the Scriptures a parable that shows us the mercy of God in reference to the state in which man, we, I, find myself. If we come here to Matthew 18:23, this is a profound parable which plays out before our understanding something very clear if we will learn the parable:

> Therefore is the kingdom of heaven likened unto a certain king, which would take account of his servants. And when he had begun to reckon, one was brought unto him, which owed him ten thousand talents. But forasmuch as he had not to pay, his Lord commanded him to be sold, and his wife, and children, and all that he had, and payment to be made. The servant therefore fell down, and worshipped him, saying, Lord, have patience with me, and I will pay thee all. Then the Lord of that servant was moved with compassion, and loosed him, and forgave him the debt.

This servant had been very unfaithful in his duty and he had come to a point where he had been so unfaithful that he owed his Lord 10,000 talents. One Roman talent weighed about 32.3 kilograms, and this was measured in silver. The servant's debt was 323,000 kilograms of silver. On the 15th of February 2013, one kilogram of silver was worth approximately US$963.86. And so this man owed his lord US$310 million.

Now, at the average Australian wage, it would take you, ever since the day that Noah was born to pay off that debt; about 4,930 years of full time employment. Could you pay that debt? Do you have that long? This man had dug such a hole for himself that he could not get out of it – there was no way he could ever pay that debt. But, the Lord of the servant was moved with compassion and loosed him and forgave him the debt.

Of course, he had insisted, "Yes yes, I'll pay it," and don't we do that? I'll be obedient; "all that the Lord hath said will we do." Can we do it? We cannot do it. And there is the description of our experience. We owe God a holy life, but we don't have it to give. So what does God do? – He offers to forgive us.

Now do you know what it means to forgive? To forgive is to *give-for*. So when God forgives sin, there is an exchange. He takes away the sin, and gives something else for that sin.

If we come here to Galatians 1:3-4, we read of that exact description here:

> Grace be to you and peace from God the Father, and from our Lord Jesus Christ, Who gave himself for our sins, that he might deliver us from this present evil world, according to the will of God and our Father.

He "gave Himself for our sins." He *gave for our sins Himself*, and took our sins.

Again here in Romans 3:23-26, a similar contemplation of the practical realities of forgiveness:

> For all have sinned, and come short of the glory of God; Being justified *freely* [BECAUSE WE DON'T HAVE THAT WHICH WE NEED TO PAY IT] by his grace through the redemption that is in Christ Jesus: Whom God hath set forth to be a propitiation through faith in his blood, to declare his righteousness for the remission of sins that are past, through the forbearance of God; To declare, I say, at this time his righteousness: that he might be just, and the justifier of him which believeth in Jesus.

"To declare His righteousness for the remission of sins that are past" – to forgive. And how far does that go in application? I believe we hang our helpless souls upon the truths contained here in *Steps to Christ*, p.62. If it wasn't for this reality, we would have no hope:

> It was possible for Adam, before the fall, to form a righteous character by obedience to God's law. But he failed to do this, and because of his sin our natures are fallen and we cannot make ourselves righteous. Since we are sinful, unholy, we cannot perfectly obey the holy law. We have no righteousness of our own with which to meet the claims of the law of God. But Christ has made a way of escape for us. He lived on earth amid trials and temptations such as we have to meet. He lived a sinless life. He died for us, and now He offers to take our sins and give us His righteousness. If you give yourself to Him, and accept Him as your Saviour, then,

sinful as your life may have been, for His sake you are accounted righteous. Christ's character stands in place of your character, and you are accepted before God just as if you had not sinned. [1]

These words mean nothing to somebody who doesn't know their sinfulness; but if you have had glimpses of the wretchedness of your heart, and if you have seen the mess that you have made of your life, these words are vitality to the soul. To know that we can stand before the holy God – who consumes sin with just a glance – to stand before Him, just as if we had not sinned, is a far, far greater relief than when the tax man says we don't have to pay our tax.

And this went so far as 2 Corinthians 5:21 where it says, that He made Christ to not just take our sins, but to *be sin* for us, that we might be made the righteousness of God in Him.

But God doesn't stop there does He? He doesn't just say, "Ok, I'm going to accept you, and you are going to stand before me as though you have never sinned," but that continues in His treatment of us. From *Our High Calling*, p.52:

> Christ assumed the office of his surety and deliverer in becoming sin for man, that man might become the righteousness of God in and through Him who was one with the Father. Sinners can be justified by God only when He pardons their sins, remits the punishment they deserve, and treats them as though they were really just and had not sinned, receiving them into divine favor and treating them as if they were righteous. [2]

So when God forgives us our sins, He does more than just considers them gone – He actually treats us as though we never even did them! Might not mean much to you now, or maybe it does, but these words will be everything to you when you find yourself at the bottom of the pit – that God would treat me, a sinner, as though the very life was as His own Son? Can you say, "Amen!" to that? Does not your soul just say, "Praise the Lord!"? We have only covered off a few little quotes and yet contained in them is the very principles of eternal life, the very kernel of hope, and without this hope, I have nothing. This is the only thing that keeps me alive in this earth. This exchange through the atonement of Jesus Christ, this abundant love of God toward me who is so undeserving; He remits the punishment I deserve. What do I deserve? Death. But not just termination – a long, protracted, painful death. That is what I deserve. But God remits that punishment and treats us as though we had not sinned.

Now it is important that we lay hold of this and cling to it with the tenacity that no matter how powerfully the billows of those temptations beat against us that we won't let it go. And as we proceed for the remainder of the hour, remember that – remember what God's promise is to you – because we never finished the story in the parable of the servant. And I want to say that I am not sharing this this morning for anyone else but my own self. What I am sharing is for me – because I am continually walking a very fine line and I am continually having to deal with issues in my heart that keep coming up again and again; and if I do not deal with them once and for all through that which we are looking at today, I am going to lose my eternal life and I am going to receive the punishment that I deserve. So today the Lord is talking to me and if you hear His voice talking to you, well, that's none of my business. He is talking to *me*.

Return to Matthew 18:23 and this time reading onto verse 35:

> Therefore is the kingdom of heaven likened unto a certain king, which would take account of his servants. And when he had begun to reckon, one was brought unto him, which owed him ten thousand talents [$310,000,000]. But forasmuch as he had not to pay, his Lord commanded him to be sold, and his wife, and children, and all that he had, and payment to be made. The servant therefore fell down, and worshipped him, saying, Lord, have patience with me, and I will pay thee all. Then the Lord of that servant was moved with compassion, and loosed him, and forgave him the debt. But the same servant went out, and found one of his fellowservants, which owed him an hundred pence...

A "pence" was four grams of silver. And so a hundred pence (400 grams of silver) was worth $240 on the 15th February, 2013. What's that compared to $310,000,000?

> ...and he laid hands on him, and took him by the throat, saying, Pay me that thou owest. And his fellowservant fell down at his feet, and besought him, saying, Have patience with me, and I will pay thee all. And he would not: but went and cast him into prison, till he should pay the debt. So when his fellowservants saw what was done, they were very sorry, and came and told unto their Lord all that was done. Then his Lord, after that he had called him, said unto him, O thou wicked servant, I forgave thee all that debt, because thou desiredst me: Shouldest not thou also have had compassion on thy fellowservant, even as I had pity on thee? And his Lord was wroth, and delivered him to the tormentors, till he should pay all that was due unto him. So likewise shall my heavenly Father do also unto you, if ye from your hearts forgive not every one his brother their trespasses.

Our sermon today is titled with a question and the question that I need to ask myself in the light of God's word today is: "*Are My Sins Forgiven?*" Have my sins really, really been forgiven? Am I really justified? Come to Luke 6:36-38:

> Be ye therefore merciful, as your Father also is merciful. Judge not, and ye shall not be judged: condemn not, and ye shall not be condemned: forgive, and ye shall be forgiven: Give, and it shall be given unto you; good measure, pressed down, and shaken together, and running over, shall men give into your bosom. For with the same measure that ye mete withal it shall be measured to you again.

"Forgive, and you shall *be* forgiven." What happens if you don't forgive? Well, Jesus tells us how we ought to pray in Matthew 6:9-15. If we come there, we are advised not just as to how to pray but what kind of a spirit it is that we are to have when we come before God with our needs of mercy and forgiveness:

> After this manner therefore pray ye: Our Father which art in heaven, Hallowed be thy name. Thy kingdom come. Thy will be done in earth, as it is in heaven. Give us this day our daily bread. And forgive us our debts, as we forgive our debtors. And lead us not into temptation, but deliver us from evil: For thine is the kingdom, and the power, and the glory, for ever. Amen. For if ye forgive men their trespasses, your heavenly Father will also forgive you: But if ye forgive not men their trespasses, neither will your Father forgive your trespasses.

Are my sins forgiven? The question actually is, have I forgiven my friends and family? That is the question. With the same measure that you meet – *as* we forgive those that have sinned against us, in the *same manner* will God forgive us. What kind of a forgiveness have you given? So what kind of a forgiveness have you got? Come back again to that parable. Matthew 18:33-35:

> Shouldest not thou also have had compassion on thy fellowservant, even as I had pity on thee? And his Lord was wroth, and delivered him to the tormentors, till he should pay all that was due unto him. So likewise shall my heavenly Father do also unto you, if ye from your hearts forgive not every one his brother their trespasses.

To forgive from where? From the heart. Now you have got to be very careful there because the heart is deceitful above all things and it can make you think, "No, there's nothing between me and my brother; nothing between me and my sister." But your heart has pulled the wool over your eyes and as time goes on, little roots of bitterness start to come up and you come to realise, if you will, that you actually haven't forgiven them. Why? Because our forgiveness is not as God's forgiveness. "Shouldest thou not have had compassion on thy fellow servant *even as* I had pity on thee?" – in the same manner of forgiveness as God had forgiveness for us?

How complete does God tell us that our forgiveness for others is supposed to be? Today – "OK, I forgive you," and tomorrow they come and say, "I'm sorry." "OK, I forgive you." And then at the end of the day, "I'm sorry," – "I forgive you." And then again and again – what do we do? We get annoyed and think, Well if you really cared you would stop doing it! And a little grudge comes up in the heart.

Matthew 18:21-22:

> Then came Peter to him, and said, Lord, how oft shall my brother sin against me, and I forgive him? till seven times? Jesus saith unto him, I say not unto thee, Until seven times: but, Until seventy times seven.

How many times is that? 490 times. Is there a 490 in the Scriptures? 490 years? 70 weeks of Bible prophecy, a day for a year? And very close to the end of those 490 years what did Jesus say? Luke 23:34:

> Then said Jesus, Father, forgive them; for they know not what they do.

487 years of total despite to His Spirit, to His prophets. They persecuted and killed them and still so many years later – "I forgive you." And then right at the end of that 490 years, come over to Acts 7:59-60:

> And they stoned Stephen, calling upon God, and saying, Lord Jesus, receive my spirit. And he kneeled down, and cried with a loud voice, Lord, lay not this sin to their charge. And when he had said this, he fell asleep.

Now I think that Christ was telling the disciples, "You be as patient with your brethren as I have been with your nation." Was it God that cast off the Jews? No. He never cast them off. They cast God off. And those that were amongst the Jews that were part of that nation that repented, He received them. So no, not seven times, but as often as they ask to be forgiven, forgive them.

Forgive them even as God forgave you – in the same manner. When God forgives us, we stand before him as though we have never sinned; and He *treats* us as though we have never sinned. So when my brother offends against me, what is forgiveness? We are to account that they *never sinned against me*.

Yes? Isn't that the forgiveness that God gives you – if you will? If you will give that forgiveness to your brother or sister? Anything short of that toward them, God will not give it to you.

So this beautiful *Steps to Christ* quote that we read where this exchange takes place and we can stand before God completely righteous is not real toward you unless it is your attitude towards your bother. While we cherish a root of bitterness in our hearts and refrain from considering that the offence was never even committed – our sins are *not* forgiven. And I find that very, very scary.

Christ's Object Lessons, p.251:

> "But if ye forgive not men their trespasses, neither will your Father forgive your trespasses." Matthew 6:15. Nothing can justify an unforgiving spirit. *He who is unmerciful toward others shows that he himself is not a partaker of God's pardoning grace.* In God's forgiveness the heart of the erring one is drawn close to the great heart of Infinite Love. The tide of divine compassion flows into the sinner's soul, and from him to the souls of others. The tenderness and mercy that Christ has revealed in His own precious life will be seen in those who become sharers of His grace. But "if any man have not the Spirit of Christ, he is none of His." Romans 8:9. He is alienated from God, fitted only for eternal separation from Him. [emphasis supplied] [3]

We get on our knees in the morning, don't we, and we say, "Oh, Father." Umm, if we have not the spirit of Christ, the spirit of divine compassion, we are none of His.

> It is true that he may once have received forgiveness; but his unmerciful spirit shows that he now rejects God's pardoning love. He has separated himself from God, and

is in the same condition as before he was forgiven. He has denied his repentance, and *his sins are upon him as if he had not repented.* [emphasis supplied] [3]

So he stands before God, just as if he *had* sinned – because he has. So, the question is: are your sins forgiven?

No. that's the wrong question. The question is: are *my* sins forgiven?

Come to another parable. Forget your brethren. Forget what they have done to you. Come and read this parable in Luke 18:10-14 – another parable that we seem to get so much hope and comfort from – but deeper yet:

> Two men went up into the temple to pray [TWO MEN WENT TO CHURCH]; the one a Pharisee, and the other a publican. The Pharisee stood and prayed thus with himself, God, I thank thee, that I am not as other men are, extortioners, unjust, adulterers, or even as this publican. I fast twice in the week, I give tithes of all that I possess. And the publican, standing afar off, would not lift up so much as his eyes unto heaven, but smote upon his breast, saying, God be merciful to me a sinner. I tell you, this man went down to his house justified rather than the other: for every one that exalteth himself shall be abased; and he that humbleth himself shall be exalted.

Who went home justified? Who went home with his sins forgiven? Well let's read it in the original from the Young's Literal Translation. The original reads like this:

> `Two men went up to the temple to pray, the one a Pharisee, and the other a tax-gatherer; the Pharisee having stood by himself, thus prayed: God, I thank Thee that I am not as the rest of men, rapacious, unrighteous, adulterers, or even as this tax-gatherer; I fast twice in the week, I give tithes of all things--as many as I possess. `And the tax-gatherer, having stood afar off, would not even the eyes lift up to the heaven, but was smiting on his breast, saying, God be propitious to me--the sinner! I say to you, this one went down declared righteous, to his house, rather than that one: ...'

Who was declared righteous? The one who said that he was "a" sinner? "*THE*" sinner! And if he is "the" sinner, what is everybody else? They are righteous!

Ellet J. Waggoner enlarges this very simply yet very beautifully from *The Present Truth*, UK Edition, August 16, 1894:

> "The Sinner."-The literal rendering of the publican's prayer is, "God be merciful to me, the sinner." See margin of Revised Version. That presents the most marked contrast to the prayer of the Pharisee, who saw everybody's sins except his own. *The publican saw himself as the only sinner.* That is the characteristic of true conviction of sin. He who has learned of the Lord, will *see himself to be so great a sinner that he cannot imagine anyone else as bad as himself.* [emphasis supplied] [4]

What did Apostle Paul say? "I am the chief of sinners" (1 Timothy 1:16). *In*

Heavenly Places, p.23, the Spirit of Prophecy echoes these words:

> When you receive the words of Christ as if they were addressed to you personally, when each applies the truth to himself as if he were the only sinner on the face of the earth for whom Christ died, you will learn to claim by faith the merits of the blood of a crucified and risen Saviour. [5]

What are we claiming? Well, we have been claiming what we can according to our faith and understanding, but we need to go deeper yet. And until we will consider ourselves as the only sinner on the face of the whole earth for whom Christ died – not until then – will we really be claiming the merits of the blood of a crucified and risen Saviour.

Let's re-read our Scripture reading in 1 John 1:9:

> If we confess our sins, he is faithful and just to forgive us our sins, and to cleanse us from all unrighteousness.

To confess my brother's sins? To say, "Lord, they've thrown a stumbling block in my path; Lord they're so annoying." NO. We are to confess "*our*" sins because we are to be as though we are the only one who has something to confess. And every body else who has sinned against me – they never sinned against me.

But it's not easy though is it? Because human beings are very fragile and we scar easily. It's so easy for our sensitive little souls to be hurt and the wounds are so deep and, "How can I ever forget what they have done to me? I see the scars, I see the effects in my life and you want me to treat them as though they never did it against me and in my own mind to consider it doesn't exist?" The world says, "Forgiven, but not forgotten." God says *that* is *not* forgiving. To forgive is to *forget*, and until we will forget, we are not forgiven.

Doesn't Jesus say that "I will remember their sins no more?" (Jeremiah 31:34). When He forgives us, He forgets. And if you forget something, well, it's like it never happened, you forgot all about it – it never existed. And until I can have this attitude to my brethren and sisters, my sins are not forgiven. But, more than just forgetting, I need to treat them as though they never sinned; as though they never hurt me.

Do you love God? We're not so fast to say it now are we? Come to 1 John 4:20:

> If a man say, I love God, and hateth his brother, he is a liar: for he that loveth not his brother whom he hath seen, how can he love God whom he hath not seen?

The Adventist Home, p.47:

> True affection will overlook many mistakes; love will not discern them. [6]

Do you love God? Not if you don't love your brother, and *love will not even discern the many mistakes of another.*

And if I cannot discern their mistakes, then they're a saint aren't they? They're righteous! And I will treat them as such and then God will treat me as such.

Come to Philippians 2:3-5:

> Let nothing be done through strife or vainglory;...

If you think that everyone else is better than you, you are not going to strive are you? You are not going to be vain because you are a "worm and no man" (Psalm 22:6).

> ...but in lowliness of mind let each esteem other better than themselves. Look not every man on his own things, but every man also on the things of others. Let this mind be in you, which was also in Christ Jesus: Who, being in the form of God, thought it not robbery to be equal with God.

But said "I am a worm and no man" and esteemed others better than Himself. This is the mind of Christ. When He took the sins of the whole world upon Himself *He really took the sins of the whole world upon Himself!* Meaning that He was "*THE*" sinner and everybody else had not sinned. Let this mind be in you which was also in Christ Jesus.

Are my sins forgiven? The Lord really calls me to consider, to search my heart. You can cut the tree down, you can cut the weeds out, but you are left with the roots and they need to be dealt with too. Hebrews 12:14-15:

> Follow peace with all men, and holiness, without which no man shall see the Lord: Looking diligently [LOOKING WHERE? LOOKING IN YOUR OWN HEART] lest any man fail of the grace of God; lest any root of bitterness springing up trouble you, and thereby many be defiled.

It's there under the surface but then in the right environment, it shoots forth. Until then you didn't know that it was there. You could be harbouring something against someone for many many years, and then right there, just as probation is about to close, in the last second, the Devil can come in with that stimuli, that right provocation and because we haven't dealt with it, it will come up and you're lost; I'm lost. Almost saved means to be not wholly saved, but wholly lost.

Is this a hard saying? I mean just picture it: there's this publican, and over there this Pharisee has paraded himself in front of everyone. Have you ever felt that the church is full of Pharisees? Do you find Pharisees a stumbling block in your church? O I hate Pharisees. I do. And do you know why I hate Pharisees? Because I am a Pharisee and Pharisees don't get along with Pharisees.

But if I want to experience forgiveness as God promises me, I need to consider them as a saint, everybody else as a saint, better than my own self.

Are my sins forgiven? *Not* if I haven't forgiven you. This is a hard saying and may God help me to hear it. AMEN.

Revisiting 1888

Part 1
PROGRESSION OF LIGHT

August 31, 2013

DURING the General Conference session in 1893 Alonzo T. Jones gave the following testimony:

> A sister told me not long ago that before that time four years ago she had just been lamenting her estate and wondering how in the world the time was ever going to come for the Lord to come if He had to wait for His people to get ready to meet him. For she said the way she had been at it–and she had worked as hard as anybody in this world, she thought–she saw that she was not making progress fast enough to bring the Lord in any kind of reasonable time at all, and she could not make out how the Lord was going to come.

> She was bothered about it, but she said when the folks came home from Minneapolis and they said, "Why the Lord's righteousness is a gift; we can have the righteousness of Christ as a gift, and we can have it now." "Oh," said she, "That made me glad; that brought light, for then I could see how the Lord could come pretty soon. When He Himself gives us the garment, the clothing, the character, that fits us for the judgment and for the time of trouble, I could then see how he could come just as soon as He wanted to." "And," said she, "it made me glad, and I have been glad ever since." [1]

Would you like to be glad? I would like to find the answer to the same problem that she had. Is it not true that as we consider our standing before the Lord both in a corporate sense and in a personal sense, we are not very much encouraged when we are willing to be honest with ourselves and with God? This sister had the same issue, she saw that the Lord would be coming soon but how could they ever be ready? But as her parents came home from Minneapolis they had something to comfort her with. And as I went through that personal testimony and was able to relate with it in many respects it ignites in me a strong desire to know what it was that buoyed her spirit up, to know what it was she found in answer, what it was that was presented by the messengers of God in 1888.

Did you know there was no transcript of what was delivered by Ellet J. Waggoner in 1888? Since that time both he and Jones have published many books. But have you ever noticed how hard it is to actually get your hands on those books? They are very rare books. They are not easy to come across. Books like *The Everlasting Covenant*. The Adventist Church in America never printed that book. They refused to print that book because it was written by Ellet J. Waggoner. The *General Conference Bulletins 1893, 1895* and *1897* are rare to find in a hard copy. *Glad Tidings, Lessons on Faith, The Consecrated Way*. These precious gems that have the elements of 1888 encapsulated within their pages are very hard to find. I thank the Lord that they can now be found on the internet in a digital format and also on audio. But have you ever wondered why there is such a great lack of their writings?

In *Manuscript Releases* Vol.16, p.104, Ellen White tells us why:

> Why do not brethren of like precious faith consider that in every age, when the Lord has sent a special message to the people, all the powers of the confederacy of evil have set at work to prevent the word of truth from coming to those who should receive it? [2]

That's the problem. In 1888 and in Jones' and Waggoner's continued ministries during the following decade, there was a *special message*. And because it was a special message, all the powers of the confederacy of evil had set at work to prevent the word of truth from coming to those who should receive it. Because it is so hard to find those books and it requires effort and expense, we generally don't expend much energy in seeking out those books to read them for ourselves, do we?

This hour I would like to spend some time on realising how important their writings and their message actually was. I was recently listening to an Adventist minister and he said that we should read Jones and Waggoner for ourselves and not accept another man's interpretation of them. Indeed did not the Apostle Paul when preaching the gospel say, Be as the Bereans, go and read the word for yourself whether these things be so? I believe that it is good advice. However, because the writings of Ellen White are much more readily available we find it easier to search for the hidden truth in her writings. And why shouldn't that be? Indeed we should. She was the inspired messenger of the Lord. But when considering Jones and Waggoner it is important for us to consider what the inspired writer actually says in regard to their message and to follow her counsel and advice.

There is an issue, however, with Jones and Waggoner that many Adventists have, and that has to do with their later history and subsequent falling away from the church. There is a temptation to consider that their writings are not as important as perhaps they might be. But Ellen White says the following regarding Jones' and Waggoner's Message in *Manuscript Releases*, Vol.16, p.107:

> Should the Lord's messengers, after standing manfully for the truth for a time, fall under temptation, and dishonour Him who has given them their work, will that be proof that the message is not true? No, because the Bible is true. "To the law and to the testimony; if they speak not according to this word, it is because there is no light in them." Sin on the part of the messenger of God would cause Satan to rejoice, and those who have rejected the messenger and the message would triumph; but it would not at all clear the men who were guilty of rejecting the message of truth sent of God. [3]

The Spirit of Prophecy says here that if they fell away, the message was still a message that was sent of God. Same book, starting on page 105:

> God will send His words of warning by whom He will send. And the question to be settled is not what person is it who brings the message; *this does not in any way affect the word spoken.* "By their fruits ye shall know them." [emphasis supplied]

> Truth is often preached by one who has not experienced its power; but it is truth nevertheless, and is blessed to those who, drawn by the Spirit of God, accept it. But when the truth is presented by one who is himself sanctified through it, it has a freshness, a force, that gives it a convincing power to the hearer. The truth, in its power upon the heart, is precious, and the truth addressed to the understanding is clear. Both are needful--the word and the inward testimony of the Spirit.

So what about Jones' and Waggoner's message then?

> In regard to the testimony that has come to us through the Lord's messengers, we can say, we know in whom we have believed. We know that Christ is our righteousness, not alone because He is so described in the Bible, but because we have felt His transforming power in our own hearts. [4]

So the 1888 Message was not a message delivered by people who had not experienced the very thing they were preaching. It was delivered by men who understood the reality of what they were conveying, men who could address the truth both to the understanding and to the heart and therefore a transforming power could be felt.

From *Manuscript Releases*, Vol.11, p.257 comes what I consider to be a very touching confession...

> We have travelled all through to the different places of the meetings that I might stand side by side with the messengers of God that I knew were His messengers, that I knew had a message for His people. I gave my message with them right in harmony with the very message they were bearing. What did we see? We saw a power attending the message. [5]

That's a revelation isn't it? Here is one who is inspired by God who would travel all over the country side just to be able to stand by the side of Brothers Jones and Waggoner and share in the ministry and the delivery of the precious message with them.

Elsewhere she actually describes that it was her *privilege* to present the word side by side with them. With who? Those whom she *knew were His messengers,* whom she knew had a message for God's people. And on page 283 of the same volume she says:

> The Lord is speaking through His delegated messengers. [6]

Would you like to hear the word of the Lord? Well, the Lord was speaking through His delegated messengers. And if the Lord was speaking through His delegated messengers then it is my belief that we need to take their messages very seriously. I want to emphasise a particular point this morning as to how important it is that we do familiarise ourselves with their messages.

In the *1888 Materials*, p.1814 it says:

> The Lord has raised up Brother Jones and Brother Waggoner to proclaim a message to the world *to prepare a people to stand in the day of God...* [emphasis supplied]

Do you want to be prepared to stand in the day of God? These men had a special message for that work.

> ...The world is suffering the need of additional light to come to them upon the Scriptures,--additional proclamation of the principles of purity, lowliness, faith, and the righteousness of Christ. This is the power of God unto salvation to every one that believeth. [7]

Why was it that God raised them up? Because the world was suffering the need of additional light.

In the *1888 Materials*, p.608:

> The question is, has God sent the truth? Has God raised up these men to proclaim the truth? I say, yes, *God has sent men to bring us the truth that we should not have had unless God had sent somebody to bring it to us.* God has let me have a light of what His Spirit is, and therefore I accept it, and I no more dare to lift my hand against these persons, because it would be against Jesus Christ, who is to be recognized in His messengers. [emphasis supplied] [8]

Now that's a powerful statement. That is a statement from the authority. God has sent these men to bring a truth that we would not have had unless God had sent them.

And therefore on p.954 of the same book:

> To accuse and criticise those whom God is using, is to accuse and criticise the Lord, who has sent them. [9]

Now these are very interesting quotes as we proceed in our study. Here was a great emphasis placed by the Spirit of Prophecy that there was a message that needed to come, that needed to be brought to the church.

Now here's an interesting one from *Manuscript Releases*, Vol.5, p.219:

I have had the question asked, What do you think of this light that these men are presenting? Why, I have been presenting it to you for the last forty-five years--the matchless charms of Christ. This is what I have been trying to present before your minds. When Brother Waggoner brought out these ideas in Minneapolis, *it was the first clear teaching on this subject from any human lips I had heard,* excepting the conversations between myself and my husband. I have said to myself, It is because God has presented it to me in vision that I see it so clearly, and they cannot see it because they have never had it presented to them as I have. And when another presented it, every fibre of my heart said, Amen. [emphasis supplied] [10]

Now she has just, in these previous quotes we read, stated that the world is suffering the need of additional light, and that unless God has sent men to bring that truth they never would have had the truth. Yet in this particular quote she says, "I have been presenting it to you for the last 45 years." This is what I have been trying, she says, to present before your minds. It's food for thought isn't it? And it's one of those things I find very hard to get my head around. In *Selected Messages*, Vol.3, p.168, she actually says that even though she had been presenting it all of those years, very few had responded, and even then only by assent!

As I had a burden on my heart to share what I'm sharing this morning I was up most of the night totally scrapping everything that I would work on because it's not something that's very easy to make sense of. Here is the Spirit of Prophecy stating that "I have been giving you this message for the last 45 years." She says, "If the Lord did not send men to bring it to us, *we would not have had it.*" Then she said that it was the "first clear teaching on this subject from any human lips I had heard."..."it is because God has presented it to me in vision that I see it so clearly, and they cannot see it because they have never had it presented to them as I have."

But there is another statement here in *Selected Messages*, Vol.3, p.172:

When I stated before my brethren that I had heard for the first time the views of Elder E.J. Waggoner, some did not believe me. I stated that I had heard precious truths uttered that I could respond to with all my heart, for had not these great and glorious truths, the righteousness of Christ and the entire sacrifice made in behalf of man, been imprinted indelibly on my mind by the Spirit of God? Has not this subject been presented in the testimonies again and again? When the Lord had given to my brethren the burden to proclaim this message I felt inexpressibly grateful to God, for I knew it was the message for this time. [11]

Ellen White said, "I have been sharing this for the last 45 years and has it not been presented in the Testimonies again and again?" Then comes a second hand account from J.S. Washburn. And he signed it to say it was true and he recounts Ellen White speaking to him here as follows:

"E. J. Waggoner can preach righteousness by faith more clearly than I can." "Why,

Sister White," I said, "Do you mean to tell me that E.J. Waggoner can preach it better than you can with all your experience?" Sister White replied, "Yes. The Lord has given him special light on that question. I have been wanting to bring it out more clearly but I could not have brought it out as clearly as he did. But when he brought it out at Minneapolis, I recognised it."

Very interesting isn't it? Very interesting... And as we continue in this sermon and as we consider what we have read so far, please do not take me as making of none effect the Spirit of Prophecy, because Ellen White writes that the last grand deception for God's people is that Satan will make the writings of the Spirit of Prophecy of none effect. And I'm not doing that. But, if the Spirit of Prophecy is going to declare that the Lord spoke through Jones and Waggoner then I want to hear that voice of the Lord, don't you? We are not to live by bread alone but by every word that proceeds out of the mouth of God. So while the Spirit of Prophecy is paramount to our last day experience, there is a relevance with the messages of Jones and Waggoner for us as well. But we want to approach this subject from a particular angle.

Selected Messages, Vol.1, p.19, being very careful not to make of none effect the Spirit of Prophecy:

> Human minds vary. The minds of different education and thought receive different impressions of the same words, and it is difficult for one mind to give to one of a different temperament, education, and habits of thought by language exactly the same idea as that which is clear and distinct in his own mind. [12]

When Ellen White was set apart from the Lord to be His messenger, did she lose her personal individuality? No. She still had her own mind of different education and different thought. Her mind varied to the minds of everybody else in the church. And it is difficult for one mind to give to one of a different temperament, education, and habits of thought, by language, exactly the same idea as that which is clear and distinct in his own mind. So while she had it clear in her mind, it was difficult for others to understand what she was saying. She said: "I am trying to communicate this." But likewise for the brothers Jones and Waggoner; their minds also varied. So there were difficulties in certain individuals' understanding of what they had to say.

Reading on from page 21 of the same book:

> There is variety in a tree, there are scarcely two leaves just alike. Yet this variety adds to the perfection of the tree as a whole.

> In our Bible, we might ask, Why need Matthew, Mark, Luke, and John in the Gospels, why need the Acts of the Apostles, and the variety of writers in the Epistles, go over the same thing?

> The Lord gave His word in just the way He wanted it to come. He gave it through different writers, each having his own individuality, though going over the same

history. Their testimonies are brought together in one Book, and are like the testimonies in a social meeting. They do not represent things in just the same style. Each has an experience of his own, and this diversity broadens and deepens the knowledge that is brought out to meet the necessities of varied minds. The thoughts expressed have not a set uniformity, as if cast in an iron mold, making the very hearing monotonous. In such uniformity there would be a loss of grace and distinctive beauty.

The Creator of all ideas may impress different minds with the same thought, but each may express it in a different way, yet without contradiction. The fact that this difference exists should not perplex or confuse us. It is seldom that two persons will view and express truth in the very same way. Each dwells on particular points which his constitution and education have fitted him to appreciate. The sunlight falling upon the different objects gives those objects a different hue.

Through the inspiration of His Spirit the Lord gave His apostles truth, to be expressed according to the development of their minds by the Holy Spirit. But the mind is not cramped, as if forced into a certain mold. [13]

That is very explanatory isn't it, that there are different minds that need to be reached? And those different minds will receive the delivery of the word in different styles. Same word, no contradiction, but a different manner of delivery. And it is so with God even in the Bible: Matthew, Mark, Luke and John. It's the same story, nothing contradictory but a perfect whole when you put them together. Every aspect is covered. If you're a highly intelligent person you might perhaps find the works of Luke to be more appealing because he wrote as a physician and he was very concise in the way he wrote it. Whereas Mark seems a little more relaxed in the delivery of his accounts that he gives; each working to a perfect whole. And so God gave Jones and Waggoner a particular experience in order that they may communicate the truth in a particular way. Ellen White had seen it in vision and therefore she was able to communicate it according to the best of her understanding in the way she had received it in vision. Jones and Waggoner had received it through in-depth study of the word of God, not through the revelation that Ellen White had.

In the *1888 Materials*, p.281 she says here:

The religion of Jesus Christ has not been as clearly defined as it should be, that the souls who are seeking for the knowledge of the plan of salvation may discern the simplicity of faith. In these (Jones' and Waggoner's) meetings this has been made so clear that a child may understand that it is an immediate, voluntary, trustful surrender of the heart to God. [14]

The way that Jones and Waggoner presented it, it was made to be so clear that a child could understand it.

The *1888 Materials*, p.1689:

> For a few years in the past, and especially since the Minneapolis meeting, truths have been made known that have been of great value to the world and to the people of God. The way has been made so plain that honest hearts cannot but receive the truth. [15]

Now I have a question. Was there a problem with the way in which Ellen White communicated what she understood? Was she unclear in her presentation? Was she speaking in gibberish so that no one could understand it? What was the problem? Well, the problem was with those who read and heard her words.

We read this before but now we want to read the last half of it.

Selected Messages, Vol.1, p.19:

> Human minds vary. The minds of different education and thought receive different impressions of the same words, and it is difficult for one mind to give to one of a different temperament, education, and habits of thought by language exactly the same idea as that which is clear and distinct in his own mind. Yet to honest men, right-minded men, he can be so simple and plain as to convey his meaning for all practical purposes.

So if the listener is right-minded and honest, he will understand the meaning. And we know from the Scriptures that these things are spiritually discerned (1 Corinthians 2:14).

> If the man he communicates with is not honest and will not want to see and understand the truth, he will turn his words and language in everything to suit his own purposes. He will misconstrue his words, play upon his imagination, wrest them from their true meaning, and then entrench himself in unbelief, claiming that the sentiments are all wrong. [16]

The Scriptures say he will do it and not even realise it because "the heart is deceitful above all things and desperately wicked; who can know it?" (Jeremiah 17:9).

So first beguiling themselves that they have an honest heart, but in reality not really wanting to admit the truth, they will not receive the message in the way it was intended. So "he will misconstrue his words, play upon his imagination, wrest them from their true meaning, and then entrench himself in unbelief, claiming that the sentiments are all wrong."

They will miss the point, like the Jews. *They* missed the point. They had the Word Himself in the very midst of them. But did they know how to read Him? They completely read Him wrong. And we see this all down through history from the beginning of the church in this world. From the Garden of Eden there was the simple gospel preached. The first sermon ever preached "enmity". That should have been the only sermon that ever needed to be preached (Genesis 3:15). Abraham understood it. In his own experience He understood the sacrifice of Christ. And when his children came to Mount Sinai God was seeking to ratify with the Hebrews the Abrahamic Covenant.

In fact let's read it there. Come to Exodus 19 for these things are written for our examples and for our admonition, upon whom the ends of the world are come (1 Corinthians 10:11).

Here in Exodus 19:3-6:

> And Moses went up unto God, and the Lord called unto him out of the mountain, saying, Thus shalt thou say to the house of Jacob, and tell the children of Israel; We have seen what I did unto the Egyptians, and how I bare you on eagles' wings, and brought you unto myself. Now therefore, if ye will obey my voice indeed, and keep my covenant, then ye shall be a peculiar treasure unto me above all people: for all the earth is mine: And ye shall be unto me a kingdom of priests, and an holy nation. These are the words which thou shalt speak unto the children of Israel.

God here was seeking to ratify the same covenant that He had with Abraham. Abraham said, AMEN! to the promise of God. And God said, You are righteous. But what did the Children of Israel say? Verse 8:

> And all the people answered together, and said, All that the Lord hath spoken *we will do*.

"*We* will make ourselves to be priests." "*We* will make ourselves to be a holy nation." And they had very quickly forgotten their short journey through the wilderness. When they came to the Red Sea, they couldn't save themselves. When they came to the waters of Meribah, they couldn't save themselves.

And the Lord "ADDED" the Ten Commandments. God had no original intention of speaking the 10 Commandments at Mount Sinai.

From *Patriarchs and Prophets*, p.264 comes this astounding statement:

> If man had kept the law of God, as given to Adam after his fall, preserved by Noah, and observed by Abraham, there would have been no necessity for the ordinance of circumcision. And if the descendants of Abraham had kept the covenant, of which circumcision was a sign, they would never have been seduced into idolatry, nor would it have been necessary for them to suffer a life of bondage in Egypt; they would have kept God's law in mind, and *there would have been no necessity for it to be proclaimed from Sinai or engraved upon the tables of stone.* And had the people practiced the principles of the Ten Commandments, there would have been no need of the additional directions given to Moses. [emphasis supplied] [17]

But what was the problem? They misconstrued the promises of God. They said "*we* will do it" and so they received the law and the sanctuary service. But how did they understand *that*? Did they misinterpret that too? They did, didn't they?

In 2nd Chronicles, the very last chapter, it says that because they were disobedient and they broke His law, God had to send them prophets because they missed the point of the books of Moses. So God sent prophets to encourage them and to aid them in understanding the law of God, and the meaning of the sacrificial system. But did they listen to the prophets? No, they killed them. And so the Interpreter came and lived it all out in His own life. Did they read *Him* aright? No they crucified Him. Did God write them off when they crucified His Son? No. God gave them another three years, and there on that very day they sealed their doom. Stephen, condemned before the Sanhedrin, explains the entire Old Testament. They didn't understand it did they? They stoned him. So then God sent the apostles and the New Testament because the Old Testament wasn't understood aright. Then how did the church receive the New Testament? Did they understand it? No they didn't.

Testimonies, Vol.5, p.664:

> If you had made God's word your study, with a desire to reach the Bible standard and attain to Christian perfection, you would not have needed the Testimonies.

So they missed the point of even the New Testament.

> It is because you have neglected to acquaint yourselves with God's inspired Book that He has sought to reach you by simple, direct testimonies, calling your attention to the words of inspiration which you had neglected to obey, and urging you to fashion your lives in accordance with its pure and elevated teachings.

> ...Additional truth is not brought out; but God has through the Testimonies simplified the great truths already given and in His own chosen way brought them before the people to awaken and impress the mind with them, that all may be left without excuse.

Now can you see the mercy of God in this progression of light through the ages? What did God need to send the Spirit of Prophecy and the Testimonies for? God has through the Testimonies simplified the great truths already given. But they needed to be made more simple because the people weren't putting in the effort to understand them. God therefore wanted to make sure that there was no excuse.

The very next paragraph says:

> The very essential principles of godliness are not understood because there is not a hungering and thirsting for Bible knowledge, purity of heart, and holiness of life. The Testimonies are not to belittle the word of God, but to exalt it and attract minds to it, that the beautiful simplicity of truth may impress all. [18]

God had to send the Spirit of Prophecy to make things more simple because man was getting both less intelligent and shall we say more slack (lazy) as well. And so God was seeking to give man every advantage he could.

Testimonies to Ministers, p.91:

> The Lord in His great mercy sent a most precious message to His people through
> Elders Waggoner and Jones. This message was to bring more prominently...

What does prominently mean? More obvious.

> This message was to bring more prominently before the world the uplifted Saviour,
> the sacrifice for the sins of the whole world. It presented justification through faith
> in the Surety; it invited the people to receive the righteousness of Christ, which is
> made manifest in obedience to all the commandments of God. Many had lost sight
> of Jesus. They needed to have their eyes directed to His divine person, His merits,
> and His changeless love for the human family. [19]

What did God have to do? They were missing the point of the Spirit of Prophecy
so God had to send it again and make it even more obvious. To try and give the people
every advantage and opportunity they could to understand God's word.

Are we any different today? The members of the church back then in a sense were
so slow of mind and so easily distracted from focusing their mental energy on studying
the word of God for themselves that God had to feed it to them in a bottle. He had to
speak to them in baby language. And how long ago was that? 120 years ago.

We need it simple don't we? Even more simple than they needed it in 1888. So how
relevant to us today are those channels of God's communication? The truth presented in
a language so simple that even a child could understand it and the honest in heart could
not miss it, and so that those who weren't honest in heart would have no excuse?

I really appreciate this meditation. The reason I appreciate it and the reason why
we first sung hymns about the love of God is because this tells us that God loves us.
This tells us how daft (slow) we really are. He wants to save us. The light delivered
there, in the promise of *enmity*, right there in the Garden of Eden, *that* was enough. But
God didn't stop there. Time and time again He has given us opportunity to understand
His word. Simpler and simpler He has made it. And He does that because He knows He
needs to because we're not getting any smarter. It's not evolution, it's *devolution*.

Let's come at it from another angle, just before we close.

Another reason why it is so important for us to become familiar with Jones and
Waggoner for ourselves.

In the *1888 Materials*, p.133 Ellen White says this:

> That which God gives His servants to speak today would not perhaps have been
> present truth twenty years ago, but it is God's message for this time. [20]

So twenty years prior to that time period it may not have been present truth. But in
that time it was God's message *for that time*. Why? Because of what was taking place

in the world and in the governments. Sunday Laws were very close to being passed. If they had received the message in 1888, Stephen Haskell quotes Ellen White as saying that they would have been in the kingdom two years* from then. So everything was just ready to go and the honest in heart knew it. They knew it! They saw that this was the message of God for that time. Is our time any more urgent than that time?

1888 Materials, p.1814:

> The Lord has raised up Brother Jones and Brother Waggoner to proclaim a message to the world to prepare a people to stand in the day of God. [21]

How soon is that day of God? Do you want to stand? Well God gave them a message to help them to get ready to stand. But the church rejected it. So what happened in the world? Well, *things slowed down*. And what happened in the church?

Signs of the Times, April 19, 1900, para.9:

> God designs that the message of redemption shall come to His people as the latter rain; for they are fast losing their connection with God.

So God gave it to them in baby speak and they still missed it. "They are fast losing their connection with God."

> They are trusting in men, and glorifying men, and their strength is proportionate to the strength of their dependence. *We are to know more than we know at the present time.* [emphasis supplied]

This is in the year 1900, so the message of righteousness by faith had already been proclaimed for the previous twelve years. And then she says "We are to know more than we know at the present time."

> We are to comprehend the deep things of God. There are themes to be dwelt upon which are worthy of more than a passing notice. [22]

Now can you see where we are and what the Lord is going to have to do for us? Shall we say, "*foetus*-speak"?

God has to speak to us even more simply today than He did back then. Because if the church missed the point back then, then God is going to give His people an even greater simplification of it.

1888 Materials, p.1689:

> The way has been made so plain that honest hearts cannot but receive the truth. But there are still treasures to be searched for. Let the shaft which has begun to work the mine of truth sink deep, and it will yield rich and precious treasures. [23]

* See note on page 261

So there is still a lot of truth for our day to come to us – a lot of truth. And it will come even more simple than it was in 1888 because God needs to speak to us according to our needs.

Now here is the important thing. If there is truth yet, then there is much more we are yet to know than in 1900. It was a very important principle.

Christ's Object Lessons, p.127:

> *In every age there is a new development of truth, a message of God to the people of that generation.* [supplied]

So that is what I just said. There was a message for them at that time, and that was the 1888 message.

We need to know more than that. There is a message of God to the people of *our* generation. But how do we find that message?

> The old truths are all essential; new truth is not independent of the old, but an unfolding of it. It is only as the old truths are understood that we can comprehend the new.

Only as we understand the message of righteousness by faith. Only as we can understand the message that God sent His people through Jones and Waggoner will we comprehend the message for our generation. No matter how simple it is, we will miss it if the old truth is not understood.

> When Christ desired to open to His disciples the truth of His resurrection, He began "at Moses and all the prophets" and "expounded unto them in all the scriptures the things concerning Himself." Luke 24:27. But it is the light which shines in the fresh unfolding of truth that glorifies the old. *He who rejects or neglects the new does not really possess the old.* For him it loses its vital power and becomes but a lifeless form. [emphasis supplied] [24]

In every age there is a new development of truth, a message of God to the people of that generation. There is a new development of truth for God's people in *this* generation. But we need to understand the truth of the previous generations. If God spoke plainly through Jones and Waggoner how much more plainly will He need to speak to us today? But if we don't know the plainness of speaking through them, we cannot understand their messages. It doesn't matter how simple God gives it to us today. In fact, the reality is we will think it's *too* simple. And because it's too simple we will reject it, when really it's a message of love because God knows we need it simple.

Many churches today are ashamed of the writings of Ellet J. Waggoner and Alonzo T. Jones, and there are very few ministers who will actually read them from the pulpit. Let us not be ashamed of their writings. Let us not be afraid to dig deep for hidden treasure in their writings and to use them in our own ministries. Admittedly they weren't infallible, but these things will be spiritually discerned and if you're honest in heart, you will understand it.

And if you have found perhaps things are a little hard to understand in the Spirit of Prophecy, well here's your answer. God knows that you might find it hard at first so He gave us something more basic, something more simple, and He did that because He loves us and He doesn't want us to be lost. He wants us to have every opportunity.

Now I really praise the Lord because as confusing at first as these subjects may appear to be, even trying to get our head around what we studied this hour, it really is a message of love because God is doing everything He can and He will not let us go even until – what point do the Scriptures say? – to the *uttermost* (Hebrews 7:25).

So may the Lord help us to receive every every ray of light in whatever way that He gives us. This is my prayer. AMEN.

Revisiting 1888

Part 2

THE LAW

September 7, 2013

IN our sermon last week we commenced an investigation into the message and the messengers of 1888. This week we want to revisit the 1888 Message and here is a very well known statement from *Testimony to Ministers*, p.91 which is frequently used as a summarising statement from the Spirit of Prophecy regarding the message by Elders Waggoner and Jones. It says here:

> The Lord in His great mercy sent a most precious message to His people through Elders Waggoner and Jones. This message was to bring more prominently before the world the uplifted Saviour, the sacrifice for the sins of the whole world. It presented justification through faith in the Surety; it invited the people to receive the righteousness of Christ, which is made manifest in obedience to all the commandments of God. Many had lost sight of Jesus. They needed to have their eyes directed to His divine person, His merits, and His changeless love for the human family. All power is given into His hands, that He may dispense rich gifts unto men, imparting the priceless gift of His own righteousness to the helpless human agent. This is the message that God commanded to be given to the world. It is the third angel's message, which is to be proclaimed with a loud voice, and attended with the outpouring of His Spirit in a large measure. [1]

It is a very summary statement. As we examined last week, Elders Waggoner and Jones were sent by God. They were raised up by God to deliver a particular message to bring more prominently before the world the uplifted Saviour, to make more obvious the love of God. As we had followed down through the ages of human nature, God gives a message but that message isn't always clearly understood and appreciated. And so as the end of the world back then was approaching, they needed something to be made very obvious in the experience of the church, and also the world was in need of a revelation of the love of God.

And here Ellen White said:

Many had lost sight of Jesus. They needed to have their eyes directed to His divine person, his merits.

They had lost sight of Jesus. They actually needed someone to point the finger and say, "Look this direction, here is Jesus." They needed someone to make it plain. It's interesting to read the very following paragraph:

> The uplifted Saviour is to appear in His efficacious work as the Lamb slain, sitting upon the throne, to dispense the priceless covenant blessings, the benefits He died to purchase for every soul who should believe on Him. John could not express that love in words; it was too deep, too broad; he calls upon the human family to behold it. Christ is pleading for the church in the heavenly courts above, pleading for those for whom He paid the redemption price of His own lifeblood. Centuries, ages, can never diminish the efficacy of this atoning sacrifice. The message of the gospel of His grace was to be given to the church in clear and distinct lines, that the world should no longer say that Seventh-day Adventists talk the law, the law, but do not teach or believe Christ. [2]

This is fascinating. Many had lost sight of Jesus within the Seventh-day Adventist Church, but they were *Seventh-day Adventists*. And what was the defining point of their religion? It was the fourth commandment embraced there in the Ten Commandments. So the church was distracted. It had brought itself to a point where it was making the law, the law, to be the all important factor in salvation; therefore they needed a message to bring Jesus back into the picture.

In the *1888 Materials*, p.560, Ellen White writes very clearly here:

> As a people, we have preached the law until we are as dry as the hills of Gilboa that had neither dew nor rain. We must preach Christ in the law, and there will be sap and nourishment in the preaching that will be as food to the famishing flock of God. We must not trust in our own merits at all, but in the merits of Jesus of Nazareth. Our eyes must be anointed with eye-salve. We must draw nigh to God, and he will draw nigh to us, if we come in his own appointed way. O that you may go forth as the disciples did after the day of Pentecost, and then your testimony will have a living ring, and souls will be converted to God. [3]

And again in *Selected Messages*, Vol.1, p.388. She wrote this in 1894; this is quite a profound statement:

> A legal religion has been thought quite the correct religion for this time. [4]

What kind of religion? The law, we've got to get the law right. We've got to get the Sabbath right and everything that pertains to the keeping of the Sabbath, the fine details, we have to get it right.

> A legal religion has been thought quite the correct religion for this time. But it is a mistake. The rebuke of Christ to the Pharisees is applicable to those who have lost

from the heart their first love. A cold, legal religion can never lead souls to Christ; for it is a loveless, Christless religion. [4]

And again in *Selected Messages*, Vol.3, p.168, a very telling statement:

> The faith of Jesus has been overlooked and treated in an indifferent, careless manner. It has not occupied the prominent position in which it was revealed to John. Faith in Christ as the sinner's only hope has been largely left out, not only of the discourses given but of the religious experience of very many who claim to believe the third angel's message. [5]

These statements portray a very clear picture of the condition of the church in the days of 1888. They were caught up in the law. They were so caught up in this preparation for Jesus to come, that they had to get everything in their lives right, but Jesus was left out of the picture.

Sanctification – is sanctification important? Absolutely! But is justification just as important? Sanctification had eclipsed the reality of justification. They were more focused on the practical things than the spiritual things. And today are we any different?

We can fall into the same danger. God is calling for a *reformation* of our lives. Reform means: *to make a change*. To be a *reformer* means to be constantly making changes, constantly improving; and we are called to be reformers, to make changes, to be improving. But do we get so caught up on the sanctification part that we forget the justification part? Can we get so caught up in trying to reform our lives, our diet, how we dress, down to the minutest details that we forget about love and forgiveness?

Church experiences are very telling aren't they? The Pharisees tithed the mint and the cumin. And Jesus says, "You should have done this, yes, but not have neglected the weightier matters of the law which are judgment, mercy and faith" (Matthew 23:23).

We are so prone to be working so hard to fine-tune our diet and our garments whilst at the same time we cherish enmity against our brethren. So prone to focus on a sanctified life forgetting that first we need to be forgiven and that I can only be forgiven as I forgive others.

The law was preached by the Adventist church until they were as dry as the hills of Gilboa. Are we any more moist? What is your church experience? What is mine?

The words of Christ in Matthew 5:23-24 are very plain and they are words for us today. God was seeking in 1888 to bring the church back to this particular point. They were running ahead. And were they not running ahead with even the Spirit of Prophecy?

You know Jesus said to the Jews of old, "Ye search the Scriptures for in them ye think you have eternal life." What did He mean by that? Christ meant that they were searching the Old Testament, seeking for all of the little minute points of detail so they could make a regulation out of it in their lives; that as they could identify a requirement of God, they would then be able to go and do it and boost themselves up in their self-esteem. But then they became Pharisees, harsh and judgmental.

Ellen White said that the church in her day was reliving the very experience of the Jews in Christ's day. She was constantly rebuking people for taking her testimonies and seeking to make laws and requirements out of them. They were searching her writings because in them they thought they had eternal life; that in reading it and doing it they would be saved.

But here in Matthew 25:23-34 is a principle:

> Therefore if thou bring thy gift to the altar, and there rememberest that thy brother hath ought against thee; Leave there thy gift before the altar, and go thy way; first be reconciled to thy brother, and then come and offer thy gift.

God doesn't want the outward appearance. He wants a heart that reflects His own heart; a heart that is full of His love; a heart that forgives others as that heart itself has been forgiven. God says, "Why are you focusing so much on getting everything so right when you've still got a problem with your brother or with your sister?" God says to sort that out first. Sort that out first and *then* your garments will be beautiful. Because I don't look on the outside, I look on the inside. However, as we studied last week, it is so true that no matter how many times God tells us, we miss the point. Last week we read from *Manuscript Releases*, Vol.5, p.219 regarding the message of Jones and Waggoner:

> I have had the question asked, what do you think of this light that these men are presenting? Why, I have been presenting it to you for the last forty-five years--the matchless charms of Christ. This is what I have been trying to present before your minds. [6]

For how long had she been preaching that message? For forty five years. And yet it is written there that God had to raise up men to bring the message more prominently before the people to make it clear and plain; because it didn't matter how much Ellen White preached it and taught it. In fact, she says that it's all through the Testimonies. The people were missing the point. They missed it. They were too preoccupied with the law, too preoccupied with trying to save themselves, trying to get righteousness out of the law.

Last week we touched on a very important aspect of the law, and perhaps as I mentioned it you might have thought, *That's interesting*, and that was that God *never* intended on giving the law. God actually never intended on giving the law there on Mount Sinai.

We read from *Patriarchs and Prophets,* p.364. Here it is very clear:

> If man had kept the law of God, as given to Adam after his fall, preserved by Noah, and observed by Abraham, there would have been no necessity for the ordinance of

circumcision. And if the descendants of Abraham had kept the covenant, of which circumcision was a sign, they would never have been seduced into idolatry, nor would it have been necessary for them to suffer a life of bondage in Egypt; they would have kept God's law in mind, and there would have been no necessity for it to be proclaimed from Sinai or engraved upon the tables of stone. And had the people practiced the principles of the Ten Commandments, there would have been no need of the additional directions given to Moses. [7]

Note: "If they had kept the law as it was observed by Abraham."

How did Abraham keep the law? Well, he believed God didn't he? He believed that whatever God had said, God himself would fulfil it. So God said of Abraham, "He is righteous. He is my friend." But the Jews didn't keep that covenant. They were too busy trying to save themselves, were they not?

I pray that as we follow it through you will see this in your own experience because Ancient Israel is Modern Israel and we are no different. So then why was the law given at Mount Sinai?

Now this is an interesting point, because if the Lord had no intention of giving the law at Sinai why do we make that law at Sinai so much our focus? Why are we always trying so hard to keep that stony law? Is there something for us to learn in the fact that God actually had no intention of giving it? Indeed there is. But why did He give it? Come to Deuteronomy chapter 5 because we want to take a look at this.

You know it wasn't until I went through Jones and Waggoner that I realised and discovered that God didn't actually want to give the Hebrews the Ten Commandments at Sinai. And Jones and Waggoner make this very plain in their writings. So picking up on their argumentations in Deuteronomy 5:1-7:

> And Moses called all Israel, and said unto them, Hear, O Israel, the statutes and judgments which I speak in your ears this day, that ye may learn them, and keep, and do them. The Lord our God made a covenant with us in Horeb. The Lord made not this covenant with our fathers, but with us, even us, who are all of us here alive this day.

Now you will notice, if you pause there, that the covenant made at Horeb was a different covenant to the one made with Abraham, Isaac and Jacob. It was a new covenant in the sense that it was not like the old one delivered to the fathers.

> The Lord talked with you face to face in the mount out of the midst of the fire, (I stood between the Lord and you at that time, to show you the word of the Lord: for ye were afraid by reason of the fire, and went not up into the mount;) saying, I am the Lord thy God, which brought thee out of the land of Egypt, from the house of bondage. Thou shalt have none other gods before me.

And he continues to recite the commandments that were given at Mount Sinai in Deuteronomy 5:22:

> These words the Lord spake unto all your assembly in the mount out of the midst of the fire, of the cloud, and of the thick darkness, with a great voice: and he added no more. And he wrote them in two tables of stone, and delivered them unto me.

He *added* no more. So what He had already been stating in the reading of the law was what? It was *added*. The 10 Commandments at Horeb, which is Mount Sinai were added. They were an addition. Why was it added? Galatians 3:19 tells us why the law was added:

> It was added because of transgressions.

Why? Because of transgressions.

In our Scripture reading this morning we read Romans 5:20. It says:

> Moreover the law entered, that the offence might abound.

So the law was added because of transgression. Now we want to enlarge that this morning and understand what the transgression was. If God had no intention of giving the Ten Commandments at Mount Sinai then what was it that went wrong that caused God to add it? What was the transgression at Sinai?

We're going to take a few quotes out of a book by Ellet J. Waggoner called *The Everlasting Covenant*. This is a very important book because many do not realise what its source material was. There are many who mourn the fact that there were no transcriptions taken in the General Conference Session of 1888. From 1893 onward, and even 1891, there were transcriptions taken; but in 1888 there was no record of what Ellet J. Waggoner delivered there in Minneapolis. And so there are many who mourn the fact and say, "Well, we don't even know what he taught at Minneapolis, so how do we know whether the church accepted it or not?" That's a poor excuse because Waggoner did not forget what he shared there.

On the 31st December, 1895 Waggoner wrote a letter to Ellen White in which he says:

> I have had a book much on my mind ever since the first winter I taught in Battle Creek 1889-1890. I began to write the manuscript three years ago. I have rewritten all that I first wrote and have rewritten more from time to time but have been hindered much.

So his mind was stimulated by what he shared in 1888. And his mind continued to develop the truth and he shared it, and clarified it as he had opportunity to present it. However he says, "I have been hindered much in preparing this book..."

This I do not regret as the delay has resulted in making the subject more clear to my own mind.

"Making the subject more clear to my mind..." Now Ellen White wrote as we read last week that in 1888, the subject was delivered so clearly that even a child could understand it. And yet here he's not sorry that he's written more and more of the manuscript and scrapped so much of it because it was getting clearer in his mind.

> I might say that I wrote forty pages of typed manuscript that winter but have thrown it away long since as the subject has opened up more clearly. It is on the everlasting covenant for God's promises to Israel. I have lately been able to write more on it and the light shines so clearly now that I feel the Lord would have me finish it at once. I am hoping to be freed from routine work soon long enough to enable me to finish it. When it is finished I will send a copy to Australia for examination.

This book was never actually printed until the 1900's and even then it was only printed in England. He sent a copy of the manuscript to the church in America, and the book committee sat on it for a very long time and then rejected it. *The Everlasting Covenant* was never printed in America, but this book was the development and unfolding of the 1888 Message.

Waggoner did not permit himself to be discouraged. He was the editor of a magazine or paper called *The Present Truth* and he decided to run these portions of manuscript as articles in the magazine. From the middle of 1896 through to the middle of 1897, he ran the articles on a weekly basis. And those papers were scattered around the world, as the papers of the Adventist church were at that time. On August, 26th 1898, Ellen White wrote to E.J. Waggoner from Australia:

> I write to you now because I want you, (and W.C. White is of the same mind too), to visit us in Australia. We think "Present Truth" the best paper published by our people. [8]

Ellen White referred to *The Present Truth* containing these articles on the Everlasting Covenant as the best paper ever published by the Seventh-day Adventist Church at the time. And in 1902 A.G. Daniels wrote to W.C. White regarding the book.

Now these few short moments may sound like a book review but it's more than that. If you want to find Waggoner's messages from 1888 in clarity, you will find them in that book. This is exactly what A.G. Daniels had to say about it:

> I do not know whether you have ever given this book a careful examination or not. Its name "The Everlasting Covenant", suggests its scope. It leads us to the very heart of the great gospel of Christ. It opens up God's plan of saving the world by grace through faith in Christ. It strikes that key note of the Reformation, namely, justification by faith. It shows weakness and folly of the covenant of works. The book really deals with the great question that so agitated our people at Minneapolis

and so far as I know is the only masterpiece that has been written on this subject since the Minneapolis meeting.

Much has been written on this subject for our papers by Sister White, Brother Waggoner and Brother Jones but "The Everlasting Covenant" is the only large work dealing with the great theme that has been produced. The work has been printed about two years but it has never been circulated among our people outside of England. A few copies have been sent to the United States but only a few. Those who have read the book agree in pronouncing it a most excellent production.

And then he sends a post script:

I failed to refer to the fact that there is more a less influence being exercised in the central and western states against the light that came to us in Minneapolis. I believe we are doing our people a positive injury by keeping the light away from them. They are not reading on this subject and ministers in whom they suppose they should have confidence are giving them error and darkness for truth and light, there is no question about this. Some of them are strongly arrayed on the side of those who opposed the light at Minneapolis. It is a fact that some of our younger ministers are not free to preach righteousness by faith as fully as they desire to, they have told me this. I am deeply convinced that something ought to be done to place a flood of light.

He saw that there was a need of a flood of light in the homes of the people. He then says:

I know of no better book to do this outside of the Bible than Brother Waggoner's book.

I have found *The Everlasting Covenant* to be a powerful book. If there are things in the Scriptures that you have found hard to understand, you need to read that book. It's like a set of keys that will unlock so many seemingly apparent contradictions in the Scriptures. It's a book that will explain so many things. But it is a book, as we studied last week regarding the writings of Jones and Waggoner, that the evil one seeks to keep away from our attention.

Now before we read some excerpts from that book come to Exodus 19:1-6. Come to Mount Sinai before the law was added and see if we can detect the transgression that called forth the entrance of the law. Remember these Scriptures are written for our admonition:

In the third month, when the children of Israel were gone forth out of the land of Egypt, the same day came they into the wilderness of Sinai. For they were departed from Rephidim, and were come to the desert of Sinai, and had pitched in the wilderness; and there Israel camped before the mount. And Moses went up unto God, and the Lord called unto him out of the mountain, saying, Thus shalt thou say to the house of Jacob, and tell the children of Israel; Ye have seen what I did unto the

Egyptians, and how I bare you on eagles' wings, and brought you unto myself. Now therefore, if ye will obey my voice indeed, and keep my covenant, then ye shall be a peculiar treasure unto me above all people: for all the earth is mine: And ye shall be unto me a kingdom of priests, and an holy nation. These are the words which thou shalt speak unto the children of Israel.

These are the words that God told Israel through Moses when they came to Mount Sinai.

I want to read now from *The Everlasting Covenant* where Waggoner says:

Note how God dwelt upon the fact that He Himself had done all that had been done for them. God had delivered them from the Egyptians and He had brought them to Himself. That was the thing which they were continually forgetting as indicated by their murmurings. They had even gone so far as to question whether the Lord was among them or not. And their murmurings always indicated the thoughts that they themselves could manage things better than God could.

Is that not a true description there of the behaviour of the Israelites in the wilderness? God constantly brought them into straight places where they couldn't save themselves. Yet all they did was murmur and complain and when God made it right they just wanted to take things into their own hands and go home. They thought, *we can do it better than God can.* So God was dwelling first on the fact that *He* had done these things.

God had brought them by the mountain path to the Red Sea and into the desert where there was no food or drink and had miraculously supplied their wants in every instance to make them understand that they could live only by His Word. [9]

Now note that He said, "The covenant, My covenant," the covenant that God made with Abraham.

The covenant which God made with Abraham was founded on faith and trust. "Abraham believed God, and it was counted unto Him for righteousness." So when God, in fulfillment of that covenant, was delivering Israel from bondage, all His dealing with them was calculated to teach them trust in Him, so that they might in truth be the children of the covenant. [10]

A careful reading of Exodus 19:1-6, *will show that there is no intimation that another covenant was then to be made.* Indeed, the evidence is to the contrary. The Lord referred to His covenant--the covenant long before given to Abraham-- and exhorted them to keep it, and told what would be the result of their keeping it. [emphasis supplied] [11]

What would be the result? They would be a peculiar treasure, a kingdom of priests, a holy nation.

The covenant with Abraham was, as we have seen, a covenant of faith, and they could keep it simply by keeping the faith (simply by taking God at His Word, believing what God said). God did not ask them to enter into another covenant with Him, but only to accept His covenant of peace, which he had long before given to the fathers. [11]

The proper response of the people therefore should have been what?

The proper response of the people therefore would have been, "AMEN! Even so oh Lord let it be done to us according to thy will." [12]

This is what Waggoner writes should have been the proper response.

On the contrary what did the people say? "All that the Lord hath spoken *we will do*. And Moses returned the words of the people unto the Lord" (Exodus 19:8).

They said, "We will do it! We will make ourselves a holy nation, a righteous nation. We will keep the law of God, we will meet your requirements."

Reading on in Waggoner:

On the contrary they said, "All that the Lord hath spoken we will do;" and they repeated their promise, with additional emphasis, even after they had heard the law spoken. It was the same self-confidence that led their descendants to say to Christ, "What shall we do, that we might work the works of God?" *Think of mortal men presuming to be able to do God's work!* Christ answered, "This is the work of God, that ye believe on Him whom He hath sent." Even so it was in the desert of Sinai, when the law was given and the covenant made. [emphasis supplied] [12]

Now that's a powerful sentence. We don't think of that often do we? We think exactly the same way they did. That there's God's work and I've got to go and do it. "Think of mortal men presuming to be able to do God's work!"

Even so it was in the desert of Sinai when the law was given and the covenant made... The great sin of the Children of Israel was unbelief; trust in self rather than in God. [13]

Why was the law added? Because of unbelief. Because they said, "We will do it." And so God said, "OK, here's My Ten Commandments." Waggoner continues:

Their assuming the responsibility of working the works of God, showed lack of appreciation of His greatness and holiness.

Now, do we fall into the same danger today where we think that we have to go and keep the Commandments of God? We strive so hard not to lie. We try so hard to keep the Sabbath day. We take it upon ourselves to do it and that shows lack of appreciation for His greatness and holiness.

It is only when men are ignorant of God's righteousness, that they go about to establish their own righteousness, and refuse to submit themselves to the righteousness of God.

Are you trying to establish your own righteousness? It's because you're ignorant. You're ignorant of God's righteousness.

> Their promises were good for nothing, because they had not the power to fulfill them. The covenant, therefore, which was based on those promises was utterly worthless, so far as giving them life was concerned. All that they could get from that covenant was just what they could get from themselves, and that was death.

We think we can do everything so well don't we? We think we know how to tie our hair. We think we know what to put in our cupboards. But all that we can get is that which we can get from ourselves and that was death.

> To trust in it was to make a covenant with death, and to be at agreement with the grave. Their entering into that covenant was a virtual notification to the Lord that they could get along very well without Him; that they were able to fulfill any promise He could make. [14]

> But God did not give them up, "for He said, Surely they are My people, children that will not lie; so He was their Saviour." He knew that they were moved by impulse in making that promise, and that they did not realize what it meant. They had a zeal for God, but not according to knowledge. He had brought them out of the land of Egypt, that He might teach them to know Him, and He did not become angry with them because they were so slow to learn the lesson. [15]

Praise the Lord that He's not like us. Do we get angry with each other when we're slow to learn the lesson? Do we get angry with ourselves when we are slow to learn the lesson?

> Because of their ignorance of the greatness of His holiness, which ignorance was expressed by their promise to do the law, God proceeded, by the proclamation of the law, to show them the greatness of His righteousness, and the utter impossibility of their working it out. [16]

How did they receive it? They said "Yes! Yes! We will do it." The Lord was giving them the law to help them realise the folly of the covenant they had just made: that they would make *themselves* His peculiar treasure. Are we any different to Israel of old?

The word of God comes to us and we are so quick to say, "Yes, yes, I'll do it." There at Sinai God was anxious to give them the covenant He made with Abraham and He came to them and said "I will work in you both to will and do of my good pleasure." And they responded: "Yes my Lord, we will work out our own salvation." Back to front isn't it? We look at God's requirements and standards right down to the minutiae of life and we think that we can work it out ourselves. And we try very hard don't we? We try and try and try. But it doesn't matter how many times we bash our head against the brick wall, do we ever learn? Well, we *need* to learn don't we? And we need to learn the very things that God was trying to communicate in 1888.

Last week I shared a testimony with you that Alonzo T. Jones gave in 1893. I want to read it again because I believe we can all relate with it:

> A sister told me not long ago that before that time four years ago she had just been lamenting her estate and wondering how in the world the time was ever going to come for the Lord to come if He had to wait for His people to get ready to meet him. For she said the way she had been at it--and she had worked as hard as anybody in this world, she thought--she saw that she was not making progress fast enough to bring the Lord in any kind of reasonable time at all, and she could not make out how the Lord was going to come.

Does that sound like your mind, your experience? I love it when I read things written down because it saves me writing out my own thoughts. Somebody's already written them out for me.

> She was bothered about it, but she said when the folks came home from Minneapolis and they said, "Why the Lord's righteousness is a gift; we can have the righteousness of Christ as a gift, and we can have it now." "Oh," said she, "That made me glad; that brought light, for then I could see how the Lord could come pretty soon. When He Himself gives us the garment, the clothing, the character, that fits us for the judgment and for the time of trouble, I could then see how he could come just as soon as He wanted to." "And," said she, "it made me glad, and I have been glad ever since." Brethren, I am glad of it too, all the time.

> Now there is sense in that thing today. You know we have all been in that same place. You know the time was when we actually sat down and cried because we could not do well enough to satisfy our own estimate of right-doing; (Now that's a candid statement) and as we were expecting the Lord to come soon, we dreaded the news that it was so near; for how in the world were we going to be ready? [17]

Yes I know the experience. We all know the experience.

So wherefore then the law? Back to the book *The Everlasting Covenant, p.303:*

> A pertinent question, and one that is fairly answered. ...Conviction necessarily precedes conversion. The inheritance could be obtained only through righteousness, although it was wholly by promise; for righteousness is the "gift of grace." But in order that men may appreciate the promises of God, they must be made to feel their need of them. The law, given in such as awful manner, was for the purpose of letting them know how impossible it was for them to get its righteousness by their own strength, and thus to let them know what God was anxious to supply them with. [18]

God was anxious to supply them with what? They needed righteousness, holiness and God was anxious to give it to them. Is He any less anxious today? I believe more so today because soon those winds of strife will be released. So Jesus is crying, "My blood! My blood!"

Are the Ten Commandments important? Absolutely! Without the Ten Commandments we might as well not call ourselves Seventh-day Adventists because it's all part of the law of God. But we cannot do it the way in which we have been getting at it. It will not work.

In 1888 they were trying so hard to fit themselves for Christ's second coming by the law, so they needed this message. If you are trying hard to fit yourself by the law of God this is the very message you need. God was trying to tell them that you are going about it in the wrong way. Now if you were doing something the wrong way wouldn't you be happy for someone to tell you, *"This is the right way"*? That is what God was trying to do in 1888. He was trying to relieve from their backs a great burden of stress. We ourselves are so prone to bear the same burden. We keep trying and trying thinking that somehow, somewhere in myself, I can find the very thing that will satisfy the claims of the law; and we think that all these standards of dress and of diet are going to make us look *pretty* before that law. But what did we read? We read that the very reason why the law of God was given at Mount Sinai was to show them how *ugly* they were: wretched, miserable, poor, blind and stark naked. Yet, they cried, "The law! The law! The law!"

The law was given to help us realise how utterly incapable we are of reaching its standards. We are slow to realise that though, aren't we? We're slow to realise that we can't get it the way we're going about it. You know it is true that we have what we call the cycle or the operation of the Old and the New Covenant, where we start out well, distrusting our own heart, and we rely on the strength of God, and we go ahead and have a victory. But then in that self- exaltation of victory we forget all about Christ and fall back again. Then we wallow in the mud for a little while – that law, that school-master, that conviction – and realise we *can't.*

That law leads us back to Christ so we lay hold of Christ's hand and off we go, the victory is ours, and then we forget again, take our eyes off Christ, and back down we go. And then we hear the law, the school-master, we feel the cane and it smites and it hurts, it stings, but oh, that's right, Christ is my source of strength. And so we go back again; we put self under, we have a victory and then what happens? Well the cycle needs to stop doesn't it? This operation of the Old and the New Covenant needs to reach a point where we cease to make the same mistakes. Cease to depend upon ourselves and try and work out our own salvation. The cycle can't go on forever can it? One of these days we actually need to learn the lesson. That's why we go through the cycle – *to learn.* May God help us if we're not learning! We need to learn – and we need to learn soon – that I cannot save myself. I myself cannot take those standards of God and keep them. *I can't!* And until that really dawns on us and clicks in our heads, we're going to fall flat on our face again and again and again. And we're going to get discouraged, we're going to go into depression, we're going to start lashing out at fellow brethren in the church and we're not going to be happy. None of us will be happy until we make this breakthrough. And yes the 1888 Message was a break through.

Stephen Haskell quotes Ellen White as saying that the Lord would have come in two years* from the time of the Minneapolis Conference. Two years! Now in the testimony that we just quoted from Jones, here is a lady who has testified that as she looks at herself and everyone else around her, she thinks there's no way we're going to be ready. The Spirit declares that they would have been ready in one year because that two years includes one year of probation being closed and the outpouring of the plagues. It was a message that would have prepared them for Christ's Second Coming within twelve months: signed, sealed and waiting for delivery.

Do we need a message like that today? We desperately need a message like that today. Desperately! Study the experience currently in the Middle East, particularly regarding Syria. Do you know there is a very clear path to the fulfilment of Daniel 11:45? And there's only one thing standing in the way from stopping its fulfilment. And that is the blood of Christ still pleading for us to learn these lessons quickly, because it will not take much at all.

In 1888 there was only the *proposition* of a Sunday bill going through the American government. Who would have thought that within twelve months that could have turned into world-wide *persecution* of Sabbath keepers? It would have happened overnight! So we need to learn it and we need to learn it very quickly. We need to stop missing the point in life's experiences.

Time and time again God is permitting us to fall flat on our faces to learn that we cannot do it and we need him to fulfill His covenant. We need Him to work in us to will and to do. And so I want to use Alonzo T. Jones to spell it out for us just in case life's experiences aren't sharp enough on the point. God spells it out for us. And yet I must confess myself: it doesn't matter how many times I read it, how many times I think about it, I'm still very prone to missing the point. But we're going to read it and these words are profound. These words are incredible; these words are the answer.

This comes from the *1893 General Conference Bulletins.* And here he delivered these words. And it is really sad to see that even though he delivered these words in such clarity, and that the congregation there listening (the congregation was the *ministers*) became so actively involved in answering the questions he proposed, yet they still missed it! They still missed it. But let's read it:

> Now let us see the whole story. "The law entered that the offence might abound," in order that we might find the more abundant grace abounding right there in all those places, and the grace abounds "through righteousness unto eternal life by Jesus Christ our Lord." Then what did the law enter for? [Voice: "To bring us to

the Lord."] What did the law enter for? [Voice: "To bring us to Christ."] Yes. Don't you see? Then whenever anybody in this world uses the ten commandments-when any sinner in this world uses the ten commandments for any other purpose than to reach Jesus Christ, what kind of a purpose is he putting them to? [Congregation: "A wrong purpose."] He is perverting the intent of God in giving the law, isn't he? [Congregation: "Yes sir."] To use the law of God with men for any other purpose, therefore, than that they may reach Christ Jesus, is to use the law in a way that God never intended it to be used.

Oh, we will use that law to judge our brethren won't we? We are quick to take the law as a guide for their lives and say they are guilty of this and they are guilty of that. No, God never intended the law to be used for any other purpose than that they may reach Jesus Christ. Oh, that's a skill I really pray the Lord Jesus will help us to use. To use the law to even help our brethren get to Christ. Not to crush, kill and destroy them, but to bring them to that relationship with Jesus.

Well, the law then brings us to Christ. That's certain. What for? [Congregation: "That we may be justified."] What does the law want of you and me? Does it make any demands of us before we reach Jesus Christ? When the law finds us, does it want anything from us? [Congregation: "It wants righteousness."] What kind? [Congregation: "Perfect righteousness."] Whose? [Congregation: "God's."] God's righteousness? [Congregation: "Yes."] Just such righteousness alone as God manifests in his own life, in his own way of doing things? [Congregation: "Yes."] Will that law be content with anything less than that from you and me? Will it accept anything less than that, a hair's breadth less? [Congregation: "No."] If we could come within a hair's breadth of it-that's too far short; we miss it.

Turn to Timothy, and Paul tells us what the law wants out of you and me and what it wants in us, too. 1 Tim. 1:5: "Now the end (the object, the aim, the intent, the purpose) of the commandment is charity." What is charity? [Congregation: "Love."] What kind of love? [Congregation: "The love of God."] "Out of a pure heart." What kind of a heart? [Congregation: "A pure heart."] "And of a good conscience." What kind of a conscience? [Congregation: "Good."] "And of faith unfeigned." That is what the law wants to find in you and me, isn't it? Will it accept you and me with anything less than that which it demands--perfect love, manifested "out of a pure heart, a good conscience, and of faith unfeigned"? No, never. Well, that is simply perfection, that it demands.

Well, now, have we--has any man in the world--any of that kind of love to offer to the law of God? [Congregation: "No."] Has any man naturally that kind of a conscience? [Congregation: "No."] No, sir. Well, then, the law makes that demand of every man on the earth tonight, no difference who he is. He makes it of you and me; he makes that demand of people in Africa and of all the people on the earth, and he will not accept anything less than that from anyone of them. But, we are talking about ourselves tonight. So, the law comes to you and me tonight and says: "I want charity; I want perfect love--the love of God. I want to see it in your life all the time. And I want to see it manifested out of a pure heart and through a good conscience and unfeigned faith." That is where we are.

""Well," says one, "I have not got it. I have done my best."

Have you ever felt that you haven't got it, but I'm doing my best?

But the law will say, "that is not what I want. I don't want your best. I want perfection. *It is not your doing I want anyhow; it is God's I want.* It is not your righteousness I am after; I want God's righteousness from you. It is not your doing I want. I want God's doing in your life." That is what the law says to every man. [emphasis supplied]

Did you hear that? I want every man to hear that. Instead of trying to strive so hard to render to the law my own righteousness, my own right-doing, lets learn how to have the right-doing of God in our lives because that's what the law wants.

Then, when I am shut off thus at the very first question and even then when I said I did my best, then I have nothing more to say. Is that not what the Scripture says: "That every mouth may be stopped." It does just that, does it not?

But there comes a still small voice saying, "Here is a perfect life; here is the life of God. Here is a pure heart; here is a good conscience. here is unfeigned faith." Where does that voice come from? [Congregation: "Christ."] Ah, the Lord Jesus Christ, who came and stood where I stand in the flesh in which I live. He lived there. The perfect love of God was manifested there. The perfect purity of heart manifested there. A good conscience manifested there, and the unfeigned faith of the mind that was in Jesus Christ is there.

Well, then, He simply comes and tells me, "Here, take this." That will satisfy, then, will it? [Congregation: "Yes."] The life manifested in Jesus Christ, that will satisfy the law. The purity of heart that Jesus Christ gives--that will satisfy the law. The good conscience that He can create, that will satisfy. The unfeigned faith which He gives--that will satisfy. Will it? [Congregation: "Yes."]

Well then is that not what the law wants all the time? It is Jesus Christ that the law wants, is it not? [Congregation: "Yes."] That is what the law wants: that is the same thing which it calls for in the fifth of Romans, is it not? But why does it call for it in connection with me? It calls for Christ in me, because the law wants to see that thing in me. Then is not the object of the law of God, the gospel of Christ alone? "Christ in you the hope of glory?" Ah, that is so.

Oh then the message of the righteousness of God which is by faith in Jesus Christ, brings us to, and brings to us, the perfect fulfillment of the law of God...

Is that what you want? Well, it's what we need. The message of the righteousness of God which is by faith in Jesus Christ brings it to us.

> So then when we have Jesus, when we have received Him by faith and the law stands before us or we stand before it and it makes its wondrous demand of charity, we can say, "Here it is. It is in Christ and He is mine!"

> Then, just as Steps to Christ tells us, we can come to Jesus now and be cleansed and stand before the law without one touch of shame or remorse. [*Steps to Christ*, p.51] Good. Brethren, when I have that which makes me at perfect agreement with the law of God, then I am satisfied, and cannot help but be glad that I am satisfied. [19]

Do you really realise what it is that we just read? Do you realise the simplicity of what we just read? If we will believe that, we have the answer to all of our problems. We have the answer to all of our lawful strivings because we don't have in ourselves what the law wants. We can't do it! But Jesus can and Jesus did. And that's what the law wants. It wants God's righteousness. It's not my righteousness anyway. And if you ask me, that takes a lot of stress off my back because I try so hard to keep the law of God but I always fall flat on my face. I can never make that law happy. But there it is, there is a life, it's already there. It's Jesus Christ. He became us. Christ in us. If we believe it, if we receive it, the stress is gone. The judgmentalism is gone, the hurt, the pain, the sorrow, the suffering is all gone. And you know, within two years we'll be in the kingdom and we want that don't we? Or maybe in two years God's people would be in the kingdom but *we* missed it again. One last chance!

Alonzo T. Jones gives a beautiful story, depiction, here of two parties arriving at the gates of heaven and I have to read these because it is so beautiful.

> And in that day there are going to be two parties there. There are going to be some there when the door is shut, and they will want to go in, and they say, " Lord, open to us. We want to come in." And someone comes and asks, "What have you done that you should come in? What right have you to enter the inheritance here? What claim have you upon that?" "Oh, we are acquainted with you. We have eaten and drunk in thy presence, and thou hast taught in our streets. Yes, besides that we have prophesied in thy name. In thy name we have cast out devils and in thy name we have done many wonderful works. Why, we have done many wonderful things. Lord, is not that evidence enough? Open the door."

> What is the answer? "Depart from me, ye that work iniquity." What did they say? "We have done many wonderful works. We have done them. We are all right. We are righteous. We are just. Exactly right. Therefore we have a right to be there. Open the door." But "we" does not count there, does it?

> There is going to be another company there that day--a great multitude that no man can number--all nations and kindreds and tongues and people, and they will come up to enter in. And if anyone should ask them that question, "What have you done that you should enter here? What claim have you here?" The answer would be:

"Oh, I have not done anything at all to deserve it. I am a sinner, dependent only on the grace of the Lord. Oh I was so wretched, so completely a captive and in such a bondage that nobody could deliver me but the Lord Himself; so miserable that all I could ever do was to have the Lord constantly to comfort me, so poor that I had constantly to beg from the Lord; so blind that no one but the Lord could cause me to see; so naked that no one could clothe me but the Lord Himself. All the claim that I have is what Jesus has done for me. But the Lord has loved me. When in my wretchedness I cried, He delivered me. When in my misery I wanted comfort, He comforted me all the way. When in my poverty I begged, He gave me riches. When in my blindness I asked Him to show me the way, that I might know the way, He led me all the way and made me to see. When I was so naked that no one could clothe me, why, He gave me this garment that I have on, and so all I can present, all that I have to present as that upon which I can enter, any claim that would cause me to enter, is just what He has done for me. If that will not pass me, then I am left out, and that will be just too. If I am left out, I have no complaint to make. But, oh, will not this entitle me to enter and possess the inheritance?"

But he says, "Well, there are some very particular persons here. They want to be fully satisfied with everybody that goes by here. We have ten examiners here. When they look into a man's case and say that he is all right, why then he can pass. Are you willing that these shall be called to examine into your case?" And we shall answer, "Yes, yes, because I want to enter in, and I am willing to submit to any examination, because even if I am left out I have no complaint to make. I am lost anyway when I am left to myself."

"Well," says he, "we will call them then." And so those ten are brought up and they say, "Why, yes, we are perfectly satisfied with him. Why, yes, the deliverance that he obtained from his wretchedness is that which our Lord wrought; the comfort that he had all the way and that he needed so much is that which our Lord gave. The wealth that he has, whatever he has, poor as he was, the Lord gave it, and blind, whatever he sees, it is the Lord that gave it to him. And he sees only what is the Lord's. And naked as he was, that garment that he has on, the Lord gave it to him. The Lord wove it, and it is all divine. It is only Christ. Why, yes, he can come in."

And then, brethren, there will come over the gates a voice of sweetest music, full of the gentleness and compassion of my Saviour--the voice will come from within, "Come in, thou blessed of the Lord." [Congregation: "Amen."] "Why standest thou without?" And the gate will be swung wide open, and we shall have "an abundant entrance into the everlasting kingdom of our Lord and Saviour Jesus Christ." [20]

Do you want that entrance? Stop looking to yourself. Stop looking to your brethren. Start looking to that precious message of the righteousness of Christ and we will find an abundant entrance.

May God help us to do that is my prayer. AMEN.

Revisiting 1888

Part 3
RIGHTEOUSNESS BY FAITH

September 14, 2013

Time is running short. It is running *very* short and it is only the Lord in His mercy that is holding back those winds of strife. Over the past two weeks we have been revisiting 1888 and last week we read several particular statements intimating that if the message of 1888 was received as God intended, it would have done a very quick work. And I referred to this statement made by Stephen Haskell who quotes Ellen White as saying:

> I saw that Jones and Waggoner had their counterparts in Joshua and Caleb as the Children of Israel stoned the spies with literal stones of sarcasm and ridicule... I saw that you wilfully reject what you know to be truth just because it was too humiliating to your dignity. I saw some of you in your tents mincing and making all manner of fun of these two brethren. I also saw that if you had accepted their message we would have been in the kingdom two years from that date but now we have to go back into the wilderness and there stay forty years. [see note on page 261] [1]

Two years from the date that the message was first given in 1888, they would have been in the kingdom. And as we understand last day prophecies, the outpouring of the plagues and the close of probation, that would have given just one year for their message to perfect a people to stand in the Day of God without an intercessor.

It would have needed to have been a very powerful message, and as we looked at it last week we saw that the testimony of the Spirit was that the church had been preaching the law, the law, until they were as dry as the hills of Gilboa. And Alonzo T. Jones in 1893 made this particular statement regarding the law and the entrance of the law and the purpose of the law; something which the Adventist Church in 1888 had not fully understood as had not the Israelites at Mount Sinai. And here in the *1893 General Conference Bulletins* he stated this:

> Now let us see the whole story. "The law entered that the offense might abound," in order that we might find the more abundant grace abounding right there in all

those places, and the grace abounds "through righteousness unto eternal life by Jesus Christ our Lord." Then what did the law enter for? [Voice: "To bring us to the Lord."] What did the law enter for? [Voice: "To bring us to Christ."] Yes. Don't you see? Then whenever anybody in this world uses the ten commandments--when any sinner in this world uses the ten commandments for any other purpose than to reach Jesus Christ, what kind of a purpose is He putting them to? [Congregation: "A wrong purpose."] He is perverting the intent of God in giving the law, isn't He? [Congregation: "A wrong purpose."] He is perverting the intent of God in giving the law, isn't he? [Congregation: "Yes, sir."] To use the law of God with men for any other purpose, therefore, than that they may reach Christ Jesus, is to use the law in a way that God never intended it to be used. [2]

A very bold statement isn't it, that the law is to be used for just one purpose and that is to get to Jesus Christ? Not for judging our brethren and sisters, not as something we ourselves feel we need to go and keep, but no, to get to Jesus.

Two years later at the General Conference Session of 1895 Alonzo T. Jones made an even bolder statement:

And man who is trying to seek life in keeping the Ten Commandments and teaching others to expect life by keeping the Ten Commandments that is yet even the ministration of death. [3]

"*The ministration of death.*" To tell others to expect life by keeping the Ten Commandments is to be a minister of death. These are very bold words.

However the Spirit of Prophecy in *Faith and Works,* p.18 resounds a very similar thought and here her words emphasise this fact:

There is not a point that needs to be dwelt upon more earnestly, repeated more frequently, or established more firmly in the minds of all than the impossibility of fallen man meriting anything by his own best good works. Salvation is through faith in Jesus Christ alone. [4]

Salvation is through faith in Jesus Christ alone. It doesn't matter how much you try and keep the Ten Commandments or how much you *do* keep the Ten Commandments it will not merit you anything.

In Romans chapter 10, Apostle Paul wrote to the church in Rome, and there he spoke of the Jews as being ignorant of God's righteousness and going about to establish their own righteousness. Last week we saw that that's the very thing that the Hebrews sought to do at Mount Sinai. God had promised them that He would make them a holy nation, but they said "We will do it. We will make ourselves holy." And when God spoke the Ten Commandments they said "All that you have said *we* will do it." They were ignorant of God's righteousness.

We saw last week that the law is the transcript of God's character. It is the expression of His righteousness, His right-doing. And that law which they thought that they could do was given that they would realise that they could *not* do it; because that law wanted *God's* righteousness, *God's* right-doing, *God's* perfection.

In the *1893 General Conference Bulletins* that we read from last week, Alonzo T. Jones gave this beautiful description of how when the law comes to us, it comes to us and says, "I want righteousness, I want a perfect life," but, it doesn't want *our* righteousness.

The Scriptures declare our righteousness is as filthy rags. The law wants God's righteousness and was not that the very reason why Jesus came? The Scriptures declare that "He made Himself of no reputation" (Philippians 2:7), and some of the versions read that He "annihilated Himself". He came and completely emptied Himself (Philippians 2:7) and said "I can of mine own self do nothing" (John 5:30). But who did the works? Who did He say did the works? "My Father, he doeth the works" (John 10:37-38). So Christ came and stood in our place completely emptied of Himself. And the Father worked His righteousness within Him, and that was the gift of Jesus Christ, th*e gift of the righteousness* (Romans 5:17), the right-doing of God.

From *1893 General Conference Bulletins* where we read there last week:

> So then when we have Jesus, when we have received Him by faith and the law stands before us or we stand before it and it makes its wondrous demand of charity, we can say, "Here it is. It is in Christ and He is mine!" [5]

Did you know the Scriptures say that it is a *"gift of righteousness?"* God has given it to us! He has sent His Son so that we can take His Son, make Him our own; and when the law of God comes and says, "I want a perfect life," we can take His Son, believe in His merits, appropriate His merits to ourselves and that law is perfectly satisfied. And the testimony in regard to the message given there at Minneapolis was that:

> When He Himself gives us the garment, the clothing, the character, that fits us for the judgment and for the time of trouble, I could then see how He could come just as soon as He wanted to. [6]

Because it was a gift! God has done everything for them and God just wanted them to appropriate that gift to themselves. It was indeed a message that could prepare the people of God in a very quick time – *a very quick time*. But as we saw, they were in a state of confusion; they were all bound up with the law, the law. Even though Ellen White had been preaching the same truth for forty five years, they had been missing the point. And so God had to send Jones and Waggoner with a very unique experience and way of communicating the message, to try and aid them in understanding the simplicity of it all. And it's interesting to note to what degree of simplicity Alonzo T. Jones actually came to in the presentation of the subject of righteousness by faith.

I want to read to you again from the *1893 General Conference Bulletins*. And the speaking and the simplicity here probably couldn't get any plainer on the subject of righteousness by faith. You will indeed find this to be very interesting:

> For what saith the Scripture? Abraham believed God and it was counted unto him for righteousness." What does that say? Abraham believed God and it it i-t, what? [Congregation: "Faith."] It, what? [Congregation: "Believed God."] His believing God--what did that amount to? [Congregation: "Righteousness."] Who counted it to him for righteousness? [Congregation: "God."] Well, did God make a mistake? [Congregation: "No."] Whether we understand it or not, the Lord did it, and He did right in doing it. He was perfectly just. He said so. We were not in the doing of it; we did not have the plan to lay. We could not have done it if we had tried anyway. Let us let Him have His own way, I say again, brethren, and when we let Him have His own way and we are in His own way, it will be all right, and we need not be a bit afraid.

> What was counted to Abraham for righteousness? He believed God, and God said, "You are righteous, Abraham. "Now that is said three times in that little short space. What was it that was counted to him for righteousness? His believing God. It, i-t, it. [7]

> "What shall we say then that Abraham our father, as pertaining to the flesh, hath found? For if Abraham were justified by works, he hath whereof to glory; but not before God." [8]

> "For what saith the Scripture? Abraham believed God, and it was counted unto him for righteousness. What was it that was counted unto Abraham for righteousness? [Congregation: "He believed God."] When God said a thing, Abraham believed it. He said "that is so." What was it that the Lord said to him? Let us turn and read, because that is important to us. Gen. 15:4-6." [9]

Let us read that Scripture because what Alonzo T. Jones is doing here is just simply reading the word of God as a little child. And are we not told that we must become as little children in order to enter the kingdom of heaven? Genesis 15:4-6

> And, behold, the word of the Lord came unto him, saying, This shall not be thine heir; but he that shall come forth out of thine own bowels shall be thine heir. And he brought him forth abroad, and said, Look now toward heaven, and tell the stars, if thou be able to number them: and he said unto him, So shall thy seed be. And he believed in the Lord; and he counted it to him for righteousness.

Returning to Jones:

> Now do you believe that Abraham became righteous in just that way? [Congregation: "Yes."] Honestly now, do you? [Congregation: "Yes, sir."] Do you know he did? [Congregation: "Yes."] The Lord called Abraham out and said, Look at the stars and tell the number of them, so shall thy seed be. Abraham said, "Amen." That is the Hebrew, Abraham said, "Amen." And the Lord said, "You are right."

Now do you know that it was as simple a transaction as that? Was it just like calling you and me out of this tabernacle and the Lord saying to us, See the stars? Tell the stars if thou be able to number them. Yes, so shall such and such be. And we say, "Amen." And He should say, "You are righteous." Suppose the Lord called you and me out tonight. No, He can do it without calling us out. He called Abraham out doors to show him the stars, but He can show us sins without calling us out doors. Has He shown you a great many sins? Has He? [Congregation: "Yes."] Now He says, If thou be able to number them, "they shall be white as snow." What do you say? [Congregation: "Amen."] Then what does the Lord say? [Congregation: "You are righteous."] Are you? [Voice: "Yes."] Do people become righteous as easy as that? Is it as simple a transaction as that? [Congregation: "Yes."] Amen. Thank the Lord! Now let us turn again to the 4th of Romans and get the particular verse where this is told. Rom. 4:23, 24: "Now it was not written for his sake alone, that it was imputed to him, but for us also, to whom it shall be imputed, if we believe on him that raised up Jesus our Lord from the dead." [10]

See the plain speaking of the Scriptures which is for us today? Reading on:

What the Lord said to Abraham, Abraham believed. And what He says to you and me, you and I believe, then we get the same results. It is not some particular thing that the Lord says, that we must believe in order to be righteous; whatever He says, believe it, and then He says, "you are right."

I would like to know whether it is not so, that when the Lord says a thing He is right? [Congregation: "Yes."] Then when I say that is so, am I not right? [Congregation: "Yes."] What in the world hinders me from being right? Can you tell? I will say it again: When the Lord says a thing, is He right? [Congregation: "Yes."] He is right in saying it; then when I say "that is so"; when I say "Amen"; when I say "be it so"; when I say "yes, that is so," then am I not right? Yes. Am I not right just as certainly as He is? Certainly. Can even He say I am wrong? [Congregation: "No."] He says a thing, and I say the same thing; can He say I am wrong? [Congregation: "No."] When you say the same thing, can He say that you are wrong? [Congregation: "No."] Well then, when we are in such a situation that the Lord Himself cannot say that you and I are wrong, I would like to know what in the world is the reason we are not right? And believing God puts us in just that situation, as He did Abraham. I would like to know what can keep us out of heaven then? What can keep us out of the kingdom of God then? [10]

That's a good question isn't it? What can keep us out of the kingdom of God then?

The only thing that can keep you and me out of the kingdom of God is to tell the Lord that He lies, and if you and I will stop that business we will get into heaven all right. That is just what people need to do, to stop telling the Lord that He lies. "He that believeth not God hath made him a liar." But whoever would make God a liar is a liar himself, and liars cannot get into the kingdom of God. "Without are liars" and all those other people referred to in Rev. 21:8, 27, and 22:15. Then the thing we want to do is to stop lying. Let us quit right now. Stop lying. No difference what the Lord says, you say, "That is so." [10]

Wow! There is a plainness of speech there that is rarely heard in the world today. If God says it, and you believe it, according to Alonzo T. Jones you're righteous and it's that simple. Really? How do you think the church of that day would have responded to a message like that? You know I believe they would have pulled out the following quote from 1886. And here Ellen White writes in *Bible Commentary*, Vol.6, p.1073:

> God requires at this time just what He required of the holy pair in Eden, perfect obedience to His requirements. His law remains the same in all ages. The great standard of righteousness presented in the Old Testament is not lowered in the New. It is not the work of the gospel to weaken the claims of God's holy law, but to bring men up where they can keep its precepts.

> The faith in Christ which saves the soul is not what it is represented to be by many. "Believe, believe," is their cry; "only believe in Christ, and you will be saved. It is all you have to do." While true faith trusts wholly in Christ for salvation, it will lead to perfect conformity to the law of God. Faith is manifested by works. And the apostle John declares, "He that saith, I know him, and keepeth not his commandments, is a liar" [11]

Do you think they could have responded with such a statement as that? Because there was Alonzo T. Jones saying Abraham simply believed God and he was saved, he was made righteous. Does it not sound similar to what Ellen White is reciting here from the pulpits of many churches today? *Believe; just believe and that is all that you have to do.* Was Jones wrong or was Jones right? What did Ellen White have to say in regard to the very plain speaking of Alonzo T. Jones? She wrote him a letter and in that letter she gave him some counsel and I want to read to you that letter:

> Brother A. T. Jones, I wish to call your attention to another matter. I was attending a meeting, and a large congregation were present. In my dream you were presenting the subject of faith and the imputed righteousness of Christ by faith. You repeated several times that works amounted to nothing, that there were no conditions. The matter was presented in that light that I knew minds would be confused, and would not receive the correct impression in reference to faith and works, and I decided to write to you. You state this matter too strongly. There are conditions to our receiving justification and sanctification, and the righteousness of Christ. I know your meaning, but you leave a wrong impression upon many minds.

> While good works will not save even one soul, yet it is impossible for even one soul to be saved without good works. God saves us under a law, that we must ask if we would receive, seek if we would find, and knock if we would have the door opened unto us. Christ offers Himself as willing to save unto the uttermost all who

come unto Him. He invites all to come to Him. "Him that cometh to me I will in no wise cast out.' You look in reality upon these subjects as I do, yet you make these subjects, through your expressions, confusing to minds. And after you have expressed your mind radically in regard to works, when questions are asked you upon this very subject it is not laying out in so very clear lines in your own mind that you can not define the correct principles to other minds, and you are yourself unable to make your statements harmonize with your own principles and faith.

The young man who came to Jesus with the question, "Good Master, what thing shall I do, that I may have eternal life?" and Christ saith unto him, 'Why callest thou me good? There is none good but one, that is God: but if you wilt enter into life keep the commandments,' He saith unto him, 'Which?' Jesus quoted several, and the young man said unto him, 'All these things have I kept from my youth up; what lack I yet?' Jesus said unto him 'If thou wilt be perfect, go and sell that thou hast, and give to the poor, and thou shalt have treasure in heaven: and come and follow me,' Here are conditions, and the Bible is full of conditions.

But when the young man heard that saying, he went away sorrowful: for he had great possessions.' Then when you say there are no conditions, and some expressions are made quite broad, you burden the minds, and some cannot see consistency in your expressions. They cannot see how they can harmonize these expressions with the plain statements of the Word of God. Please guard these points. These strong assertions in regard to works, never make our position any stronger. The expressions weaken our position, for there are many who will consider you an extremist, and will loose the rich lessons you have for them, upon the very subjects they need to know.

Christ said, 'If any man will come after me, let him deny himself, and take up his cross daily, and follow me.' I feel such an intense interest that every soul shall see, and understand and be charmed with the consistency of the truth. The evidence of our love to Christ is not pretension; but practice. My brother it is hard for the mind to comprehend this point, and do not confuse any mind with ideas that will not harmonize with the word. Please to consider that under the teaching of Christ many of the disciples were lamentably ignorant; but when the Holy Spirit that Jesus promised, came upon them and made the vacillating Peter the champion of faith. What a transformation in his character. But do not lay one pebble for a soul that is weak in the faith to stumble over, in over-wrought presentations or expressions. Be ever consistent, calm, deep, and solid. Do not go to any extreme in anything, but keep your feet on solid rock. O precious, precious Saviour. 'He that hath my commandments and keepeth them, he is it that loveth me, and he that believeth me shall be loved of my Father, and I will love him, and will manifest myself to him.' [12]

This letter was written to Alonzo T. Jones in respect to messages that he was communicating. Interesting isn't it? We just read previously from Alonzo T. Jones where he said "Just believe, if God says it, whatever it is that he says just say Lord, Amen it is so, and you are righteous. God will count you as fit for His kingdom." And here Ellen White gave him a warning: *Be very, very careful what you say.*

It's interesting there that she actually says: "I know your meaning, you look in reality upon these subjects as I do."

So was he wrong? No. He was not wrong. His meaning was right. What he meant to convey was the same reality that Ellen White believed and taught herself. But then she says:

> Please consider that under the teaching of Christ many of the disciples were lamentably ignorant.

There was the problem. Ellen White could understand what he was communicating, but the others were getting confused. They had difficulties harmonising his messages with the way they previously read the word of God. The law, the law, the law was what they had been focusing on their whole Christian experience. Then along comes Alonzo T. Jones who says if you are going to try and keep the law, and you are going to tell people they're going to be saved by keeping the law, you're a minister of death. And they got very uncomfortable, very uncomfortable indeed.

What was the issue? The issue was that the people were "lamentably ignorant". She said, "You look in reality upon the subject as I do but please be careful not to lay one pebble for a soul that is weak in the faith to stumble over."

They were not yet ready to understand the simplicity of the message. His meaning was correct but he was misunderstood. And the problem is very clearly defined here in *Faith and Works*, p.18. Ellen White wrote this in 1890:

> The danger has been presented to me again and again of entertaining, as a people, false ideas of justification by faith. I have been shown for years that Satan would work in a special manner to confuse the mind on this point. The law of God has been largely dwelt upon and has been presented to congregations, almost as destitute of the knowledge of Jesus Christ and His relation to the law as was the offering of Cain. I have been shown that many have been kept from the faith because of the mixed, confused ideas of salvation, because the ministers have worked in a wrong manner to reach hearts. The point that has been urged upon my mind for years is the imputed righteousness of Christ. I have wondered that this matter was not made the subject of discourses in our churches throughout the land, when the matter has been kept so constantly urged upon me, and I have made it the subject of nearly every discourse and talk that I have given to the people."
>
> In examining my writings fifteen and twenty years old [I find that they] present the matter in this same light--that those who enter upon the solemn, sacred work of the ministry should first be given a preparation in lessons upon the teachings of Christ

and the apostles in living principles of practical godliness. They are to be educated in regard to what constitutes earnest, living faith. [13]

What was the problem? The problem was that the ministers had been working in a wrong manner. They had not educated the people in regard to what constitutes earnest, living faith.

So as soon as Alonzo T. Jones came along and said, "Believe! Believe as Abraham believed," they misunderstood him. What did Alonzo T. Jones mean when he said believe? Ellen White said, "I know your meaning, it's exactly what I agree with but the way you're expressing it the people are getting confused." And the people were getting confused because they didn't understand what he meant when he taught what faith was.

In 1899 Alonzo T. Jones makes it very clear what he meant when he speaks of Abraham's believing:

> Faith is the expecting the word of God to do the thing which that word speaks, and the depending upon the word only to accomplish the thing which that word speaks."

> Abraham is the father of all them which be of faith. The record of Abraham, then, gives instruction in faith—what it is, and what it does for him who has it.

> What shall we say, then, that Abraham our father, as pertaining to the faith, has found? What saith the Scripture?

> When Abram was more than eighty years old, and Sarai his wife was old, and he had no child, God "brought him forth abroad, and said, Look now toward heaven, and tell the stars, if thou be able to number them: and he said unto him, So shall thy seed be."

> And Abram "believed in the Lord; and he counted it to him for righteousness." Gen. 15:5, 6. Abram accepted the word of God, and expected by the word what the word said. And in that he was right. [14]

In fact, turn to Romans 4:18-22. The apostle spells it our very clearly for us here:

> Who against hope believed in hope, that he might become the father of many nations, according to that which was spoken, So shall thy seed be. And being not weak in faith, he considered not his own body now dead, when he was about an hundred years old, neither yet the deadness of Sarah's womb: He staggered not at the promise of God through unbelief; but was strong in faith, giving glory to God; And being fully persuaded that, what he had promised, he was able also to perform. And therefore it was imputed to him for righteousness.

What did Alonzo T. Jones say? "Abram accepted the word of God, and expected by the word what the word said. And in that he was right."

When God came to him and said so shall thy seed be, Abraham's faith was a belief that God would fulfil His word.

We know the Scripture in Isaiah: "My word shall not return unto me void but it shall accomplish the thing whereunto I sent it" (Isaiah 55:11).

Abraham's faith lay hold of that reality, that *"it"* – *"the word"* would produce the very thing itself. And so back to this message of righteousness by faith. We meet the law. We realise that the righteousness of God contained in the law is something that we do not have to give. It's not in our selves and yet we see our miserable lives and we see that everything we do is full of iniquity. And we cry out, "Oh, who shall deliver me from the condemnation of this law?!" I don't have what it wants. I've just got these filthy garments. They're my own right-doing! Then Jesus comes to us and He says, "Here, here is my life, a perfect life, a life which is full of the workings of God. Take it, believe it, believe that it's yours." And if we will do that, if we will do it, then *Steps to Christ*, p.62 says.

> Christ's character stands in place of your character, and you are accepted before God just as if you had not sinned. [15]

Is that not how we find forgiveness? God comes to us: "I forgive you. Here is my Son, a propitiation for the remission of sins that are past." And what do we do? Well, we believe it don't we? We don't bother waiting for a happy flight of feelings because we know that feelings will not justify us. Feelings will not bring us forgiveness. We've only got one option and that is to say, *"Ok Lord.* Thank you."

And in *Steps to Christ*, p.50, Ellen White describes exactly that:

> From the simple Bible account of how Jesus healed the sick, we may learn something about how to believe in Him for the forgiveness of sins. Let us turn to the story of the paralytic at Bethesda. The poor sufferer was helpless; he had not used his limbs for thirty-eight years. Yet Jesus bade him, "Rise, take up thy bed, and walk." The sick man might have said, " Lord, if Thou wilt make me whole, I will obey Thy word." But, no, he believed Christ's word, believed that he was made whole, and he made the effort at once; he willed to walk, and he did walk. He acted on the word of Christ, and God gave the power. He was made whole.

> In like manner you are a sinner. You cannot atone for your past sins; you cannot change your heart and make yourself holy. But God promises to do all this for you through Christ. You believe that promise. You confess your sins and give yourself to God. You will to serve Him. Just as surely as you do this, God will fulfill His word to you. If you believe the promise,--believe that you are forgiven and cleansed,--God supplies the fact; you are made whole, just as Christ gave the paralytic power to walk when the man believed that he was healed. It is so if you believe it. [16]

She is speaking just as plainly as Alonzo T. Jones here isn't she?

Do not wait to feel that you are made whole, but say, "I believe it; it is so, not because I feel it, but because God has promised. [16]

And God supplies the fact!

Now the big issue with Alonzo T. Jones' plain speaking was that they couldn't see past the justification point. They could see the declaration of Christ's righteousness for the remission of sins that are past. That's fine. But what did we read before? We read that there are conditions, there is a change, there is a practical holiness that needs to be evident in the life. And Jones' message didn't seem to harmonise with that. But Ellen White said, "I know what you mean, that is exactly the way that I understand it as well."

One thing today that Christianity is so quick to forget or overlook is what righteousness is. Righteousness is right-doing. So when we speak of righteousness by faith we're not just talking about an aura of holiness or just a sense of holiness or just a legal transaction. We are talking about something that is practical in the life itself. It was a message given in 1888 which was *right-doing by faith*. But because the people didn't understand how it was that faith works they choked on Jones' words.

Colossians 2:6 communicates to us the very basic principle. We have received Jesus Christ – how? By taking God at His word and simply believing that He means what He says, and He will produce the fact.

As ye have therefore received Christ Jesus the Lord, so walk ye in him.

How do you receive forgiveness for your sins? By taking God at His word. By believing that He will fulfil His word to you. So just as ye have received Christ, so walk ye in Him. Continue to take God at His word. God gives you the promise. Rely and depend upon Him to supply the fact!

Christ's Object Lessons, p.61:

Our part...

And don't we want to know what our part is because God's not going to do everything for us. It's described as a co-operation where God works and man works. Well what is man's works? It is to receive God's word and to hold it fast.

Our part is to receive God's word and to hold it fast, yielding ourselves fully to its control, and its purpose in us will be accomplished. [17]

What is our part? To believe! To believe that the word of God will accomplish the thing itself. And so when the law of God comes to us and it says, "Thou shalt have no other god's before me," it's a promise, it's the word of God with a power in it to accomplish *itself* in our lives. Then when it comes and it says, "Thou shalt not lie," we are to receive that word as having power in itself to keep us from lying. In *The Desire of Ages* Ellen White refers to Psalms 119:11 as Christ speaking:

Thy word have I hid in my heart that I might not sin against thee.

"Thy word have I hid in my heart that I might not sin," because that word itself would accomplish the fact itself. And when Jesus was tempted in the wilderness what was His answer? "*It is written.*" And that was His defence. That was His power to overcome because the faith of Jesus, which was the same faith that Abraham had, took God at His word, believed that God would keep His word.

And one of the very last articles Ellen White ever wrote for any publication comes from the *Bible Training School*, June 1, 1915, para.1, the very year that that she died. She writes here regarding faith:

> The work of faith means more than we think. It means genuine reliance upon the naked word of God...

Means what? "Genuine reliance on the naked word of God."

> By our actions we are to show that we believe that God will do just as He has said. [18]

By what? By our actions. We are called to live a holy life. We can because God has promised to keep us holy; He has promised that we will have no other gods before Him; He has promised that we shall not lie; He has promised that we shall not covet. This is His word and if we believe it, then by our actions we will show we believe God will do just as He has said.

> The wheels of nature and of providence are not appointed to roll backward nor to stand still. We must have an advancing, working faith, a faith that works by love and purifies the soul from every vestige of selfishness. It is not self, but God, that we must depend upon. We must not cherish unbelief. We must have that faith that takes God at His word. [18]

"Faith that takes God at His word." If we will have *that* faith, if we will have a faith that will say "*Amen!*" to whatever God says, God will call us righteous because that word is going to produce the thing.

The other thing that Apostle Paul writes in Romans chapter four is that God counts those things that aren't as though they are. So in the one year of probation that was given to the church God knew that the word would produce the thing because it doesn't return unto Him void.

It was interesting, as I was preparing this particular sermon today, I kept on wanting to go down in my mind in the research and study of different aspects of the whole message, justification, sanctification, etc. But each time I tried to do so I kept on coming up against a block and that block was that it is righteousness by *faith*.

It doesn't matter how clear we might be on all of the other subjects, if we haven't understood faith, when God comes to us as clearly as He did through Alonzo T. Jones in 1893, what will our reaction be? *Hmmm, I'm not too sure about that*, and we'll pull out the same quote from 1886. Why? Because we haven't understood what it means to *believe*.

Review and Herald, October 18, 1898, para.7 Ellen White writes:

> At nine o'clock I attended a meeting of the students in the school chapel. About eighty were present, and the room was full. An hour was occupied in reading, and in talking to them about the necessity of their understanding how to exercise faith. This is the science of the gospel. The Scripture declares, "Without faith it is impossible to please God." The knowledge of what the Scripture means when urging upon us the necessity of cultivating faith, is more essential than any other knowledge that can be acquired. We suffer much trouble and grief because of our unbelief, and our ignorance of how to exercise faith. We must break through the clouds of unbelief. We cannot have a healthy Christian experience, we cannot obey the gospel unto salvation, until the science of faith is better understood, and until more faith is exercised. There can be no perfection of Christian character without that faith that works by love, and purifies the soul. [19]

What is more essential than any other knowledge? Did you know what it means to exercise faith? You know the question was asked by the jailor to Apostle Paul: "What must I do to be saved?" What did Apostle Paul say? "Believe on the Lord Jesus Christ and thou shalt be saved." Believe, only believe! Yes, but we need to understand what the Scriptures mean when they say, *"believe"*.

The Lord gave his people a precious message through Elders Jones and Waggoner but the church never received the message. Not just because of the human pride in the ministers; but the members of the church missed out on it because they had not been educated in regard to the very fundamental principles of faith.

Selected Messages, p.145:

> Said the angel, "Some tried too hard to believe..."

Is this your problem? Do you get confused at what it means to believe when the word of God says "believe"?

> Some tried too hard to believe. Said the angel "Faith is so simple, ye look above it. [20]

Have we been doing that our whole entire life? Could it be that today we are missing the point simply because we don't understand the science of faith? After all, the message was righteousness by *faith*. We can focus so much on righteousness and all the *right-doing* but "without faith it is impossible to please God" (Hebrews 11:6).

Of the 1888 Message, Ellen White wrote in the *1888 Materials*, p.281:

> The religion of Jesus Christ has not been as clearly defined as it should be, that

the souls who are seeking for the knowledge of the plan of salvation may discern the simplicity of faith. In these meetings [the meetings of Jones and Waggoner] this has been *made so clear that a child may understand that it is an immediate, voluntary, trustful surrender of the heart to God*--a coming into union with Christ in *confidence*, affectionate obedience to do all His commandments through the merits of Jesus Christ. It is a decisive act of the individual, committing to the Lord the keeping of the soul... [emphasis supplied]

Committing to who? The Lord. It is the trusting of the fulfilling of His word.

...It is the climbing up by Christ, clinging to Christ, accepting the righteousness of Christ as a free gift. The will is to be surrendered to Christ. Through faith in the righteousness of Christ is salvation. [21]

In our first message we looked at how the Lord needs to speak to us more and more simply. But if God comes to us today and He speaks more simply than He did in 1893, would we miss it simply because we haven't educated ourselves in regard to faith?

May God help us to come to the point where we know by experience that God means what He says. He Himself will do what He says. Don't the Scriptures say that "it is God that worketh in you both to will and do of His good pleasure?" (Philippians 2:13). And what does it say before that? "Work out your own salvation with fear and trembling" (Philippians 2:12). So what is our part? The working out of our salvation is to lay hold of the word of God; to resign ourselves to *Its* workings and whatever the Lord says we can say, "Amen, let it be," and *God* will supply the fact.

Next week we will take this formula and we will apply it to the truth for this generation. But until then may God help us to be as little children – if Daddy says so, then it is so. AMEN.

Revisiting 1888

Part 4
LIGHT FOR OUR GENERATION
September 21, 2013

JESUS is coming again; but the Scriptures and the Spirit of Prophecy make it very plain that when He comes very much depends on His people. It is written that "Christ is waiting with longing heart to see His own beautiful character perfectly reproduced in His people and when He sees that He will take them home" (paraphrased from *Christ's Object Lessons*, p.69). This world is not our home – we sing that in many hymns. We certainly do not find this world to be a comfortable place do we? We would like to be removed from this earth would we not? Indeed.

Well, this week is our closing study on revisiting 1888. Over the past three weeks we have examined small portions of the Jones and Waggoner message. And we have also dealt with some of the major issues as to why they are not fully appreciated today. It is my prayer that this study today will not be the end of something but rather a culmination of the last three Sabbaths; to inspire us to actually begin something; to begin to familiarise ourselves with that "precious message" delivered in 1888 and the following years.

As we heard last week, it was a message that would accomplish a work in a very short time – a *very* short time – within a few years, Ellen White states in several quotes. And the testimony that Alonzo T. Jones gave there in 1893 I believe is a very powerful testimony, that as there was this sister in the church looking at herself and looking at the church, she thought, *How are we ever going to be ready for Jesus to come?* And then when she heard the 1888 Message she found the answer to the problem that we all have, and her words were:

> ...that when he himself gives us the garment, the clothing, the character that fits us
> for the judgment and for the time of trouble I could then see how he could come just
> as soon as he wanted to. [1]

One year? Three years? Three months? One week? Can we limit God? But we do

– by not believing what He has written. They were given a year or two and that would have been all that they would have needed to be fitted for translation. Today we have no guarantee that we even have that long. It is written here in *Early Writings*, p.67:

> Said the angel, "Deny self; ye must step fast." Some of us have had time to get the truth and to advance step by step, and every step we have taken has given us strength to take the next. But now time is almost finished, and what we have been years learning, they [the new converts] will have to learn in a few months. They will also have much to unlearn and much to learn again. [2]

Not years. Months!

And in *The Great Controversy*, p.612 Ellen White speaks of the outpouring of the latter rain and of the people of God going forth with the loud cry. And of the opposition that rises against it, she says:

> Notwithstanding the agencies combined against the truth, a large number take their stand upon the Lord's side. [3]

A large number have yet to be called out from the world and from the various churches. At what time? When the word of God goes forth with power. When the latter rain is pouring out upon God's people, a large number will have but a few months to be fitted for translation.

Is it any wonder then, as we read there in our very first study in *Christ's Object Lessons*, p.127 that it is true that there is a message today needed, a greater clarification, crystallisation of even that which they had in 1888:

> In every age there is a new development of truth, a message of God to the people of that generation...

We are no longer the generation of 1888, we are the generation next in line and there is a message of God to the people of this generation. However, she says:

> ...The old truths are all essential; new truth is not independent of the old, but an unfolding of it. [4]

It is only as the old truths are understood that we can comprehend the new. So only as we know the Jones and Waggoner message will we appreciate the message for our day. Only as we understand a message that could prepare God's people within a year or two will we come to understand and comprehend a message that can do it in a few *months*.

We often like to rely upon a particular statement – "Sanctification is the work of a lifetime" (*Christ's Object Lessons*, p.65). Well I'm sorry, we do not have a life-time. Maybe we ourselves could have missed the point and are just as ignorant of salvation as those are who will hear the truth at the last second. Maybe we ourselves have much to learn and much to unlearn in just a few short months. We need a message today that will cut short the work of God in righteousness; a message that will fit us for translation in a very short time – a *very* short time.

I want to have a quick review of the past few weeks and I want to use the following two statements from the Spirit of Prophecy:

Faith and Works, p.18:

> There is not a point that needs to be dwelt upon more earnestly, repeated more frequently, or established more firmly in the minds of all than the impossibility of fallen man meriting anything by his own best good works. [5]

Two weeks ago we read that in 1888 God had to send the church a message to break them out of this: *the law, the law, the law,* mentality; where Ellen White says they had preached the law until they were as dry as the hills of Gilboa. So Waggoner brought the truth of the law in Galatians, that the law was *"added"* because man took the law of God as a command when God intended it as a promise. God intended the law to cause man to realise that he can't keep it. The very next sentence says:

> Salvation is through faith in Jesus Christ alone. [5]

And therefore if salvation is though faith in Jesus Christ alone, we read this quote taken from *Review and Herald*, October 18, 1898 par. 7 which echoes our study last week:

> The knowledge of what the Scripture means when urging upon us the necessity of cultivating faith, is *more essential* than any other knowledge that can be acquired. We suffer much trouble and grief because of our unbelief, and our ignorance of how to exercise faith. We must break through the clouds of unbelief. We cannot have a healthy Christian experience, we cannot obey the gospel unto salvation, until the science of faith is better understood. [emphasis supplied] [6]

So whilst it must be constantly brought home to us, dwelt upon earnestly, repeated frequently, established firmly in our minds that we cannot keep the law – not in our own merits, in our own strength, or in our own best good works – then we need to understand *faith*. It's just as important that we understand the *science of faith*. And so this was the message that God was seeking to convey in 1888, seeking to prepare a people to be ready for Christ to come *through faith in Jesus Christ alone.*

Today I believe we are no different. Is it not true that when the law of God comes to us and when it says, "I want righteousness," do we not say, "Just wait a moment, I'm getting there. Just one moment; give me a lifetime and I'll have it all sorted then because sanctification is the work of a life-time. And just there on my death-bed I'll be all sealed and I'll be ready. But until then I'll do my best, I'll try hard." This was the mentality of the church in 1888. That's the mentality of many Christians today.

This next quote comes from *1893 General Conference Bulletins* by Alonzo T. Jones:

> "Well," says one, "I have not got it. I have done my best." But the law will say, "that is not what I want. I don't want your best. I want perfection. It is not your doing I want anyhow; it is God's I want. It is not your righteousness I am after; I want God's righteousness from you. It is not your doing I want. *I want God's doing in your life."* [emphasis supplied] [7]

You know I really praise God for those words. I really do, because until I read those words for myself I was trying so hard in my own strength to keep the law and thinking that by my own personal obedience I can merit salvation; that as I see the standards of God, as I dress as God instructs, as I eat as God instructs then He will be pleased with me. Well what do the Scriptures say in Hebrews? "Without faith it is impossible to please God" (Hebrews 11:6). Because there it also says in Romans that "What is not of faith is sin" (Romans 14:23). Therefore if faith is not bringing the perfect working of God into my life, if it is not faith that causes God to dress me, causes God to feed me, if it is not God doing those works, it's filthy garments, *filthy garments*. If we are doing it all in our own strength we are Pharisees and we will crucify the Son of God afresh in His believers upon this earth.

God was trying to convey this to His church in 1888: that you need a power outside of yourself; you cannot merit anything by your own best good works. And you know, I got so much relief when I realised the law actually doesn't want my obedience. It causes me to now stop looking within myself for the answers. Stop relying on myself, but now to start praying, *Alright, Lord teach me how to LET you do it in me.* And the answer is found there in the messages of Jones and Waggoner to the point there that it is so simple even a child may understand. But they missed it back then, didn't they?

And we have examined a process down through the ages where God has to keep making the truth more and more simple. And so the light for our generation needs to be a truth that is even simpler than the Jones and Waggoner message. There needs to be an even greater crystallisation of the righteousness by faith message.

It is true as we sang in the hymn, Jesus is coming again. And He is coming again very soon, and before He comes He will cease His intercession in the Most Holy Place, and we will need to stand before God without an intercessor. To stand before God; to stand before the law without sin, individually, singly and alone. The law will come to us that day just as it comes to us now and will say, "I want a perfect life." But friends, the Scriptures are very plain that the wages of sin is death. Do you have a perfect life? Well maybe by the time you've been sealed and settled into the truth both intellectually and spiritually so that you cannot be moved, then maybe, from then on you will cease to sin. But that law wants a perfect existence. *A perfect existence!* And the reality is that if we do not have a perfect existence to present to that law today and in that day, we will receive the plagues; we will suffer the wrath of God.

Churches today like to teach a *vicarious* sacrifice. And we often think that the justification that God gives us is just an imputation where Jesus Christ is our substitute and He covers us. Is that not taught in Adventism today: that the righteousness of Christ is as an umbrella and we are hiding under that umbrella still committing our secret sins? If we do not have a perfect life to give to the law, a life that is our own life personally, individually, we are dead. This is *clear logic*.

I want to ask you a question: if a man went to trial and he was judged to be guilty of man-slaughter, and the sentence of condemnation was the death-sentence, how would the law of this country react if someone perfectly innocent came along and said, "I will die in his stead"? How would the law of this country react? It would say, "Not a chance – no! That man committed the act; that man has to pay the penalty."

There is no way that any legal system on this earth will permit an innocent person to die in the place of someone convicted of a terrible crime and yet you will hear anecdotes like that in the churches though, won't you? That such and such a man was on death row and someone came along and took his place. No! It doesn't work like that, and such a story does not actually give us the answer to our problem because we need a perfect existence, not just something that's going to be a blanket covering the sins of our past.

If we think that the law of God is going to excuse and accept a vicarious sacrifice, we don't appreciate the law of God as we should. If man's law will not permit a guilty sinner to go free – and God's law is infinitely more righteous and just – then when the law comes to you and me personally and it demands a perfect life from you *personally*, if you don't have that to give, you're dead and buried. But you won't be buried in the church courtyard because you died in shame!

If the law of man will not permit a substitute, then the law of God will not permit a substitute because it's too holy, too just, and too good. So how then can we stand in that day? Well the law of God wants a perfect life, a perfect existence, and by *existence* it means a perfect life from the day that we are born to the day that we die, a life totally full of obedience. But what kind of obedience? *God's* right-doing. Do you have that to give?

Well I'm very happy to be able to tell you today that you do. We personally, individually, do have a life that we can present to the law of God which is perfectly full of the right-doing of God from the day we were born to ever-after – if you will believe it. If you will believe what? "It". If we will believe "It". Whatever promise God makes for us, if we will believe "It", He will supply the fact and He will count us as righteous.

I want to read this from *Steps to Christ*, p.62:

> The condition of eternal life is now just what it always has been,--just what it was in Paradise before the fall of our first parents,--perfect obedience to the law of God, perfect righteousness. If eternal life were granted on any condition short of this, then the happiness of the whole universe would be imperilled... Since we are sinful, unholy, we cannot perfectly obey the holy law. We have no righteousness of our own with which to meet the claims of the law of God. [8]

After quoting this, Alonzo T. Jones in *1893 General Conference Bulletins* says:

> That is so. Then how in the world are we ever going to have eternal life?

Good question.

> Ah! "the gift of God is eternal life through Jesus Christ our Lord." But we have got to have "perfect righteousness" before we can have that gift, don't you see? Oh then, just like the Lord, He comes and says, "Here, in Christ, is perfect righteousness; here is perfect obedience to the law of God from birth to the grave; you take that and that will fully meet the condition on which alone anyone can have eternal life." [9]

Do you believe it? Believe it friends, because this is the only way we can have eternal life.

> All right. Are you not glad of it? [Congregation: "Yes."] I am so glad of it that I don't know what else to do than to be glad. Oh, He wants me to have eternal life. I haven't a thing to merit it; I haven't a thing that will meet the condition upon which alone it can be granted. Everything that I have would ruin the universe if He should grant me eternal life upon it. Well, He can't do that; but He wants me to have eternal life; He wants me to have it so bad that He died that I might have it. [Congregation: "Amen!"] And oh, then again I say, it is just like God, who is love, as He is, He comes and says, Here, in Christ, is perfect obedience from the first breath you ever drew, until the last one, and you take Him and His righteousness and then you have got the other." That is the condition. Good! Good! Yes, sir. [9]

There it is! In Christ is a perfect existence. But how personal is that? The law of God wants perfect obedience from individuals. The law of God wants perfect obedience from Camron.

Just echoing Alonzo T. Jones here in *Steps to Christ*, p.62:

> Christ has made a way of escape for us. He lived on earth amid trials and temptations such as we have to meet. He lived a sinless life. He died for us, and now He offers to take our sins and give us His righteousness. [10]

Now when you read the word righteousness, read the word as it means: *"right – doing"*, acts, works, fruit. So He offers to take our sins and give us His right-doing.

> If you give yourself to Him, and accept Him as your Saviour, then, sinful as your life may have been, for His sake you are accounted righteous. Christ's character stands in place of your character and you are accepted before God just as if you had not sinned. [10]

But the law of God won't accept a substitute as we consider a substitute to be. So how does this work? How personal does the righteousness of Christ apply to each one of us? Is it just a legal, judicial thing or is it more than that?

Last week we looked at righteousness by faith and what was faith? We read here from *The Bible Training School*, June 1, 1915, para 1, one of the very last articles Sister White ever wrote for a paper:

> The work of faith means more than we think. It means genuine reliance upon the naked word of God. By our actions we are to show that we believe that God will do just as He has said... We must not cherish unbelief. We must have that faith that takes God at His word... Without faith (a faith that will rely upon a plain statement of the word) it is impossible to please God. [11]

So if we want to know how it is that the righteousness of Christ is mine, we need to read God's word exactly as it reads and believe it, whatever it says. He has come to us and said, "Here, in Christ, is perfect obedience." But that law wants perfect obedience from ourselves personally, not just judiciously.

Here in the very first part of Hebrews 7:26 is our answer – if you have faith.

> For such an high priest [Jesus Christ] became US.

"Became us." Will you read that word as you read it? Will you receive that word as it says? Jesus Christ became *US*.

The Desire of Ages, p.390:

> In His promises and warnings, Jesus means me... God so loved the world, that He gave His only-begotten Son, that I by believing in Him, might not perish, but have everlasting life. The experiences related in God's word are to be MY experiences. Prayer and promise, precept and warning, are mine. [12]

So Jesus became who? Don't be afraid to say it friends. If you have faith you can say that Jesus became *me*; because when God says such a High Priest became "us", He became us in the sense that He would have died if there was only one person to die for; and He relates with us as though there's nobody else – God means "me". Me!

Let's enlarge this. Come to Hebrews 4:15. We want to look at this in light of the *1888 Message* and the message as it developed over the following years.

> For we have not an high priest which cannot be touched with the feeling of our infirmities but was in all points tempted like as we are, yet without sin.

That's the kind of life we're needing isn't it? A life that can go through all the temptation, can be touched with all the misery of this world, but is yet without sin.

Alonzo T. Jones in the *1895 General Conference Bulletins* makes these particular comments on that verse. Listen very carefully:

> He could not have been tempted in all points like as I am if He were not in all points like as I am to start with. Therefore it behooved Him to be made *in all points like me,* if He is going to help me where I need help. I know that right there is where I need it. And oh, I know it is right there where I get it. Thank the Lord! There is where Christ stands and there is my help.

> "We have not a high priest which cannot be touched"--two negatives there; have not a high priest which cannot be touched. Then what do we have on the affirmative side? We have a high priest who can be touched with the feeling of our infirmities--my infirmities, your infirmities, our infirmities. Does He feel my infirmities? Yes. Does He feel your infirmities? Yes. What is an infirmity? Weakness, wavering, weakness--that is expressive enough. We have many of them. All of us have many of them. We feel our weaknesses. Thank the Lord, there is One who feels them also--yea, not only feels them but is touched with the feeling of them. There is more in that word "touched" than simply that He is reached with the feeling of our weaknesses and feels as we feel. He feels as we feel, that is true, but beyond that He is "touched"; that is, He is tenderly affected; His sympathy is stirred. He is touched to tenderness and affected to sympathy and He helps us. This is what is said in the words, "touched with the feeling of our infirmities." Thank the Lord for such a Saviour!

> But I say again, He cannot be tempted in all points like as I am unless *He was in all points like I am to start with.* He could not feel as I do unless *He is where I am and as I am.* In other words, He could not be tempted in all points as I am and feel as I feel unless *He was just myself over again.* The word of God says: "In all points like as we are." [emphasis supplied] [13]

Did you lay hold of that? He cannot be tempted in all points as I am unless He was in all points like as I am. And He cannot feel what I feel unless He is where I am and as I am. That makes perfect sense doesn't it? Because I respond to certain stimuli in my environment around me. Life's experiences create trials, tribulations and stir up infirmities. But wouldn't He need to be right where I am, in exactly the same situation in order to meet and feel the same challenges that I am feeling?

Now say, if you and I were to drive down the road and there's a billboard and on that billboard there's some kind of temptation; in order for Jesus Christ to be tempted in all points like as I am, He needs to be driving down the road at that same time, at that same place, tempted with the same billboard. Does that make sense? It really does. It really does make sense. Because unless He is where I am and as I am He cannot be tempted in all points like me. And unless He is myself over again, without sin, then there is not a perfect life that is my life that I can give to the law. I will enlarge that.

Reading on in *1895 General Conference Bulletins* a few pages down:

> In Jesus Christ there is furnished in completeness all that man needs or ever can have in righteousness, and all there is for any man to do is to choose Christ and then it is his. [14]

You want the righteousness of Christ? You want God's perfect doing in your life? All you need to do is choose Christ and then it's yours.

> So then as the first Adam was We, the second Adam is We. In all points He is as weak as are we. Read two texts: He says of us, "Without me ye can do nothing." Of Himself He says: "Of mine own self I can do nothing."
>
> These two texts are all we want now. They tell the whole story. To be without Christ is to be without God, and there the man can do nothing. He is utterly helpless of himself and in himself. That is where the man is who is without God. Jesus Christ says: "Of mine own self I can do nothing." Then that shows that the Lord Jesus put Himself in this world, in the flesh, in His human nature, precisely where the man is in this world who is without God. He put Himself precisely where lost man is. He left out His divine self and *became we.* And there, helpless as we are without God, He ran the risk of getting back to where God is and bringing us with him. It was a fearful risk, but, glory to God, He won. The thing was accomplished, and in Him we are saved. [emphasis supplied] [14]

Are you following this? I really pray that you are following this because this was the 1888 Message that needs to crystallise in our understanding – that Jesus Christ became our own-selves and as our own-selves He lived a perfect life. Who was He? He was we. He was me. His life, His perfect life, was our life individually, personally. Every single one of us has the right to say, "Jesus lived *my* life," and I pray that we will have the faith to say it, believe it, and live like we believe it.

When the law comes to me and says, "I want a perfect life," and it's not going to accept a substitute, we don't need a substitute because there is Jesus Christ who became me. His life was the life of Camron and from the day Jesus Christ was born, through all eternity, He who became we lived a perfectly holy life. And so individually we can say to the law, "Here is a perfect life, here is Camron's perfect life and it's full of the right-doing of God."

You know the word atonement, it's more than just an appeasing of the wrath of God, at-one-ment, AT ONE – ONE – He became we. But the question is: will you take God at His word? Will you? If we will, then as we are so prone to look back in our lives and see only sin and remorse; it drags us down doesn't it? Well, we can see what God says; we read there in *Steps to Christ* that we will stand there "just as if we had not sinned", because Jesus Christ who became we never sinned, and as God looks upon

Jesus Christ He sees us – because He became us. He sees Jesus meeting every single temptation and trial we have ever had in our lives and having a complete victory. And if He didn't do it for each of us individually we could never be justified. Never, never ever be justified. The law will not permit it. But as we look back and see how it is that Christ has conquered everything in our past, then we can look forward as well and we can look in the present moment. And because we can look in the present moment, we find Jesus has come so close to me, that He is right where I am and as I am, and whatever trial I am going to meet with next, in order for me to be justified, He has to have already met that trial and done it right. Now that's a trial to look forward to isn't it? Because He's already had the victory! The victory's already mine if I will believe it.

You know, we often speak of the *appropriation* of the righteousness of Christ – appropriating His merits. Do you know what "appropriate" means? It simply means to make it your own, to take it personally. So when we are told to appropriate the merits of Jesus Christ we are being told to consider them as yours, yes, as yours; to believe that Jesus Christ emptied Himself and said "I can of mine own self do nothing, the Father, He is the one that doeth the works" (John 5:30, 14:10). I am to believe that what the Father worked in Him, He worked and *works* in me.

And here further from Alonzo T. Jones *1895 General Conference Bulletins*:

> If He had come into the world as He was in heaven, being God, manifesting Himself as He was there and God being with Him, His name would not have been "God with us," for He would not then have been ourselves. But He emptied Himself. He Himself was not manifested in the world. For it is written: "No man knoweth the Son but the Father"--not simply no man, but no one. No one knoweth the Son but the Father. "Neither knoweth any man the Father, save the Son and he to whomsoever the Son will reveal Him." It is not written, No man knoweth the Son but the Father and he to whom the Father will reveal Him. No. No man knoweth the Son at all, but the Father. And the Father does not reveal the Son in the world, but the Son reveals the Father. Christ is not the revelation of Himself. He is the revelation of the Father to the world and in the world and to men. Therefore, He says, "No man knoweth the Father but the Son and he to whomsoever the Son will reveal the Father." So it is the Father that is revealed in the world and revealed to us and revealed in us in Christ. This is the one thing that we are studying all the time. This is the center around which everything else circles. And Christ having taken our human nature in all things in the flesh and so having become ourselves, when we read of Him and the Father's dealings with Him, *we are reading of ourselves and of the Father's dealings with us. What God did to Him was to us; what God did for Him was for us.* And therefore, again it is written: "He hath made Him to be sin for us, who knew no sin; that we might be made the righteousness of God in Him." 2 Cor. 5:21. [emphasis supplied] [15]

Can you see the atonement here?

> "The Lord is my shepherd; I shall not want. He maketh me to lie down in green pastures; he leadeth me beside the still waters. He restoreth my soul: he leadeth me in the paths of righteousness."

> Who? Me, a sinner? one laden with sins? Will He lead me in the paths of righteousness? Yes. How do you know? He did it once. In Christ He led me in the paths of righteousness once, for His name's sake, a whole lifetime. Therefore I know that in Christ He will lead me, a sinful man, again and ever in the paths of righteousness for His name's sake. That is faith. [15]

Oh may the Lord grant us this faith!

> Taking these words as we have heard in Brother Prescott's lesson this evening, as being themselves the salvation of God which comes to us, they themselves will work in us the salvation of God itself. That is where Christ got it. When He put Himself where we are, where did He get salvation? He did not save Himself. That was the taunt, "He saved others; Himself He cannot save. . . . Let Him now come down from the cross and we will believe on Him." He could have done it. But if He had saved Himself, it would have ruined us. We would have been lost if He had saved Himself. O, but He saves us! Then what saved Him? This word of salvation saved Him when He was ourselves, and it saves us when we are in Him. He leads me in the paths of righteousness for His name's sake--*me, me!* And this in order that everyone on the earth can say in him, "He leadeth me."

> "Yea, though I walk through the valley of the shadow of death." Where was He in the twenty-second Psalm? On the cross, facing death. The twenty-third Psalm comes right in there, in proper order, you see, as He steps into the dark valley. "Though I walk through the valley of the shadow of death, I will fear no evil: for thou art with me; thy rod and thy staff they comfort me." Who? *Christ and in Him ourselves, and we know it because God did it once for us in Him. And in Him it is done still for us.* [emphasis supplied] [15]

Wow! The church really missed out back in the years following 1888 didn't they? Here in the life of Christ was a prophecy of every single one of our own lives. What God did for Christ He was doing it for us. As He worked in Christ He was working in us!

So when we see Jesus Christ asleep on a boat in the middle of the storm, what are we really to see? We are to see Him doing that as our own selves. And if you're in the middle of a storm and you will let this appreciation become your reality – Christ has already done it as you. You've already done it. No need to stress, you have already fallen asleep in the middle of the storm – so just fall asleep again!

And then as you see Christ standing before Caiaphas and you see Him being falsely accused, scorned, beaten, spat upon and not a single iota of reaction, do you know you are looking at yourself in Christ? He did that as you with all of your frailties, your infirmities, with your nervous disorders, and with your weak heart and you failures from the past that want to keep haunting you. He did it as us! Receive it as a prophecy of your own life. And yes, is it not as the Scriptures say, "a faith that is to work by love?" (Galatians 5:6). When you see what God has actually done, that he has come this close – wow! There is a perfect life, it's right there, I just have to live that life. But that God would actually come into my sinful wretchedness – what a contemplation!

You know what we're like when we see each other's sins – "Just go away, you contaminate me!" No. Jesus came literally into our very experience. Not just ours, but for every man that has ever lived in this world. But the problem is they will never avail themselves of it, never. And we can say that He has lived a perfect life for every man because does not Jesus say "whatever ye have done unto the least of these ye have done or not done it unto me" (Matthew 25:40). Can you understand it? How Jesus Christ can come and live the life of every single individual and do everything right? I don't understand it; but the Scriptures tell us in Colossians that it's a *mystery*. It's a mystery that Christ would be in us, one with us. And truly it is a hope of glory, even though there is such a short time period. It is hope because it is the answer we need.

Christ's Object Lessons, p.311:

> When we submit ourselves to Christ, the heart is united with His heart, the will is merged in His will, the mind becomes one with His mind, the thoughts are brought into captivity to Him; we live His life. [16]

Now that's plain speaking isn't it? His life: we personally live His life. There's a perfect union, an at-one-ment.

From *The Desire of Ages*, p.668:

> If we consent, He will so identify Himself with our thoughts and aims, so blend our hearts and minds into conformity to His will, that when obeying Him we shall be but carrying out our own impulses. [17]

Now have you ever been puzzled about that one? Well here's your answer. If Jesus Christ was me and now I have submitted and consented to that reality, of course I am going to be carrying out the impulses of my own heart. Obedience will only be natural. Because didn't Jesus say, "I delight to do thy will... thy law is within mine heart?" (Psalm 40:8). Whose heart was His heart? It was my heart; it was your heart; it's our heart.

In Galatians 2:20 here it is very clear:

> I am crucified with Christ...

Yes, because if Jesus Christ became me, us, when He died we died, but when He rose again, does it not say "on the third day He will raise *us* up"? (Hosea 6:2). Is that not God's promise there in the Old Testament?

Nevertheless I live...

I still have my own personal individuality.

Yet not I but Christ liveth in me and the life which I now live in the flesh I live by the faith of the Son of God who loved me and gave himself for me.

Do not those words describe it perfectly? I live but yet not I, but Christ liveth in me. And there is a lot more that I could actually share from Jones and Waggoner – a lot more. But the church missed it, *the church missed it.* Are we going to miss it today?

What they shared back then was only an introduction to the subject. It's something that we need today to make even clearer, simpler, plainer because we don't have a couple of years, we've only got a few short months!

Is there any other truth that can prepare us? Is there any other truth than that there is a life, a perfect life, it's your life, just make it your own? Can any other message prepare us for Jesus to come? If we will make this our own we may come to a fork in the road, but as we come to that fork in the road we will know just which way to go; *The Desire of Ages* tells us that (p.668); because we will pray: "Lord, you've already gone this way before me in Jesus Christ, Jesus was me, He lived my life, He's done it aright, He's gone down the right road. Amen Lord! Let it be so!"

And if we will consent and yield to that it will be our experience. We will say, "Lord, live out Thy life, which was my life, within me." And whatever it is that we are trialled with in life, Jesus is right there, He is meeting the trial right now, He's already met the trial. And indeed our prayer will be "Lord I yield to thee my life, live out Thy life within me." His victory will be our victory. And it is my prayer that God will help us to believe this, to be like a little child – if Daddy said so, then it is so.

Just because you don't understand it, don't doubt it. Have you ever wondered about 2 Corinthians 3:18? And I might go a little overtime but I make no apologies because this is the most exciting subject in the entire Scriptures. This is the only message that gives me hope, the *only* message. And for a long time I wondered about 2 Corinthians 3:18. It says here:

But we all, with open face beholding as in a glass the glory of the Lord, are changed into the same image from glory to glory, even as by the Spirit of the Lord.

Now I always puzzled about that because it says looking "as in a glass". What's a "glass"? Well, it's a mirror. What do you see when you look in a mirror? You see your own self don't you? When you look in a mirror you see the reflection of your own self.

But did you note the first part of the verse: "with open face"? And the other versions render it "without a veil."

Without the veil of *unbelief*, we see it as it really is because the Scriptures tell us plainly that God set forth His Son as a propitiation for every man. So every single man has a perfect life, a perfect existence. And when we will believe this, when this veil of doubt is removed, we will see the reality, and the reality is that when we are looking at the life of Jesus Christ – filled with the glory of the Father's perfect works – we are looking in that mirror and seeing our own life. And if we are constantly keeping that before our mind's eye – it's my life, it's MY LIFE – we will make some very quick steps because it's me, I've already done it! Obedience will become second nature.

Jesus can come just when we start believing this perfectly, and it's our choice as to when we believe it. There is a light that is needed for our generation, and there is not a single message other than this one here that needs to really clarify itself in our understanding in our practical reality. The atonement is the truth around which all other truths cluster, so that when we look at Christ and His obedience, we need to see Him being obedient as our own selves.

What if we saw Christ one hundred years ago as our example, somewhere *over there* doing everything right and we're just going to copy and imitate? Maybe a hundred years ago that might have given us sanctification because *"it's a lifetime and I'm still trying to work that one out."* But we can't afford to have Jesus over there. We can't afford to look 2000 years ago for some substitute. Jesus is coming very soon and we need to see Jesus right here, right now, standing up here preaching a perfect sermon, sitting in a chair listening to a sermon, meeting all of the distractions and having a victory.

If we claim to be justified, this is a reality because without a perfect existence there is no justification. If we don't live it, if we don't preach it, God will raise up someone else because He wants to come and He'll even get the stones to call out if He has to. We need what Ellen White calls "the electric shock of the Holy Spirit."

Testimonies, Vol.5, p.257:

> Pray that the mighty energies of the Holy Spirit, with all their quickening, recuperative, and transforming power, may fall like an electric shock on the palsy-stricken soul, causing every nerve to thrill with new life, restoring the whole man from his dead, earthly, sensual state to spiritual soundness. You will thus become partakers of the divine nature, having escaped the corruption that is in the world through lust; and in your souls will be reflected the image of Him by whose stripes you are healed. [18]

Through what? Through the electric shock of the Holy Spirit which will transform us. Have you ever looked at electricity in science? Electricity can fuse things together down to even the atomic level where things that are diametrically opposed become bonded in one substance. Through the power of the Holy Spirit He can bring to us the life of Jesus Christ – the at-one-ment of Jesus Christ.

They were afraid in 1888 that the message of Waggoner and Jones would lead people into fanaticism; they were afraid of where it was going. It will be no different today, *no different*.

Selected Messages, Vol.2. p.57:

> The baptism of the Holy Ghost as on the day of Pentecost will lead to a revival of true religion and to the performance of many wonderful works. Heavenly intelligences will come among us, and men will speak as they are moved upon by the Holy Spirit of God. But should the Lord work upon men as He did on and after the day of Pentecost, many who now claim to believe the truth would know so very little of the operation of the Holy Spirit that they would cry, "Beware of fanaticism." They would say of those who were filled with the Spirit, "These men are full of new wine."

Listen to this:

> The time is not far off now when men will want a much closer relation to Christ, a much closer union with His Holy Spirit, than ever they have had, or will have, unless they give up their will and their way, and submit to God's will and God's way. [19]

What did she say that men will want not far off? A closer union with Christ than they've ever had before! Anything that falls short of what we're studying today friends, anything that falls short of that union – we will be lost.

> The great sin of those who profess to be Christians is that they do not open the heart to receive the Holy Spirit. When souls long after Christ, and seek to become one with Him, then those who are content with the form of godliness, exclaim "Be careful, do not go to extremes." [19]

Friends, I entreat you to dig deep into this truth. I'm limited with what I can share with you and everything that I could share with you is useless unless you make it your own as you study it out for yourself.

Jones and Waggoner gave us an introduction to this beautiful truth that we so desperately need today, but unless we understand their truth we will not understand this truth today. We can be ready for Jesus to come today because we have a perfect life and that life is our life, and if we believe it, we will live like it. Just like when we say the words *by beholding we become changed*. Yes because if we are getting up in the morning or even before we get out of bed planning our day, at that very moment we will be thinking Jesus is here, Jesus is right here with me, as me, and He's living my perfect life. And if we ask the Holy Spirit to show us that perfect life, He will show us just what

I have done that day. But we will be very quick to forget this if we don't keep it before our mind's eye. We need to keep it constantly before us – *constantly.*

I can't emphasise the importance of this message any more than I have just tried.

I just want to close with Alonzo T. Jones from the *1893 General Conference Bulletin*:

> Oh, He is a complete Saviour. He is my Saviour. My soul doth magnify the Lord. My soul shall rejoice in the Lord, brethren, tonight. Oh, I say with David, come and magnify the Lord with me and let us exalt His name together. He has made complete satisfaction. There is not anything against us, brethren. The way is clear. The road is open. The righteousness of Christ satisfies. [20]

And may each of us say: AMEN.

CHRIST MY RIGHT-DOING

October 26, 2013

I would like to commence our meditation this morning by reading a few verses from Zechariah chapter 3. We are familiar with the story here in Zechariah 3:1-7. Here was a vision of Zechariah:

> And he showed me Joshua the high priest standing before the angel of the Lord, and Satan standing at his right hand to resist him. And the Lord said unto Satan, The Lord rebuke thee, O Satan; even the Lord that hath chosen Jerusalem rebuke thee: is not this a brand plucked out of the fire? Now Joshua was clothed with filthy garments, and stood before the angel. And he answered and spake unto those that stood before him, saying, Take away the filthy garments from him. And unto him he said, Behold, I have caused thine iniquity to pass from thee, and I will clothe thee with change of raiment. And I said, Let them set a fair mitre upon his head. So they set a fair mitre upon his head, and clothed him with garments. And the angel of the Lord stood by. And the angel of the Lord protested unto Joshua, saying, Thus saith the Lord of hosts; If thou wilt walk in my ways, and if thou wilt keep my charge, then thou shalt also judge my house, and shalt also keep my courts, and I will give thee places to walk among these that stand by.

Now here was Joshua the high priest, and as the high priest he was the representative of the people. And here he stood before the Lord in filthy garments. What were these filthy garments? Come to Isaiah 64:6:

> But we are all as an unclean thing, and all our righteousnesses are as filthy rags; and we all do fade as a leaf; and our iniquities, like the wind, have taken us away.

Filthy rags, filthy garments, all our "righteousnesses". In the literal reading it says all our *righteous acts*, all our righteous doings. But aren't those acts right? Are they not righteous? It's very interesting to consider that, because here God says that even he who was ordinating according to the calling of the Lord as a high-priest for the people God, even his right-doing, his ministering in his office, was as filthy garments.

We come to Daniel chapter nine. We want to read of right acts that are "righteousnesses" that are not filthy garments but that are right. In Daniel 9:13-14 we read here that everything we do, even if it is right, all our *right-doings* is as filthy garments. Here was Daniel praying as he saw the time of Israel's deliverance from captivity drawing near. And he says in his prayer:

> As it is written in the law of Moses, all this evil is come upon us: yet made we not our prayer before the Lord our God, that we might turn from our iniquities, and understand thy truth. Therefore hath the Lord watched upon the evil, and brought it upon us: for the Lord our God is righteous in all his works which he doeth: for we obeyed not his voice.

What God does is true righteousness. In the works that God does He's righteous. But our works, our right-doings is filthy garments. But if God does it, then it is right.

Come to John chapter 5. We want to examine this in the life of Christ. In John 5:30 here is One speaking who became one of us and here it says:

> I can of mine own self do nothing: as I hear, I judge: and my judgment is just; because I seek not mine own will, but the will of the Father which hath sent me.

Jesus Christ who was equal with God made Himself of no reputation and became as we are. He took upon himself sinful flesh. He was, as the book Hebrews says, made like unto his brethren in all things (Hebrews 2:17). And as we in all things cannot do anything of ourselves right, likewise Jesus Christ had to say "I do not mine own will, I do not mine own works" because the oneness between Christ and humanity put Christ in a position as the same as us, where He could not work His own works.

Come to John chapter 5:19-20, just a few verses up, here Jesus says:

> Then answered Jesus and said unto them, Verily, verily, I say unto you, The Son can do nothing of himself, but what he seeth the Father do: for what things soever he doeth, these also doeth the Son likewise. For the Father loveth the Son, and showeth him all things that himself doeth: and he will show him greater works than these, that ye may marvel.

Jesus says, "I cannot do anything of mine own self but the Father shows me what He's doing and therefore I do likewise." That translates to these words here in John 14:10:

> Believest thou not that I am in the Father, and the Father in me? the words that I speak unto you I speak not of myself: but the Father that dwelleth in me, he doeth the works.

Did you note there how Jesus says even though it was the Father that dwelt in Him doing the works, *first* the Father revealed to Him what *He* was doing. How did Christ know the working of the Father? Come back to John 5:39. Here Jesus is speaking to the Pharisees and He says:

> Search the Scriptures; for in them ye think ye have eternal life: and they are they which testify of me.

Did Jesus have the New Testament? He only had the Old Testament, and in the Old Testament the Father showed Jesus what He would work within Him. So Jesus says, "What I see the Father do, these also do I." And a simple illustration of that reality is the Messianic prophecies. Christ learned His calling by studying the Scriptures; He read in the word what God would work within Him at the given time.

And in Isaiah 55:10-11, whilst we often consider this in the light of our appreciation of God's word, it was no different for Jesus Christ:

> For as the rain cometh down, and the snow from heaven, and returneth not thither, but watereth the earth, and maketh it bring forth and bud, that it may give seed to the sower, and bread to the eater: So shall my word be that goeth forth out of my mouth: it shall not return unto me void, but it shall accomplish that which I please, and it shall prosper in the thing whereto I sent it.

So Jesus Himself searched the Scriptures because they were they which testified of Him, and as He read that word, that word accomplished within Him what God had spoken.

Psalms 119:11. Ellen White applies this verse to Jesus Christ. How was it that Jesus Christ lived a life full of the working of God?

> Thy word have I hid in mine heart, that I might not sin against thee.

The word, the Scriptures, He kept and He stored and they worked when the time was right for them to work.

And in *Christ's Object Lessons*, p.61 it speaks of this word of God and it refers to it here as "our part" but as Jesus Christ became in our place then this was His part also:

> Our part is to receive God's word and to hold it fast, yielding ourselves fully to its control, and its purpose in us will be accomplished. [1]

And therefore in *The Desire of Ages*, p.123:

> By what means did He (Christ) overcome in the conflict with Satan? By the word of God. Only by the word could He resist temptation. "It is written," He said. [2]

So He says, "I do not seek Mine own will; I don't do the working. It is the Father that works in me; it is the Father that gives Me the victory over all of these temptations." But how did the Father work? By the *word only*. "Only by the word could [Christ] resist temptation."

Come to Isaiah 55:11. We want to look at this for a moment and see how important this appreciation is that the word of God will not return unto Him void but it – *it* – will accomplish the thing where unto He sent it and prosper in it.

> So shall my word be that goeth forth out of my mouth: it shall not return unto me

void, but it shall accomplish that which I please, and it shall prosper in the thing whereto I sent it.

Let us now turn to Deuteronomy 32:1-2:

> Give ear, O ye heavens, and I will speak; and hear, O earth, the words of my mouth.
> My doctrine shall drop as the rain, my speech shall distil as the dew, as the small rain
> upon the tender herb, and as the showers upon the grass:

My doctrine, My teaching, the words that descend from My mouth, shall drop as the rain and distil as the dew. Is there a perfect connection there with Isaiah chapter 55 and this particular verse we refer to as one of the promises of the latter rain, the outpouring of the Holy Spirit, that this doctrine of God will pour upon our hearts and cause us to flourish and to bring forth fruit?

Come to Joel 2:23, a connecting verse. The word of God is as the rain that comes down. Christ's doctrine, God's doctrine, will drop as the rain.

> Be glad then, ye children of Zion, and rejoice in the Lord your God: for he hath
> given you the former rain moderately, and he will cause to come down for you the
> rain, the former rain, and the latter rain in the first month.

Here again it is speaking of rain, of waters coming from the sky and in the *Young's Literal Translation* it reads as this, and you will note the marginal reading as well:

> And ye sons of Zion joy and rejoice in Jehovah your God for he hath given to you
> the teacher for righteousness who causeth to come down to you a shower sprinkling
> and gathered in the beginning.

In the marginal reading it says: "He hath given you the teacher of righteousness according to righteousness."

A teacher of right-doing according to right-doing! And as we examine the life of Christ we see His source of right-doing, we see *the word* that worked and produced the thing itself. This appreciation of the power being in *the word itself*, to perform the thing itself, is bound up with God's doctrine in the last days, bound up with a teaching of righteousness. But note there in the *Young's Literal Translation* that He has given you this teacher for righteousness in the beginning. This comprehension that needs to be gained regarding the power of God's word is just the beginning, and then it follows on and it will produce its final effects. And this is here in Joel 2:28-29:

> And it shall come to pass afterward, that I will pour out my spirit upon all flesh;
> and your sons and your daughters shall prophesy, your old men shall dream dreams,
> your young men shall see visions:

That will be the final outpouring. But what needs to come first? The doctrine that falls as the rain and distils as the dew. Without the understanding that the word of God produces the thing itself there can be no final outpouring of the latter rain.

Before we receive the great expectation that we have, we need to understand righteousness according to righteousness as demonstrated in the life of Christ. And until we understand that, we cannot receive the Holy Spirit in all its fullness. We cannot.

Are we still in the beginning? Are we waiting and expecting for the Spirit to be poured out upon us when we still have yet to learn the very fundamentals of the word of God? Until we realise that the power of God is in the word of God *itself* to perform the thing *itself*, God cannot pour out the Spirit upon us.

The connection between those verses and Isaiah 55 are very clear on that point. Christ resisted temptation by holding fast to that word and by yielding Himself to its control.

What kind of power is in the word? Come to Genesis 1:1:

> In the beginning God created the heaven and the earth.

How did He do it? Verses 2-3:

> And the earth was without form, and void; and darkness was upon the face of the deep. And the Spirit of God moved upon the face of the waters. And God said, Let there be light: and there was light.

He *"said"* and there it was. And as you go down on these consecutive days, God "says". Come to verses 6-7:

> And God said, Let there be a firmament in the midst of the waters, and let it divide the waters from the waters. And God made the firmament, and divided the waters which were under the firmament from the waters which were above the firmament: and it was so.

And on each day God *"said"* and it was so.

The very basic fundamentals of the word of God.

The Desire of Ages, p.123. We read a small portion of this before and now we want to read it in its larger context:

> "The prince of this world cometh," said Jesus, "and hath nothing in Me." John 14:30. There was in Him nothing that responded to Satan's sophistry. He did not consent to sin. Not even by a thought did He yield to temptation. So it may be with us. Christ's humanity was united with divinity; He was fitted for the conflict by the indwelling of the Holy Spirit. And He came to make us partakers of the divine nature. So long as we are united to Him by faith, sin has no more dominion over us. God reaches for the hand of faith in us to direct it to lay fast hold upon the divinity of Christ, that we may attain to perfection of character.

And how this is accomplished, Christ has shown us. By what means did He overcome in the conflict with Satan? By the word of God. Only by the word could He resist temptation. "It is written," He said. And unto us are given "exceeding great and precious promises: that by these ye might be partakers of the divine nature, having escaped the corruption that is in the world through lust." 2 Peter 1:4. Every promise in God's word is ours. "By every word that proceedeth out of the mouth of God" are we to live. When assailed by temptation, look not to circumstances or to the weakness of self, but to the power of the word. [3]

Would you like the experience that Christ had? Where even the sophistry of Satan and your own heart cannot deceive you? Where not even in a thought will you yield to temptation? Well Christ has shown us how this is to be accomplished. Christ did not give in. But how have you been in your life? How have you been in the last year, in the last week? Thoughts – has Satan found any foothold in your thoughts? In your life? How do you feel when you look at your past life? How do you feel when you look at the last week or maybe even the last half hour while you have been sitting in here? Like Joshua the high priest would have felt standing before God? Filthy garments! But what was the promise? "Take away the filthy garments and clothe him with a change of raiment." Can we praise the Lord for those words? Absolutely we can!

Christ's Object Lessons, p.311:

> Only the covering which Christ Himself has provided can make us meet to appear in God's presence. This covering, the robe of His own righteousness, Christ will put upon every repenting, believing soul. "I counsel thee," He says, "to buy of Me . . . white raiment, that thou mayest be clothed, and that the shame of thy nakedness do not appear." Revelation 3:18.
>
> This robe, woven in the loom of heaven, has in it not one thread of human devising.

What does that mean? Not one thread of human working. This robe of Christ's righteousness is full of the right-doing of God, of God Himself working perfectly in the life of Christ.

> Christ in His humanity wrought out a perfect character, and this character He offers to impart to us.

When you read of "character" don't just read of it as something of a mental function. Character is a result of thoughts and feelings cherished. And habits are formed and the habits make up the character. The promise is that Christ wrought out a perfect character, and this character He offers to impart to us. It is a complete change of reality, change of mind occupation, change of habits, change of life!

> "All our righteousness are as filthy rags." Isaiah 64:6. Everything that we of ourselves can do is defiled by sin. But the Son of God "was manifested to take away our sins; and in Him is no sin." Sin is defined to be "the transgression of the law." 1 John

3:5,4. But Christ was obedient to every requirement of the law. He said of Himself, "I delight to do Thy will, O My God; yea, Thy law is within My heart." Psalm 40:8

"Thy word have I hid in mine heart that I might not sin against thee" (Psalm 119:11).

> "When on earth, He said to His disciples, "I have kept My Father's commandments." John 15:10. By His perfect obedience He has made it possible for every human being to obey God's commandments."

He kept his Father's commandments. What did we read regarding the word? We are to lay hold of it and keep the word. The *word* worked

> When we submit ourselves to Christ, the heart is united with His heart, the will is merged in His will, the mind becomes one with His mind, the thoughts are brought into captivity to Him; we live His life. [4]

Friends, what do we call that? We call it an atonement, AT-ONE-MENT. The life of Christ is our own life. That law requires obedience from the individual and Christ became as our own selves. And He as our own selves lived a perfect life. And this perfect life, He says, "Here, take it, this is what will satisfy the claims of the law." The life becomes merged with His life. You see how close that is? The heart with heart, the will with the will, the mind with the mind and the thoughts brought into captivity. One – one mind, one heart.

> This is what it means to be clothed with the garment of His righteousness.

Are you naked today?

> Then as the Lord looks upon us He sees, not the fig-leaf garment, not the nakedness and deformity of sin, but His own robe of righteousness, which is perfect obedience to the law of Jehovah. [4]

The robe of righteousness. His own robe of *right-doing*. Because the robe of righteousness includes practical obedience, therefore I have entitled today's sermon: "*Christ My Right-Doing.*"

We often consider this word "righteousness" in a non-practical sense. We think of it in a legal or purely character manner, but no, it equates to practical obedience as well – right-*doing*.

Steps to Christ, p.62:

> Since we are sinful, unholy, we cannot perfectly obey the holy law. We have no righteousness [no right-doing] of our own with which to meet the claims of the law of God. But Christ has made a way of escape for us. He lived on earth amid trials and temptations such as we have to meet. He lived a sinless life. He died for us, and now He offers to take our sins and give us His righteousness [right-doing]. If you give yourself to Him, and accept Him as your Saviour, then, sinful as your life

may have been, for His sake you are accounted righteous. Christ's character stands in place of your character, and you are accepted before God just as if you had not sinned. [5]

Now does that make you feel better about the week you just had? Praise the Lord for these words because when we discover who we really are, and when we discover that even my right-doing doesn't count, we're not left high and dry, we're left low and black, damp in the bottom of the pit.

But to see a life which Jesus lived which is our own life, a perfect existence that God counts as our own and He looks upon that, and doesn't see our grotty failings, it gives us so much peace doesn't it?

I really praise the Lord for it. I hang my helpless soul upon this reality. This precious ray of light amidst the darkness that comforts our souls – that even though we are so sinful, we stand before God as if we had not sinned. What do we call this? We call this justification don't we? This pardoning love of God.

From *Faith and Works*, p.100 comes a new element, this precious robe of Christ's righteousness which is so dear to us:

> But while God can be just, and yet justify the sinner through the merits of Christ, no man can cover his soul with the garments of Christ's righteousness while practicing known sins or neglecting known duties. God requires the entire surrender of the heart, before justification can take place; and in order for man to retain justification, there must be continual obedience, through active, living faith that works by love and purifies the soul. [6]

Did you catch that? In the light of those words let me ask you how you feel about the last week you just had. You know we often fall into the danger of considering justification as some blanket covering where I can go on this process of making mistakes in my sanctification walk. And we fall into the danger of thinking that it's OK if I make a mistake, I'm still covered with this robe of Christ's righteousness. But there's something here that we need to get very clear in our minds and in our experience: "*no man can cover his soul with the garments of Christ's righteousness while practicing known sins or neglecting known duties.*" In order for man to retain justification there must be continual obedience. The word of God says, "Examine yourselves, prove yourselves whether ye be in the faith except ye be a reprobate" (2 Corinthians 13:5).

Could I think that I am justified and I stand before God as though I have not sinned when I am sinning against the light that I have? Do I really stand before God as though I have not sinned? Not if I have been "*practicing known sins or neglecting know duties.*" Not if I do not have "*continual obedience.*"

Maybe you have done what I have been doing for much of my life, for much of my Christian walk, living a lie, in a false sense of security thinking it's OK. I'm justified.

I can go and do what I want to do and then learn from my previous mistakes and then come back, and everything's fine, I'm still covered by the blood of Christ. Friends, we lose our justification if we commit a known sin. And we need come back and crucify the Son of God afresh.

Read also this statement from *The Spirit of Prophecy*, Vol.4, p.299:

> But let none deceive themselves with the belief that God will accept and bless them while they are willfully violating one of his requirements. The commission of a known sin silences the witnessing voice of the Spirit, and separates the soul from God. Jesus cannot abide in the heart that disregards the divine law. God will honor those only who honor him. [7]

The Scriptures are clear: *there is no condemnation if you are in Christ Jesus*, but what fellowship hath righteousness with unrighteousness? What communion hath light with darkness? How can I think that I am in Jesus Christ when I am wilfully engaging in a known sin? I am not in Christ if I do that. I have stepped outside my justification and I need to come back and repent. And how long will it take? Notice it says there: "*the commission of a known sin silences the witnessing voice of the Spirit.*"

How long did it take Mary and Joseph to find Jesus again? Three days of painful heart-searching. How long does it take us to find renewed justification? How strong is the deception of our own heart? And when they shall say "*peace and safety*" (1 Thessalonians 5:3); let us take that in a personal sense. What kind of destruction? *Sudden* destruction because we won't expect it. Because I thought I was fine. I thought I was covered by the robe of Christ's righteousness. I thought it was OK for me to go and make some mistakes.

Yes, if you've done it in ignorance or if you've been deceived into sin the Spirit of Prophecy makes it clear, OK that's a different story. But if you have the light and you make the choice, you have done it wilfully, and you stand before God in filthy garments. So what then shall we do, because this is something that we need to learn to deal with aright in our own lives? What shall we do? How shall we come before God? Well, we read it there – in the life of Jesus we see just what to do – read the Bible as He read it.

Come to Matthew 21:20-23. I want to look at this for a moment. You know this one well. And here the angel is speaking to Joseph in the last part of verse 20:

> Behold, the angel of the Lord appeared unto him in a dream, saying, Joseph, thou son of David, fear not to take unto thee Mary thy wife: for that which is conceived in her is of the Holy Ghost. And she shall bring forth a son, and thou shalt call his name JESUS: for he shall save his people from their sins. Now all this was done, that it might be fulfilled which was spoken of the Lord by the prophet, saying, Behold, a virgin shall be with child, and shall bring forth a son, and they shall call his name Emmanuel, which being interpreted is, God with us.

The naming of Jesus was the fulfilling of the Old Testament, that He would be called Emanuel, God with us. So Emmanuel, *"God with us"*, is synonymous with Jesus who shall save them from their sins. That *"God with us"* will provide the solution to the problem of sin.

Now I want to read from Alonzo T. Jones in *1895 General Conference Bulletins* regarding these verses:

> Christ could not be God with us without becoming ourselves, because it is not Himself that is manifest in the world. We do not see Jesus in this world, as He was in heaven; He did not come into this world as He was in heaven, nor was that personality manifested in the world which was in heaven before He came.

Christ said it is nothing of Himself, "the Father... doeth the works." He revealed the Father.

> He emptied Himself and became ourselves. Then putting His trust in God, God dwelt with Him. And He being ourselves and God being with Him, He is "God with us." That is His name.

> If He had come into the world as He was in heaven, being God, manifesting Himself as He was there and God being with Him, His name would not have been "God with us," for He would not then have been ourselves. But He emptied Himself. He Himself was not manifested in the world. For it is written: No man knoweth the Son but the Father." The Father does not reveal the Son in the world, but the Son reveals the Father. Christ is not the revelation of Himself. He is the revelation of the Father to the world and in the world and to men... So it is the Father that is revealed in the world and revealed to us and revealed in us in Christ. This is the one thing that we are studying all the time.

That Christ emptied himself and the Father revealed himself through Christ. And it was as He was we, and the Father was with Him, He was "God with us".

> This is the center around which everything else circles.

This is what Alonzo T. Jones says, and we know the quote by Ellen White *"the central truth around which all other truths cluster"* (*Manuscript Releases*, Vol.12, p.33).

The atonement and the sacrifice of Jesus Christ. That Christ was as ourselves and the Father was with Christ.

> And Christ having taken our human nature in all things in the flesh and so having become ourselves, when we read of Him and the Father's dealings with Him, we are reading of ourselves and of the Father's dealings with us. What God did to Him was to us; what God did for Him was for us. And therefore, again it is written: "He hath made Him to be sin for us, who knew no sin; that we might be made the righteousness of God in Him." 2 Cor. 5:21. [8]

The Father did the works in Him and He was us. So the Father did the works in us. When He worked for Christ, He was working for you and me. This is the centre around which everything else clusters.

And if we want to rightly understand all the peripheral truths of doctrine, personal religion, etc, it's through *this* appreciation. What God did to Him He did to us, and what God did for Him was for us. What God worked in Him He worked in us. And if this is the case, is not the following verse true? Galatians 2:20 our Scripture reading:

> I am crucified with Christ:

Amen? Absolutely! Because if He became our own selves and He was crucified, then I am crucified with Christ.

Nevertheless, what happened to Jesus Christ? He rose again.

> Nevertheless I live; yet not I, but Christ liveth in me: and the life which I now live in the flesh I live by the faith of the Son of God, who loved me, and gave himself for me.

Christ now lives. And how did Christ live? By every word that proceeds out of the mouth of God. By the faith of Jesus that believes that the word would work, and yielding to the working of that word.

I want to read Alonzo T. Jones comments on this from *The Advent Review and Sabbath Herald,* October 24, 1899:

> "I AM crucified with Christ; nevertheless I live; yet not I, but Christ liveth in me: and the life which I now live in the flesh I live by the faith of the Son of God, who loved me, and gave himself for me."

> It may not be amiss to emphasize what this Scripture does say, by noting what it does not say.

> It does not say, I want to be crucified with Christ. It does not say, I wish I were crucified with Christ, that he might live in me. It does say, "I am crucified with Christ."

> Again: It does not say, Paul was crucified with Christ; Christ lived in Paul; and the Son of God loved Paul, and gave himself for Paul. All that is true; but that is not what the scripture says, nor is that what it means; for it means just what it says. And it does say, "I am crucified with Christ; nevertheless I live; yet not I, but Christ liveth in me; and the life which I now live in the flesh I live by the faith of the Son of God, who loved me, and gave himself for me."

> Thus this verse is a beautiful and solid foundation of Christian faith for every soul in the world. Thus it is made possible for every soul to say, in full assurance of Christian faith,

Isn't that what we're seeking? When we see what we've done we need an assurance. Well here it is right in the word of God.

> Thus it is made possible for every soul to say, in full assurance of Christian faith, "He loved me." "He gave himself for me." "I am crucified with Christ." "Christ liveth in me." Read also 1 John 4:15.

> For any soul to say, "I am crucified with Christ," is not speaking at a venture. It is not believing something on a guess. It is not saying a thing of which there is no certainty. Every soul in this world can say, in all truth and all sincerity, "I am crucified with Christ." It is but the acceptance of a fact, the acceptance of a thing that is already done; for this word is the statement of a fact.

> It is a fact that Jesus Christ was crucified. And when he was crucified, we also were crucified; for he was one of us. His name is Immanuel, which is "God with us"—not God with him, but "God with us." When his name is not God with him, but "God with us;" and when God with him was not God with him, but God with us, then who was he but "us"? He had to be "us" in order that God with him could be not God with him, but "God with us." And when he was crucified, then who was it but "us" that was crucified?

> This is the mighty truth announced in this text. Jesus Christ was "us." He was of the same flesh and blood with us. He was of our very nature. He was in all points like us. "It behooved him to be made in all points like unto his brethren." He emptied himself, and was made in the likeness of men. He was "the last Adam." And precisely as the first Adam was ourselves, so Christ, the last Adam, was ourselves. When the first Adam died, we, being involved in him, died with him. And when the last Adam was crucified,—he being ourselves, and we being involved in him,—we were crucified with him. As the first Adam was in himself the whole human race, so the last Adam was in himself the whole human race; and so when the last Adam was crucified, the whole human race—the old, sinful, human nature—was crucified with him. And so it is written: "Knowing this, that our old man IS CRUCIFIED WITH HIM, that the body of sin might be destroyed, that henceforth we should not serve sin."

Are you following this? This is profound! Simply reading *the word of God* as it reads. Friends, how much hope is contained in this verse? In just one verse is the power of God unto salvation, salvation that is already there if we will accept the fact.

> Thus every soul in this world can truly say, in the perfect triumph of Christian faith, "I am crucified with Christ;" my old sinful human nature is crucified with him, that this body of sin might be destroyed, that henceforth I should not serve sin. Rom. 6:6. Nevertheless I live; yet not I, but Christ liveth in me. Always bearing about in my body the dying of the Lord Jesus,—the crucifixion of the Lord Jesus, for I am crucified with him,—that the life also of Jesus might be made manifest in my body. For I who live am always delivered unto death, for Jesus' sake, that the life also of

Jesus might be made manifest in my mortal flesh. 2 Cor. 4:10, 11. And therefore the life which I now live in the flesh I live by the faith of the Son of God, who loved me, and gave himself for me.

Can you see all the other verses now coming into play? All powerfully interconnected in this blessed fact of the crucifixion of the Lord Jesus which was accomplished for every human soul?

> In this blessed fact of the crucifixion of the Lord Jesus, which was accomplished for every human soul, there is not only laid the foundation of faith for every soul, but in it there is given the gift of faith TO every soul. And thus the cross of Christ is not only the wisdom of God displayed from God to us, but it is the very power of God manifested to deliver us from all sin, and bring us to God.
>
> O sinner, brother, sister, believe it. Oh, receive it. Surrender to this mighty truth. Say it, say it in full assurance of faith, and say it forever. "I am crucified with Christ: nevertheless I live; yet not I, but Christ liveth in me: and the life which I now live in the flesh I live by the faith of the Son of God, who loved me, and gave himself for me." Say it; for it is the truth, the very truth and wisdom and power of God, who saves the soul from all sin. [9]

Say it! What did he say? He said, "*Say it forever!*" Oh friends, will we say that forever? Every day, every hour, every minute, every moment: "I am crucified with Christ!" And this is the *word of God* is it not?

Christ came in the beginning. When God came to create the earth there was just a black mass. And God said, "Let there be light," and there was light. God says, "Say this, it's My word" and just accept it!

God says that we are crucified with Christ – then it is so! But more than that Paul says, "I live, yet not I, but now I live by the faith of the Son of God." And how did the Son of God live His life? We touched on that a moment ago. He depended upon the *word*. He lived on every word that proceeded out of His mouth. And if He became as our own selves, and He died, and we died with Him, then how ought we to live with Him? Exactly the same way! Depending upon the word of God to work within us, if we will believe it, and accept the fact.

So why then do we fail and fall? Why do we then find ourselves outside the bounds of the precious gift of justification? It is because we stop believing. We doubt God, that's why. We tell him that His word is not true. That's the reality of it. We say, "God you are a liar," and we choose to sin. We *choose* to sin! Why do we choose to sin? Because at the time it's so exciting and it looks so pleasurable. We think that what sin is offering us then and there is better than what God is offering us. We doubt God's word. Because what does God's word say? Well come to Psalms 16:11. We think sin is so exciting and so pleasurable, more-so than spending time with God.

> Thou wilt show me the path of life: in thy presence is fulness of joy; at thy right hand there are pleasures for evermore.

So we tell God He is a liar or what? To think that we would rather sin and enjoy the pleasures of sin for a moment. Just a little moment. We're telling God that this is more pleasant than being with Him. We're doubting God's word. We're telling Him He is a liar. And why is it that sin has such a strong appeal to us? It's because we don't believe that we are crucified with Christ – that's why. Because if we truly believed that He was *we*, and He died, and we died with Him, then what happened to the body of this sin?

Come to Romans chapter 6 and we'll just have a quick look over these verses here. We want to look at the practical reality of this now. Because we are so easily caught up with ourselves and wanting to please ourselves with sin. Because we doubt God's word. We doubt the *power* of God's word. And in doing that we are doubting our own salvation. Romans 6:2-9:

> How shall we, that are dead to sin, live any longer therein?

If I have been crucified with Christ why am I still sinning?

> Know ye not, that so many of us as were baptized into Jesus Christ were baptized into his death? Therefore we are buried with him by baptism into death: that like as Christ was raised up from the dead by the glory of the Father, even so we also should walk in newness of life.

Of course, because as He was raised, we were raised to newness of life.

> For if we have been planted together in the likeness of his death, we shall be also in the likeness of his resurrection: Knowing this, that our old man is crucified with him,

What is crucified with him? The old man that loves sin. It was crucified with Him.

> That the body of sin might be destroyed, that henceforth we should not serve sin. For he that is dead is freed from sin.

Friends, if we are still a captive to sin, we are not dead! It's very simple. Self is still alive. We have doubted the power of God's word.

> Now if we be dead with Christ, we believe that we shall also live with him:

Now if we're dead with Christ – we have to believe that to begin with don't we? So now the action of faith continues. We believe that we shall also *live* with Him.

> Knowing that Christ being raised from the dead dieth no more; death hath no more dominion over him. For in that he died, he died unto sin once: but in that he liveth, he liveth unto God. Likewise reckon ye also yourselves to be dead indeed unto sin, but alive unto God through Jesus Christ our Lord.

What does *reckon* mean? It's an activity of the mind. You see, faith is more than a belief. It is something that engages with your thought processes. Your reality is dependent upon the functions of your mind. "Reckon yourselves also to be dead unto sin and to be alive unto God through Jesus Christ our Lord." Reckon, consider it. If Jesus says I am crucified with Christ, what are these clamours of my carnal nature? *They're a figment of my imagination.* They're just chemical reactions, electrical impulses, they're just feelings. They don't exist. According to the word of God, the *"old man"* is dead. The body of sin is dead. It is our lack of faith that causes us to fall under the deception of the Devil. Continuing on in Romans 6:12-13:

> Let not sin therefore reign in your mortal body, that ye should obey it in the lusts thereof. Neither yield ye your members as instruments of unrighteousness unto sin: but yield yourselves unto God, as those that are alive from the dead, and your members as instruments of righteousness unto God.

Yield them, just yield! And friends, if we can just understand the concept of that text, things will become much more simple to us. Because we are either serving the Devil or we are serving God. We are not ourselves. There are only two influences in this world. There is either the influence of sin or there is the influence of God. How do we give in to sin? We just yield ourselves to the influence of sin. Well, the word of God says to us that in the same manner you are yielding to sin, yield to My influence, yield to the power of the word. And that word in Romans 6:12, is *"let"*, *"let"*, *"let."*

In Isaiah 45:8 it also speaks of *"let"*:

> Drop down, ye heavens, from above, and let the skies pour down righteousness: let the earth open, and let them bring forth salvation, and let righteousness spring up together; I the Lord have created it.

Is that what we need? This righteousness to spring up in our life? Can you note the animation there of the righteousness in the life? To *let it spring forth.*

And Amos 5:24 says:

> But let judgment run down as waters, and righteousness as a mighty stream.

"Let" it come as a mighty stream. Let righteousness, *right-doing* come down as a mighty stream. It's there. It's just waiting for us to let it!

The perfect right-doing of Jesus is just waiting to come down like a mighty stream upon us because He became our own selves. His life was our own life. And it's there just waiting to come gushing into our hearts and into our practical life; to just cleanse us from the actions of sin. If we *will.*

And that *will* is the deciding factor isn't it? Whilst God has in Christ lived out a perfect life and that life was our own life, there's just one aspect that makes it completely our life and that's *our choice!* That's how it is that God can actually say, "Yes, this is your life." Because we have to *choose* for it to be our life. And friends, when we're talking about choices we're talking about *action of the will*.

Last week a quote was read from *Mind, Character and Personality*, Vol.2, p.691:

> As soon as we incline our will to harmonize with God's will, the grace of Christ stands to cooperate with the human agent;

So there it is. There's the righteousness waiting to come. But we have to *will* for it to come.

> But it (the grace of Christ) will not be the substitute to do our work independent of our resolving and decidedly acting. [10]

Decidedly acting. Remember the paralytic as Bethesda? Christ came to him and he acted on the word of Christ. And as he acted on the word of Christ, God gave the power and he was made whole.

Steps to Christ, p.51:

> In like manner you are a sinner. You cannot atone for your past sins;

Previous life, last ten years, last ten days, you can't atone for them.

> You cannot change your heart and make yourself holy. But God promises to do all this for you through Christ. You believe that promise. You confess your sins and give yourself to God. You will to serve Him. Just as surely as you do this, God will fulfill His word to you. If you believe the promise,--believe that you are forgiven and cleansed, [I LOVE THIS!] --God supplies the fact; you are made whole, just as Christ gave the paralytic power to walk when the man believed that he was healed. It is so if you believe it. [11]

Am I crucified with Christ? Believe it and God will supply the fact. You know the quote where it says we cannot empty ourselves of ourselves but we must consent, must let God do this work (Christ's Object Lessons p. 159).

But is there sin still in our life? Is there perfect obedience in our life? You may be assured that if there is no perfect obedience in your life it is because you do not really believe. That's why! You're not taking God at His word. You're not reading the word of God and receiving the word of God as having power in itself.

If there is still sin in our lives it's because we do not believe. Jesus believed and He lived a perfect life. No guile was found in His mouth. If we really believed God; if we really believed in the judgment; if we really believed in the atonement of Jesus Christ as we have studied this hour, that what God did for Him He did for us; if we really believed in the power of His word; and if we really believed in an eternal, immortal inheritance, then we would stop sinning and live a perfect life as well.

So we've got a lot of work to do haven't we? We've got some pretty hard work to do to conquer sin, haven't we?

John Bunyan in *The Work of Jesus Christ as an Advocate*, tells us yes, we do, we have a lot of hard work to do. And here he says:

> He that undertakes to believe sets upon the hardest task that ever was proposed to man; not because the things imposed upon us are unreasonable or unaccountable, but because the heart of man, the more true anything is, the more it sticks and stumbles thereat; and, says Christ, "Because I tell you the truth, ye believe me not" (John 8:45). Hence believing is called labouring, (Hebrews 4:11); and it is the sorest labour at times that any man can take in hand, because assaulted with the greatest oppositions; but believe thou must, be the labour never so hard.

Labour – there's our work – to hold fast to the word of God. Believe it! And if we believe it we will place confidence upon it, won't we? We will depend upon it. And it will produce it.

And just like Jesus sailed like the sun above it all, we will as well. But no, it wasn't easy for Him. He had to labour didn't He? "*With strong cry and tears unto him that was able to save him.*" Hebrews 5:7. He found it hard to believe as well, because He had this same heart of man, that the more true something is the harder it is to do.

Selected Messages, Vol.1, p.337:

> We shall often have to bow down to weep at the feet of Jesus...

I thank the Lord for the *Spirit of Prophecy* telling us that. It tells us that God knows we're not going to get this one right overnight. He knows that we're often going to make some mistakes.

> We shall often have to bow down to weep at the feet of Jesus, because of our shortcomings and mistakes; but we are not to be discouraged; we are to pray more fervently, believe more fully, and try again. [12]

"And try again" to do what? "Believe more fully!"

John the Revelator saw a company of people standing on the sea of glass. They kept the commandments of God and kept the faith of Jesus.

I just want to close with one more quote from Alonzo T. Jones *1895 General Conference Bulletins*; it's the faith of Jesus that we are to have:

> When He stood where we are, He said, "I will put my trust in Him" and that trust was never disappointed. In response to that trust the Father dwelt in Him and with Him and kept Him from sinning. Who was He? We. And thus the Lord Jesus has brought to every man in this world divine faith. That is the faith of the Lord Jesus. That is saving faith. Faith is not something that comes from ourselves with which

we believe upon Him, but it is that something with which He believed--the faith which He exercised, which He brings to us, and which becomes ours and works in us--the gift of God. That is what the word means, "Here are they that keep the commandments of God and the faith of Jesus." They keep the faith of Jesus because it is that divine faith which Jesus exercised Himself.

He being we brought to us that divine faith which saves the soul--that divine faith by which we can say with Him, "I will put my trust in Him." And in so putting our trust in Him, that trust today will never be disappointed anymore than it was then. God responded then to the trust and dwelt with Him. God will respond today to that trust in us and will dwell with us. [13]

There it is, if you will just lay hold of that faith. And it's already there. It's already ours. *"I live by the faith of the Son of God."* Galatians 2:20. Then the rest will come – continual obedience!

And as these people stand on the sea of glass, can you imagine all these ancient mighty saints with their great stature and gigantic intellect looking upon the short, small, weak, feeble people who perfected a character after 6000 years of sinful degradation? Do you reckon they will marvel at that? Can you imagine it? Well, I thank God so much that Jesus came right down to our level to make this possible. May it be our experience. AMEN.

A CALL TO IMMEDIATE ACTION

January 25, 2014

WHAT are you doing? Does it grate your nerves when people ask you questions like that, with a pathos like that? *What* are you doing? It's almost irritating isn't it? But I believe it's a good question. What are you doing? What am *I* doing? Why are we doing what we do? Do we really believe that Jesus is coming very soon or do we think maybe He will come in a few years?

Do we think there is time for us to start a family, grow the family, start a business, make the money, climb the corporate ladder, anything? Or maybe we enjoy our relaxation time coming home from work; work is so tiring, we just want to come home and relax. I know that's my great weakness.

But what I want to share with you this morning is something that the Lord has brought past me which He's not going to let go and He wants me to pay close attention to this particular subject. Because if I am going to pay close attention to what is happening in the world just now, and in the months that are past, God is really calling us to re-examine what we are doing.

From *Testimonies*, Vol. 5, I want to read a few statements regarding our work at this time and I say "this time" because this is what Ellen White wrote back in her day. And here we are many years on – is it not much more applicable now? I just want to read a few paragraphs, this first one comes from *Testimonies*, Vol.5, p.381:

> I am alarmed at the indifference of our churches. Like Meroz, they have failed to come up to the help of the Lord. The laymen have been at ease. They have folded their hands, feeling that the responsibility rested upon the ministers. But to every man God has appointed his work; not work in his fields of corn and wheat, but earnest, persevering work for the salvation of souls. God forbid, Elder M, that you or any other minister should quench one particle of the spirit of labor that now exists. Will you not rather stimulate it by your words of burning zeal? The Lord has made us the depositaries of His law; He has committed to us sacred and eternal truth, which is to be given to others in faithful warnings, reproofs, and encouragement. By means of railroads and steamboat lines [INTERNET?] we are connected with every part of the world and given access to every nation with our message of truth. Let us sow the seed of gospel truth beside all waters; for we know not which shall prosper, this or

that, or whether both shall be alike fruitful. Paul may plant, and Apollos water; but it is God who giveth the increase. [1]

Here we are called to scatter this truth that God has given us. But we seem to have a problem where we think, *don't cast your pearls among the swine.* We think we have the ability to make a judgment of those we interact with in this world. And we think, *nope, they're swine. Skip. Pass.* And then we shut ourselves up in a tight box thinking it's just me and my little unit of close friends or the church that I'm part of – we're the only ones and everyone else is swine (pigs).

The Scripture says, "Blessed are ye that sow beside *all* waters." Isaiah 32:20. We have no right to decide who is going to accept the message and who is not. We have a particular duty to proclaim the message and I want to have a look at this duty that we have. Reading from page 393 of the same book:

> All who put to use the ability which God has given them will have increased ability to devote to His service. Those who do nothing in the cause of God will fail to grow in grace and in the knowledge of the truth. [2]

Are you growing in grace and in the knowledge of the truth? If not, this is your problem. You're doing nothing in God's cause. And as I look over the past twelve years of my life I wonder, *could I have been more advanced?* Because I have to confess that I have been living a very selfish life. I fell into the very danger that the reformers did of old. In *The Great Controversy*, p.606 Ellen White writes of these reformers here:

> Many reformers, in entering upon their work, determined to exercise great prudence in attacking the sins of the church and the nation. [3]

Yes, don't bring a time of trouble upon yourself before it's due. Right? Is this the counsel that we have been given?

> They hoped, by the example of a pure Christian life, to lead the people back to the doctrines of the Bible. [3]

Was this your hope? It *was* mine. Have you heard it said: just go to work every day, clock-in and clock-out? Maybe give a smile to the lady at the check-out when you go to do the shopping. It doesn't matter, you don't need to put any effort into saving souls; you don't need to find somebody to study with; you don't need to take the time to labour for anyone because your *example* is the loud cry. And that loud cry is going to come forward when you stand in the courts. So you don't need to do anything now. Just go about your daily life. And then one day you'll stand in the courts and all of the true people will hear it. And they will come out. But reading on in *The Great Controversy*, p.606:

> But the Spirit of God came upon them as it came upon Elijah, moving him to rebuke the sins of a wicked king and an apostate people; they could not refrain

from preaching the plain utterances of the Bible,—doctrines which they had been reluctant to present. They were impelled to zealously declare the truth, and the danger which threatened souls. The words which the Lord gave them they uttered, fearless of consequences, and the people were compelled to hear the warning. [3]

And this is why I'm making this recording today. Because I cannot sit back any more and do nothing. We read a moment ago that those who do nothing will fail to grow in grace and in the knowledge of the truth.

A man who would lie down and refuse to exercise his limbs would soon lose all power to use them. Thus the Christian who will not exercise his God-given powers not only fails to grow up into Christ, but he loses the strength which he already has; he becomes a spiritual paralytic. It is those who, with love for God and their fellow men, are striving to help others that become *established, strengthened, settled,* in the truth. [emphasis supplied] [4]

We remember the quote that says that the seal of God is a "settling into the truth, both intellectually and spiritually, so they cannot be moved" (*The Faith I Live By*, p.287). Here is a beautiful harmonising statement. They will be settled into the truth so that they cannot be moved, by striving to help others with all of the powers that God has given them.

The true Christian works for God, not from impulse, but from principle; not for a day or a month, but during the entire period of life.

How is our light to shine forth to the world unless it be by our consistent Christian life? How is the world to know that we belong to Christ, if we do nothing for Him? Said our Saviour: "Ye shall know them by their fruits." And again: "He that is not with Me is against Me." There is no neutral ground between those who work to the utmost of their ability for Christ and those who work for the adversary of souls. Everyone who stands as an idler in the vineyard of the Lord is not merely doing nothing himself, but he is a hindrance to those who are trying to work. Satan finds employment for all who are not earnestly striving to secure their own salvation and the salvation of others. [5]

It's not enough just to be striving to secure your own salvation. You need to be living for others. Jesus Christ never lived for Himself. He gave up everything that was Him to save others. He did not make His own personal salvation His purpose in life. He saved Himself by planting Himself as a dead seed in the furrow of this world's need.

Ellen White says just a few pages over on page 464:

My heart is stirred to the very depths. Words are inadequate to express my feelings as I plead for perishing souls. Must I plead in vain? As Christ's ambassador I would arouse you to labor as you never labored before. Your duty cannot be shifted upon another. No one but yourself can do your work. *If you withhold your light, someone must be left in darkness through your neglect.* [emphasis supplied] [6]

Did you hear that? Did you pay close attention to that? This rattles me because this tells me that I have a duty, a particular duty, that no one else can do. And if I do not do my duty someone will be left out of the kingdom of God. There are individuals in this world that only can be saved by certain individuals. And if those certain individuals do not go about their God appointed duty, then the blood of those that are lost will be placed upon them because they were the only ones who could save them.

So how many souls are perishing, or have perished, because *I* have not taken up *my* duty? Can we be grateful for the blood of Jesus that we can wash our blood-stained hands in? But will that blood of Jesus always flow? And shall we suffer souls to perish around us now? Again on page 465 of the same book:

> The members of the church should individually hold themselves and all their possessions upon the altar of God. Now, as never before, the Saviour's admonition is applicable: "Sell that ye have, and give alms; provide yourselves bags which wax not old, a treasure in the heavens that faileth not, where no thief approacheth, neither moth corrupteth. For where your treasure is, there will your heart be also." Those who are fastening their means in large houses, in lands, in worldly enterprises, are saying by their actions: "God cannot have it; I want it for myself." They have bound up their one talent in a napkin and hid it in the earth. *There is cause for such to be alarmed.* Brethren, God has not entrusted means to you to lie idle nor to be covetously retained or hid away, but to be used to advance His cause, to save the souls of the perishing. It is not the time now to bind up the Lord's money in your expensive buildings and your large enterprises, while His cause is crippled and left to beg its way. [emphasis supplied] [7]

But look beyond the financial side. Look at talents and look at the abilities that God has given you – abilities to labour for souls, to study with people. You might be good at health work. What are you doing? Are you waiting for someone to get sick before you go and help them or are you seeking out those who need help? Are you talented at presenting the word of God? Do you have opportunities where you can speak to large audiences? What a talent! Are you burying it in the earth?

Is blood going to be on your hands because you've permitted the Devil to discourage you from labouring as God has called you to? All heaven! All heaven is waiting for us to take up our task, to do it! It is written that "Christ is waiting with a longing heart to see His image perfectly reflected in His people" (paraphrased from *Christ's Object Lessons*, p69.) A longing heart! And what sort of a heart did Jesus have? It was no different to yours or mine. The Spirit of Prophecy declares it was a human heart. Are you absent from a loved one? Do you sense a loss? Do you miss them? For over 2000 years Jesus Christ has been ministering in the sanctuary. He misses His people!

Christ's Object Lessons, p.415:

> The last rays of merciful light, the last message of mercy to be given to the world, is a revelation of His character of love. [8]

Now the character of the love of Jesus was not just in the workshop going about the daily tasks. As soon as He was called, as soon as the time was fulfilled, He stepped out to minister according to His ability in the role that God has placed Him in. Now, everybody's role is different, but are you in your role? Are you exercising your ability?

> The children of God are to manifest His glory. In their own life and character they are to reveal what the grace of God has done for them. [8]

What a privilege it would be to just declare to the world, "Behold you God!" (Isaiah 40:9). This whole world is on a path of philosophy that tells man there is an inherent divinity within him, and that it is being developed, and given the right time, the right environment, the right mental consciousness, man can be like superman and just rip his shirt apart and say, "I am God!"

But here we are called to lose ourselves in Jesus Christ; to fully yield ourselves to *His* working; to be the transparent medium of His glory to display. To stand before the world in character, in life, in love – behold your God! What a privilege! Further on in *Christ's Object Lessons*, p.419:

> It is the privilege of every soul to be a living channel through which God can communicate to the world the treasures of His grace, the unsearchable riches of Christ. There is nothing that Christ desires so much as agents who will represent to the world His Spirit and character. [9]

What is Christ wanting more than anything else? He is wanting you and me to say, "Lord, here I am. Use me. I empty myself by thy grace – fill me with Thy Spirit and use me."

> There is nothing that the world needs so much as the manifestation through humanity of the Saviour's love. All heaven is waiting for channels through which can be poured the holy oil to be a joy and blessing to human hearts." [9]

All heaven is just waiting, waiting! Heaven is not waiting for the whole world to be converted. Heaven is not waiting for the things that we are waiting for. Heaven is waiting for *individuals*, maybe just one or two, to say, "Me Lord, pick me."

And what kind of a work would God do with just two or three people? We know the story of Gideon's army where he started with over 20,000 men. And he was told to lead this army out to battle. But as they were going to the conflict God said to Gideon, "You've got too many people." He said, "Go and ask the soldiers, are you scared? Did you just get married? Have you just bought a house? Or have you just bought a business?" Go home, we don't want you here because you're half-hearted. Your heart is at home with your wife. It's in your business. Your land is an idol. God wants whole-hearted service!

And then they came to the river, and there was another sifting. And God said, "Gideon, pay close attention to how they drink this water." And those that really had no care for the work of God placed their face in the waters and gulped it down and just got stuck into satisfying their own sense of need.

And God said, "Gideon, pick the ones that can hardly hold the water in their hand because they're busy watching for the enemy; those who aren't putting themselves first, but rather the glory of God and the victory for His people." And they left with only with 300. Apparently only 300 against this massive multitude of people! How many people are there in the world now? Seven billion according to latest count by the United Nations. God can do it with 300! Is that all He needs – 300? Maybe He can do it with less.

Let us come to another story. This is a beautiful story. Come to the story of Jonathan here in 1 Samuel 14. This is a powerful story. Here in verse 6, they were basically under the control of the Philistines; so much so that not even an Israelite could not even possess a weapon of war, except for Jonathan and his father the king. And there was this Philistine garrison there in verses 6-10:

> And Jonathan said to the young man that bare his armour, Come, and let us go over unto the garrison of these uncircumcised: it may be that the Lord will work for us: for there is no restraint to the Lord to save by many or by few. And his armour bearer said unto him, Do all that is in thine heart: turn thee; behold, I am with thee according to thy heart. Then said Jonathan, Behold, we will pass over unto these men, and we will discover ourselves unto them. If they say thus unto us, Tarry until we come to you; then we will stand still in our place, and will not go up unto them. But if they say thus, Come up unto us; then we will go up: for the Lord hath delivered them into our hand: and this shall be a sign unto us.

That's an interesting sign isn't it? Where is your faith? Where is mine? These two young men had taken the *challenge* from the others as a sign it is time for the Lord to work. Are there challenges in this world today? Yes, they have made void the law of God. It is time for us to work. It is not time for us to get all scared, the victory is His. Verses 11-15:

> And both of them discovered themselves unto the garrison of the Philistines: and the Philistines said, Behold, the Hebrews come forth out of the holes where they had hid themselves. And the men of the garrison answered Jonathan and his armourbearer, and said, Come up to us, and we will show you a thing. And Jonathan said unto his armourbearer, Come up after me: for the Lord hath delivered them into the hand of Israel. And Jonathan climbed up upon his hands and upon his feet, and his armourbearer after him: and they fell before Jonathan; and his armourbearer slew

after him. And that first slaughter, which Jonathan and his armourbearer made, was about twenty men, within as it were an half acre of land, which a yoke of oxen might plow. And there was trembling in the host, in the field, and among all the people: the garrison, and the spoilers, they also trembled, and the earth quaked: so it was a very great trembling.

You see the Lord came into the battle and He fought side by side with Jonathan and his armour bearer. And that victory fell to the Israelites that day. God wants to work, but God loves team-work. He's not someone who likes to do things on His own.

But He needs just two people to take Him at His promise, and run with it. Just two people, that's all that's needed. But if He can have more, even better!

There is another powerful story that is contained in the Scriptures regarding a victory where God can work with a small number. And that one is Caleb and Joshua when they examined the land of Canaan. In Numbers chapters 13 and 14 we read the story of the spies that were sent into Canaan – twelve of them, one from each tribe. And they came back bearing large bunches of grapes and fruit and the produce of the land, saying, "This is a goodly land. It flows with milk and honey. But there are giants in that land, sons of Anak – we be not able to go up." And ten men, just ten men had such a testimony.

We hear that testimony today. "We be not able to go up!" We be not able to do this work that God has given me because I don't have the talent, or I don't have the money. Or I don't have a team to work with. Or perhaps you've become discouraged. You can come up with lots of excuses can't you? I know I can.

Two men – only two men – said, "We be able to go up!" and the whole multitude of Israelites wanted to stone them. *Wanted to stone them!* You know it's amazing that they would actually want to stone them. They weren't very happy with their report.

I want to read from *Testimonies*, Vol.5, p.380 once more regarding Caleb and Joshua. Now listen very carefully to this, in fact, *very* carefully please:

> While the doubting ones talk of impossibilities, while they tremble at the thought of high walls and strong giants, let the faithful Calebs, who have "another spirit," come to the front.

Are you a faithful Caleb? Come to the front!

> The truth of God, which bringeth salvation, will go forth to the people if ministers and professed believers will not hedge up its way, as did the unfaithful spies.

Now note that there are ministers and believers that will hedge up the way. As we continue with this study, remember that.

> Our work is aggressive. Something must be done to warn the world.

What am I doing? What are you doing?

> And let no voice be heard that will encourage selfish interests to the neglect of missionary fields.

Is your church motivated toward missionary work? Or does it encourage the selfish interest of, no, don't step out of your comfort zone, it's fine, just wait until you stand in the courts?

> We must engage in the work with heart and soul and voice; both mental and physical powers must be aroused. All heaven is interested in our work, and angels of God are ashamed of our weak efforts. [10]

Angels of God are ashamed of my weak efforts!

Now before I read on regarding Caleb, you might be saying, "Well, what is there I can do?" Don't ask me! Get on your knees and ask the Lord. Even women have a calling. There's a particular quote I would like to share regarding women and the need of women in this final work. And it comes here from *Daughters of God*, p.19:

> Women are needed who are not self-important, but gentle in manners and lowly of heart, who will work with the meekness of Christ wherever they can find anything to do for the salvation of souls. All who have been made partakers of the heavenly benefits [THAT INCLUDES WOMEN] should be earnest and anxious that others, who do not have the privileges which they have enjoyed, should have the evidences of the truth presented before them. [11]

What is your duty whether you're male or a female? Your duty is to present the evidences of truth before the people.

> And they will not merely desire that others should have this benefit, but will see that they do have it, and will do their part toward the accomplishment of this object. [11]

No. No excuse. God has a role for you and that role will save certain souls. If you don't take up that role those souls are lost. We return to *Testimonies*, Vol.5, p.383:

> Human agencies are to be employed in this work. Zeal and energy must be intensified; talents that are rusting from inaction must be pressed into service. The voice that would say, "Wait; do not allow yourself to have burdens imposed upon you," is the voice of the cowardly spies. [12]

Have you got people saying you don't have to do missionary work and you can just wait for the courts?

Cowards!

> We want Calebs now who will press to the front--chieftains in Israel who with courageous words will make a strong report *in favor of immediate action*. When the selfish, ease-loving, panic-stricken people, fearing tall giants and inaccessible walls,

clamor for retreat, let the voice of the Calebs be heard, even though the cowardly ones stand with stones in their hands, ready to beat them down for their faithful testimony." [emphasis supplied] [12]

We want Calebs who will now come to the front; Calebs who will make a strong report in favor of "immediate action!"

Immediate, that means *now*, not tomorrow. It doesn't mean when I've cleared that bill, that debt. It doesn't mean when I get a more comfortable home so I can have more 'head space'. It means now – "Now, Lord, use me!" And a moment later it becomes – "Now, Lord, use me!"

Alonzo T. Jones in the *1893 General Conference Bulletins*, p.181 quoted that particular statement from the Spirit of Prophecy and I want to read this. It's very powerful. Something for us to really think about:

> Who went into the land of Canaan?

You know the answer. Out of all that great multitude there, at the first attempt to enter the Promised Land, *only two souls*.

> The men who said they could go in. And because God was with them they went into the land when all the rest fell in the wilderness. They went with their perishing brethren, as they wandered because of their unbelief all the thirty-eight years. But God had promised, "You shall go in." Who will go into the land now? Has not the testimony been read to us that as Israel was on the borders of Canaan, so are we? [13]

If this is the testimony of 1893, where are we now? In 1888 they came up to the borders of the Promised Land and there were two men, Alonzo T. Jones and Ellet J. Waggoner. And as Joshua and Caleb they gave a good report. "We can go in. We can go in right now!" And the people stoned them. And the Spirit of Prophecy said, "Now we have to wander back into the wilderness."*

In 1899 Stephen Haskell quoted Ellen White as having stated the following nearly a decade earlier:

> If the people of god had Gone to work as they should have gone to work right after the Minneapolis meeting in 1888 the world could have been warned in two years and the Lord would have come.*

Within two years! It's like they would have been just like the Israelites of old and just walked straight into the Promised Land. But they had to go back into the wilderness for forty years? No, three times that, plus some – plus how much, is up to us.

God is bringing – has *brought* – His people to these borders again. There is a

---

* See note on page 261

revival taking place in Adventism of the righteousness by faith message. For many years it has been buried. Ellen White writes: that "the light... has been in a great degree kept away from the world" (*Selected Messages*, Vol. 1, 234). But God is igniting it anew and He has brought us to the borders of His promised land. Reading on in *1893 General Conference Bulletins*:

> Who shall go in? Those who "make a strong report in favor of immediate action." They will go in. God says so. It may be that the doubting, fearful ones will linger, and cause the cause of God to linger, but do not be afraid. God has promised that we shall go in; the Calebs shall go in. That is settled. [13]

So even if there is a delay and there's another forty years before Christ comes, who are those that will go in? Only those who *today*, when the Lord brings His people to the borders of the Promised Land, will say, "We can go in *now!*" Only those who are calling for "immediate action" will be those that will go in. And everybody else who, today, is not doing that work, will perish in the wilderness.

Friends, the second time that the children of Israel came to the borders of the Promised Land, there was no delay. This time, God's people will not go back into the wilderness but rather, they will cross the Jordan.

But those who do not believe that they can go in immediately will never make it in. Because if Christ would have come in two years from 1888, and this message goes forward with power as has been promised, it will do a very quick work. *A very quick work!*

And if we do not believe that it can be a quick work, if we do not *submit* to a quick work, we will be left out. Only those who call for immediate action will go in! Do you want to be found as an unfaithful servant saying, "My Lord delayeth His coming. Let me make a bit more money. Let me grow my family a bit more?"

> "When the selfish, ease-loving, panic-stricken people, fearing tall giants and inaccessible walls, clamor for retreat, let the voice of the Calebs be heard, even though the cowardly ones stand with stones in their hands, ready to beat them down for their testimony."

> What are we here for? We have had in our lessons hitherto that we are not to be afraid of all the powers in this world and the powers of the enemies that will stand against us and against the cause of God. We have seen that in the lessons here. Now this brings us to the point where we are to stand faithful to the message of God and not be afraid of cowardly Seventh-day Adventists even. That is where God wants us to stand. He wants us to know what the message is now. He wants us to give the message as it is now, and if there are those who would beat you down with stones and clubs in their hands, and revile you or anything of the kind, thank God that now is the time for "immediate action." [13]

I really pray that these words and thoughts are sinking into your mind because all God needs is just two or three faithful souls and He will run and He will accomplish the work in a very short time.

But if you do not ask the Lord *now* to use you in that final work, if you want to put if off for a couple of weeks, for a couple of months, for a couple of years... By the time you resign yourself to the Lord, it will be too late because with just a few faithful souls God will finish the work in a very short time. He will cut short His work in righteousness and it will be over before you even know it. But when it's over you will make that bitter lamentation: "The harvest is past, the summer is ended and my soul is not saved!" (Jeremiah 8:20). And many of the souls that weren't saved through what should have been your instrumentality will be accounted to your account.

Immediate action! You know there's a problem with these words "immediate action" because there are seemingly big giants. There are organisational issues that seem to be so big. How can we deal with all these church politics and get the message out? How can we deal with the lack of funds that we think we need to run the programs that we think we need to run?

In the last days money means nothing to God, *especially* in the last days. Because if the whole of heaven is just waiting to pour out His Spirit so they can do this work, God is going to give them every resource they need to finish that work. But He's only going to give it to those who have laid everything on the line. He's not going to give one cent to someone who's going to put it towards their own selfish venture. Not one cent! And I eat my own words on this because I'm still so earthly, so selfish.

And we know the statement by Martin Luther: "Even if I knew that tomorrow the world would go to pieces, I would still plant my apple tree." So we go out and plant trees and we think, *yep, I'm going to get apples off this tree next year*. Well if we really understand that the 1888 Message was a message that would do a work in two years, then wouldn't we be praying that the message will do that work today? Maybe I should be putting my money into helping spread the gospel instead of buying that apple tree for planting?

And sure, some may be saying, "Camron, you're a fanatic! Do you really think that you can hasten Christ's coming?" I've recently spoken with a number of people and they've said to me, "Ah, no. The Lord's timing is perfect. He does everything according to what is already mapped out and chartered and all of those people dying in Africa has nothing to do with you not doing your work. It's just that God sets the limit of time and when the clock hand reaches that time then we can stop dying."

One thing that I said to each of these people that spoke this to me was: the Spirit of Prophecy declares that within a few years of 1888 He could have come. So how does that equate to Christ's coming in 2018 or 2031, according to His "calculation"? No. If they had done their job back then, He would have come. If we do our job today, Christ will come.

The only bound that God has set to time is the time when He knows there are going to be a faithful few – a few that will make the *choice* for Him to come. They will say, "Lord, you promised that you could come in a very short time. We want nothing. We have nothing in this world. We claim that promise. Let's go and get this job done so you can come and take us home." And He will come! He will take them home! *But only those that call for immediate action!*

There's another issue that we tend to have though. We think, *two years! – that means one year to get ready!* And probation closes at the end of that one year. And then the time of trouble – living without an intercessor. That means I only have one year to get ready; one year to perfect a character; only one year to deal with the giants of my own heart; clamber over those walls of unbelief!

Seven years, a few years – don't take two years literally if you don't want to. But the Scriptures are clear that we are to look for and to "hasten His coming." (2 Peter 3:12). God is just waiting for us to make the choice. Whenever we make the choice, He will come.

And I have some very interesting quotes that I want to use to close our time with this. The message of Alonzo T. Jones and Ellet J. Waggoner in 1888 was a message of "immediate action." Here is a testimony given in 1893 that Jones shared in the General Conference sessions. And I believe that this particular testimony actually shows us the crux of the entire 1888 Message. He shared this with the ministers there:

> A sister told me not long ago that before that time four years ago she had just been
> lamenting her estate and wondering how in the world the time was ever going to
> come for the Lord to come if He had to wait for His people to get ready to meet him.

Good question? How will He ever come? Sanctification is the work of a life-time, right? I will receive the character of Christ. But that character of Christ is made up of thoughts, and feelings, and habits make character. So, I'm needing a bit more time to develop this right and holy character. Listen very carefully to this testimony. She had the same problem, of this mentality:

> For she said the way she had been at it--and she had worked as hard as anybody in
> this world, she thought--she saw that she was not making progress fast enough to
> bring the Lord in any kind of reasonable time at all, and she could not make out how
> the Lord was going to come. [14]

Two years! How can the Lord come in two years? God's people could never be ready – it's impossible! Especially if this message of righteousness by faith is just being revived. How can it do its work?

Well, if it's the real Message of 1888, then it will do its work within two years. And on that point I encourage you to examine those who profess to be preaching righteousness by faith. How fine-tuned is their message as a message that will do a quick work? A *quick* work!

Many preach righteousness by faith, and the faith of Jesus in the sense that Christ was our *example*. So you've got a "monkey see, monkey do" kind of business where you have to imitate it. Well, I think we need a couple of lifetimes to get that one right! So study 1888 for yourself. Read the books! And I can't emphasise that point any more strongly than READ – THE – BOOKS! It's amazing how many people I speak with who are blasé about the message of Jones and Waggoner. They just take it for granted that they know it; that their minister's preaching it. *Read the books for yourself!* Know the message for yourself! Or God is going to hold you accountable. Continuing on with the quote:

> She could not make out how the Lord was going to come. She was bothered about it, but she said when the folks came home from Minneapolis and they said,

The folks came home from Minneapolis with the message of righteousness by faith fresh in their mind and what did they have to say?

> "Why the Lord's righteousness is a gift; we can have the righteousness of Christ as a gift, and we can have it now." "Oh," said she, "That made me glad; that brought light, for then I could see how the Lord could come pretty soon. When He Himself gives us the garment, the clothing, the character, that fits us for the judgment and for the time of trouble, I could then see how he could come just as soon as He wanted to." "And," said she, "it made me glad, and I have been glad ever since." Brethren, I am glad of it too, all the time. [14]

He can come when? "Just as soon as He wanted to!" Because you see, it is a gift – "a gift!" A lot of people that have been bound up in a legal religion hear the 1888 Message, particularly Alonzo T. Jones, how he talks about the faith of Abraham and "just believe God," and I've heard it said, "That's just cheap grace."

Well, if it's cheap grace, it's still *cheap*, that means there is actually something I can buy, a couple of pennies that I can put toward my own salvation. Now the church had to come to the realisation that it was *free* grace! *Free!* That means there was nothing they could buy; nothing they could do for their salvation. Not even the widow's two mites could count. *It is a gift!*

And this testimony at Minneapolis was simply that if they would take that gift, Jesus would come – Jesus would come. Now I've found many, many ministers trying to preach righteousness by faith but they're missing something. They are missing the full understanding of that *gift*.

Before we close with a close examination into what that gift is, I'm going to leave you in suspense for a moment. And I'm going to read from *The Great Controversy*, p.609 in the chapter of the last final warning, so that you can understand that if your understanding and intellect and heart grasp the understanding of this gift, you will not let anyone take it from you. But rather you *you will run with it!*

> Different periods in the history of the church have each been marked by the development of some special truth, adapted to the necessities of God's people at that time. [15]

Isn't a gift something that we really need at this time? Whether God's people are ready or not, we can tell that this earth is about to fall to pieces and we don't have time to sanctify ourselves. *We need a gift.* We need to see something right there, right now, and I can just lay hold of it and make it my own.

> Every new truth has made its way against hatred and opposition; those who were blessed with its light were tempted and tried. The Lord gives a special truth for the people in an emergency. Who dare refuse to publish it? He commands His servants to present the last invitation of mercy to the world. They cannot remain silent, except at the peril of their souls. Christ's ambassadors have nothing to do with consequences. They must perform their duty, and leave results with God. [15]

Have you ever heard the words: "Who cares?" Well you can make it your phrase because you will run with this message that we need in these last days. And if someone wants to bombard you, trip you up, accuse you, condemn you, falsify, spread gossip about you, you can say, "Who cares!" Because we have got nothing to do with consequences. Now page 612 of the same book:

> Servants of God, with their faces lighted up and shining with holy consecration, will hasten from place to place to proclaim the message from Heaven. By thousands of voices, all over the earth, the warning will be given. [16]

Praise the Lord that it says thousands of voices because more will run with it than just one or two. But God only needs just one or two to set the ball rolling; to set an example. And what an honour it would be to have God count you as the Caleb and the Joshua that inspired the others to run with it. It could be you!

> The message will be carried not so much by argument as by the deep conviction of the Spirit of God. The arguments have been presented. The seed has been sown, and now it will spring up and bear fruit. The publications distributed by missionary workers have exerted their influence, yet many whose minds were impressed have been prevented from fully comprehending the truth or from yielding obedience. Now the rays of light penetrate everywhere, the truth is seen in its clearness, and the honest children of God sever the bands which have held them. Family connections, church relations, are powerless to stay them now. Truth is more precious than all besides. Notwithstanding the agencies combined against the truth, a large number

take their stand upon the Lord's side. [16]

Amen! I look forward to that time and I really pray that I'm part of that number and I pray that you are as well – that you will be part of that number who will lay hold of truth and not let anything take it away from you; even if you have to sever church relations, or the heart strings of the family.

Truth is more precious than all besides, and what can be more precious than the truth of the gift of Jesus Christ? And the Scriptures say that the gift of God is eternal life through Jesus Christ our Lord – the gift of eternal life (Romans 6:3).

Eternal life is a gift. Do you realise that? Sure, we are to work in co-operation with God; we are to answer our prayers as best we can. There is something that we need to do. But whatever we do, whatever duty it is that God gives us, whether it's practical or a home-life or standards or anything; never think that that it's going to merit you salvation – it cannot and it will not. So let's spend a brief time looking at this gift.

I want to very quickly show you that this is a truth that has been lost sight of. I want to share with you some of Martin Luther's words from his *Commentary on Galatians* which he wrote back in 1536 I believe. And what is written here is absolutely profound. And before I read what I was going to read I just want to see if I can find another statement. Because this is *righteousness by faith* and we seem to find a lot of people preaching *right-doing*, but not *faith*, and one without the other is sin! So we want to see what righteousness by faith is and what faith is. Now this comes from his comments on Galatians 2:20. Here he says:

> Faith must be therefore purely taught...

Now if your minister is not preaching this kind of faith – it's not faith.

> ...namely, that thou art so entirely joined unto Christ, that He and thou art made as it were one person: so that thou mayest boldly say, I am now one with Christ, that is to say, Christ's righteousness, victory and life are mine. And again, Christ may say, I am that sinner, that is, his sins and his death are Mine, because he is united and joined unto Me, and I unto him. For by faith we are so joined together that we are become members of His body, of His flesh and of His bones (Eph 5:30).

Faith must be taught that Jesus became as one's self, that He stands before the law of God and says, "I am that sinner, I will take the punishment." And it gives us the right, yes the *right*, to stand before God and say, "I am as Christ. His righteousness, His life is mine" – the gift of God.

Now to this gift! How practical is this gift? Listen to this – this is amazing! This is Martin Luther's comments on Galatians 3:13:

> So, making a happy change with us, He took upon Him our sinful person, and gave unto us [GAVE, GIFT] His innocent and victorious person; wherewith we being

now clothed, are freed from the curse of the law. For Christ was willingly made a curse for us, saying, as touching My own person, I am blessed and need nothing. But I will abase Myself and will put upon Me your person (Phil 2:7)... and will suffer death, to deliver you from death. Now, He thus bearing the sin of the whole world in our person, was taken, suffered, was crucified and put to death, and became a curse for us. But because He was a person divine and everlasting, it was impossible that death should hold Him. Wherefore he arose again the third day from the dead, and now living forever: and there is neither sin nor death found in Him any more but only righteousness, life and everlasting blessedness.

This image and this mirror...

2 Corinthians 3:18: "Beholding as in a glass the glory of the Lord." With our our faces unveiled, we see Jesus who became as our own person and had a victory over sin and took away all the condemnation. What do you see when you look in the mirror? you see yourself!

This image and this mirror we must have continually before us, and behold the same with a steadfast eye of faith. He that doth so, hath this innocency and victory of Christ, although he be never so great a sinner. By faith only therefore we are made righteousness, for faith layeth hold of this innocency and victory of Christ. Look then how much thou believest this, so much dost thou enjoy it...

The more you believe it, the more it will be your reality.

...If thou believe, sin, death and the curse to be abolished, they are abolished. For Christ hath overcome and taken away these in Himself, and will have us to believe, that like as in His own person, there is no sin or death, even so there is none in ours, seeing He has performed and accomplished all things for us.

How? Because He became as our own person, as our own selves, and He had the victory over sin and death. It's gone. And He was we.

Wherefore if sin vex thee and death terrify thee [DO YOU GET ANXIOUS AND NERVOUS ABOUT SIN – DO YOU ALWAYS WORRY ABOUT IT?], think that it is (as indeed it is) but an imagination, and a false illusion of the devil. *For in very deed there is now no sin, no curse, no death, no devil, to hurt us any more, for Christ hath vanquished and abolished all these things.* The victory of Christ is most certain and *there is no defect in the thing itself but in our incredulity.* [emphasis suplied]

In our incredulity – in our *unbelief.* Because we do not believe that Jesus became our own selves and vanquished sin and death, it still has a victory in our life. But if we will believe it, *if* we will believe it – there is no sin, there is no Devil, there is no curse, there is no death. They are all an "imagination and a false illusion."

Now I read that to you from Martin Luther and now I want to read to you from Alonzo T. Jones. And I want you to see how lost this message has been and how fully it qualifies us to call for "immediate action."

What we just read in Martin Luther shows us there is a gift, not just Christ's innocence and freedom from guilt and the forgiveness of all of our sins, but a victorious life that leads a practical existence of having constant victory over sin.

Now from study No.15 of the *1895 General Conference Bulletins* by Alonzo T. Jones, I close with these very powerful paragraphs. And you will see how amazingly they harmonise with Martin Luther. He says here:

> We are still studying the name of Christ, which is "God with us." And as stated before, He could not be God with us without becoming ourselves, because it is not Himself that is manifest in the world. We do not see Jesus in this world, as He was in heaven; He did not come into this world as He was in heaven, nor was that personality manifested in the world which was in heaven before He came. He emptied Himself and became ourselves. Then putting His trust in God, God dwelt with Him. And He being ourselves and God being with Him, He is "God with us." That is His name.

Have you ever read the name "Emmanuel" like that before? We think of it as God in Jesus who came to us. No He emptied His divine self and God dwelt in Him and we were in Christ. All of humanity was in Christ and the Father was in Christ.

> If He had come into the world as He was in heaven, being God, manifesting Himself as He was there and God being with Him, His name would not have been "God with us," for He would not then have been ourselves. But He emptied Himself. He Himself was not manifested in the world. For it is written: "No man knoweth the Son but the Father"--not simply no man, but no one. No one knoweth the Son but the Father. "Neither knoweth any man the Father, save the Son and he to whomsoever the Son will reveal Him." It is not written, No man knoweth the Son but the Father and he to whom the Father will reveal Him. No. No man knoweth the Son at all, but the Father. And the Father does not reveal the Son in the world, but the Son reveals the Father. Christ is not the revelation of Himself. He is the revelation of the Father to the world and in the world and to men. Therefore, He says, "No man knoweth the Father but the Son and he to whomsoever the Son will reveal the Father." So it is the Father that is revealed in the world and revealed to us and revealed in us in Christ.

Now revealed in us, in Christ. We are told to do a work. To say to the world – "Behold your God!" It's in the gift. The Father revealed in the Son, revealed in us, in Christ.

> This is the one thing that we are studying all the time. This is the center around which everything else circles. And Christ having taken our human nature in all things in the flesh and so having become ourselves, when we read of Him and the Father's dealings with Him, we are reading of ourselves and of the Father's dealings with us.

Past tense. Anything you are reading of Jesus Christ, you are reading of you, because He became us; He became you, He became me. And as the Father lived in Him a perfect life, He lived it in us. It's our life, it's a perfect life, it's the gift of God. Will you believe? To believe is to receive, to appropriate the merits, to make His obedience your own. And God will supply the fact. All you have to do is say "Amen" and let! And listen carefully as we proceed – you'll see that.

The great central truth is what God did in Him, He did in us, and will continue to do it today. You want to study all the reforms; you want to study all the doctrines – only through the eyes of that truth!

> And Christ having taken our human nature in all things in the flesh and so having become ourselves, when we read of Him and the Father's dealings with Him, we are reading of ourselves and of the Father's dealings with us. *What God did to Him was to us; what God did for Him was for us.* [emphasis supplied] [17]

> Weak as we; sinful as we--simply ourselves--He went through this world and never sinned. He was sinful as we, weak as we, helpless as we, helpless as the man is who is without God, yet by His trust in God, God so visited Him, so abode with Him, so strengthened Him, that, instead of sin ever being manifested, the righteousness of God was always manifested.

The right-doing of God.

> But who was He? He was ourselves. Then God has demonstrated once in the world and to the universe that He will so come to me and you and so live with us as we are in the world today and will cause His grace and His power to so abide with us that, in spite of all our sinfulness, in spite of all our weaknesses, the righteousness and the holy influence of God will be manifested to men instead of ourselves and our sinfulness.

Amen!

> In Jesus Christ as He was in sinful flesh, God has demonstrated before the universe that He can so take possession of sinful flesh as to manifest His own presence, His power, and His glory, instead of sin manifesting itself. And all that the Son asks of any man in order to accomplish this in Him is that the man will let the Lord have Him as the Lord Jesus did.

Do you need to be possessed by the Spirit of God? Well, just *let*.

> Jesus said, "I will put my trust in Him." And in that trust Christ brought to every one the divine faith by which we can put our trust in Him. And when we do so separate from the world and put our sole trust in Him, then God will so take us and so use us that our sinful selves shall not appear to influence or affect anybody, but God will manifest His righteous self, His glory, before men, in spite of all ourselves and our

sinfulness. That is the truth. And that is the mystery of God, "Christ in you, the hope of glory." God manifest in sinful flesh.

Upon this point, also, Satan discourages many. To the believing sinner Satan says: You are too sinful to count yourself a Christian. God cannot have anything to do with you. Look at yourself. You know you are good for nothing. Satan has discouraged us thousands of times with that kind of argument.

Yes true, here's this great work of God calling for immediate action and you think, I'm just a nobody. Who am I? I'm a sinner! What would God want with me? Could I ever be among His elite and faithful in the last days? Could I ever be an example to trigger off a great revival? No, you're a dreamer...

Well friends, reality starts with a dream! And if you feel that God has put it in your heart to call for immediate action, it's a dream that the Holy Spirit has given you. In Joel it says "I will put my Spirit upon them and they shall dream dreams, they shall prophecy!" (Joel 2:28,29).

But God has wrought out an argument that puts this plea of Satan all to shame, for Jesus came and became ourselves--sinful as we are, laden with the sins of the world--far more sins than there are upon me. And in Him, laden with ten thousand times more sins than ever were upon me, God has demonstrated that with one so sinful as that, He will come and live a whole lifetime and manifest Himself and His righteousness in spite of all the sinfulness and in spite of the devil. God laid help upon One who is mighty, and that help reaches us. Thank the Lord.

Brethren, that does me good. For I know that if ever anything good is to be manifested in this world where I am, it must come from some source besides myself. That is settled. But, O! the blessedness of it is, God has demonstrated that He will manifest His righteous self instead of my sinful self when I let Him have me. I cannot manifest righteousness of myself; I cannot manifest His righteousness in myself. No. I let Him have me, absolutely, overwhelmingly. Then He attends to that. He has demonstrated it so. He has demonstrated a whole lifetime what God is when He is joined with me in sinful flesh. He can do it again as certainly as He can have me.

Will you let Him have you? O, does it call for too full a surrender? No. It is becoming. How full a surrender did He make? He surrendered all Himself. Christ gave up Himself, emptied Himself. The French translation is, "He annihilated Himself." He undid Himself and sank Himself in us in order that God, instead of ourselves and His righteousness, instead of our sinfulness, might be manifested in us in our sinful flesh. Then let us respond and sink ourselves in Him, that God may still be manifest in sinful flesh.

Let us do that. We will do that! Jesus Christ never sinned His whole entire life. If we will sink ourselves in Christ immediately and stand there, we cannot sink. We will not sink. But will you believe it? Too many doubts! That's the problem!

Just closing in this next paragraph. We need a gift. That testimony of 1888 was that Christ can come just as soon as He wants to. Can we call for immediate action? Can we really, really be justified in saying the Lord can come in two years, in two months, if He wanted to?

> Christ has allied Himself with every human being, on His own part; and if every human being in the world tonight should drop everything and say, *"Yes, that is a fact; He and I are one, and He is the one,"* every soul would be saved tonight, and Christ would appear in every soul tomorrow. [emphasis supplied] [18]

And He would see His image perfectly reproduced in His people and He would come to take them home.

What are you doing? What am I doing? Such amazing revelations – so clear. Why has it been so long for me to read these books? Why has it been so long for me to learn that this world is falling apart? Don't invest your money in the world. It's nothing, it's vain, it's fake!

There is a perfect life. This life is in the Son, Jesus Christ. And even though we may remain on this earth a little bit longer, we don't have to worry because everything is already taken care of. Christ has already met the trials. The victory is already mine. Sin has already been vanquished. It doesn't exist! It's a figment of our imagination. Doubt is powerful though isn't it?

Friends, I invite you to take a close look at your life. Take a close look at your priorities in life. Do you really believe that Jesus is coming? If you believe that He is coming, and He is coming very soon, and you really believe the power of this message, you won't be putting your money in building worldly enterprises. You won't be spending your time reading the news – news is irrelevant. You may say, "Oh I am trying to see what is going on in the world." Nothing will go on in the world until you get your act together!

The winds are ready to blow! They've been ready to blow since 1888! It's just waiting for the servants of God to be sealed in their foreheads. And it's for you to make the choice – "I am one with Christ – live out that life within me." This is a call to action. And I need you to encourage me, just as much as everyone needs my encouragement. God is a team player, we are all team players. We're a body of Christ, members – plural – in particular.

May God help us to find our duties. May God help us to let go of any of these cords that are holding us back from running with this. Let's be like Caleb and Joshua, let's say, "Yes! We are able!" And friends, the second time they came up to the borders of the promised land, there was no delay. They walked straight in. And we can walk straight in! So let's do it, is my prayer. AMEN.

Mercy In My Pit of Misery

by Camron Schofield

In the darkness I did sit,
Wretched and miserable
Alone in my pit.

Above me, the thunder roared;
The wrath of an angry Lord.

A shiver went down my spine,
To think, to know, to feel,
That it's my turn this time.

"You're gonna die!"
Cried the voices in my head.
"It's time to go to hell,"
They said.

I waited, with breath abated,
For that final stroke of death.

There was a boom,
There was a flash
There was a vision of light.
Then settled once more,
My perpetual night.

But in the light, I did see,
There in my pit,
A personality.
Who could it be?

And how dare they
Invade my space.
Didn't they know this pit,
My life, was a waste?

I clenched my fists,
And got ready to fight.

Another boom,
Another flash,
Another vision of light.

Who could it be,
Down here with me?

Who could it be,
That would partake with me,
This woe, this pit,
Of misery?
This hole that I had dug,
To reap what I had sown?
To think, to know, to feel,
That I was not alone.

Who could it be,
Down here with me?

Another boom,
Another flash,
Another vision of light.

Who could it be,
Down here with me?

Another boom,
Another flash,
Another vision of light.

'Twas my sins that I did reap.
'Twas me that made my pit so deep.

And yet,
To think, to know, to feel,
That I was not alone,
Melted my heart of stone.

Who could it be,
Down here with me?

I wept, I cried,
I cried some more.
I cried until my throat was sore.

Who could it be,
Down here with me?

A hand touched my check,
And wiped away a tear.
I startled with fear.
Then a voice, I did hear.

"Be not afraid,
Neither be thou dismayed."

'Twas a voice that I did not know,
The sound of love, and not of woe.
Sweet and melodious in my ear,
Foreign to me down here.

Another boom,
Another flash,
Another vision of light

And then another boom,
Another flash,
Death's stroke drew nigh.
And yet,
Another vision of light.

In the light I did see,
A hand, reached out in pity.

And the voice,
It spake once more:
"I give to thee my hand;
Take it, hold it tight.

And I will help thee,
Through the night."

I hesitated,
And there was silence.

Another boom,
Another flash,
Another vision of light.

And there with me,
Was no personality.

Could it be,
I had delayed too long?
Could it be, that hand,
Was gone?

Billows of despair rolled over me,
And yet, a hope within.
"Lord, save me!" I cried,
And threw myself into the night.

Another boom,
Another flash,
A hand in the light!

It took hold of mine.
And I held it tight.

Another boom,
Another flash,
And I died.

Here on the mountain top I sit.
Far, far from my dismal pit.
Visions of night,
Have passed from my sight.
All that I see,
Is Jesus with me.

References

We have provided the page and paragraph references to 1893 and 1895 *General Conference Bulletins*, ISBNs: 0992507405 & 0992507413. This will be noted in square brackets: e.g. [GCB1893 269.1-270.3]

The Sweetest Words on Earth
1. Ellen G. White, *The Great Controversy*, p.642, para.3
2. Alonzo T. Jones, *General Conference Bulletins*, February 27, 1893, p.413, para.4 to p.414, para.1 [GCB1893 249.3-250.2]
3. Alonzo T. Jones, *General Conference Bulletins*, February 27, 1893, p.416, para.7 to p.417, para.3 [GCB1893 254.4-255.4]

God's Abounding Grace

Part 1 - Waking Up to the Reality
1. Ellen G. White, *Christ's Object Lessons*, p.315, para.1
1. Ellen G. White, *Steps to Christ*, p.31, para.1

Part 2 - The Gift of Jesus Christ
*Page 46: The author emphasises the fact that we ourselves do not become divine through our union with Christ: "It is not humanity reaching out to the divinity, but divinity reaching out to humanity. It was divinity that took humanity into itself. Humanity did not take divinity into itself. We do not become divine. We do not evolve to a higher state of existence. Only God is self-existent. We are not. We can never exist as God... Christ did not bring the attributes of divinity into our human nature; they are only ours as a gift when the human is united with the divinity of God. Even though we are one with Him, His attributes will never be inherent in humanity of itself" (*A Life that Measures with the Life of God*, Camron Schofield, published 2015, page 57).
1. Alonzo T. Jones, *General Conference Bulletins*, February 21, 1895, p.269, para.7 to p.270, para.3 [GCB1895 144.4-145.3]

Part 3 - Out of Myself and Into Christ
1. Ellen G. White, *Bible Commentary*, Vol.7, p.926, para.5
2. Ellen G. White, *God's Amazing Grace*, p.10, para.2
3. Ellen G. White, *1888 Materials*, p.552, para.1
4. Ellen G. White, *The Desire of Ages*, p.483, para.1
5. Ellen G. White, *The Desire of Ages*, p.687, para.3
6. Ellen G. White, *The Desire of Ages*, p.690, para.1, 2
7. Ellen G. White, *Manuscript Releases*, Vol.13, p.369, para.3
8. Ellen G. White, *Testimonies*, Vol.2, p.205, para.3

Part 4 - Ready When You Are
1. Ellen G. White, *Steps to Christ*, p.62, para.2
2. Ellen G. White, *The Desire of Ages*, p.667, para.5
3. Ellen G. White, *Christ's Object Lessons*, p.311, para.4

Part 6 - Sanctified by Faith
1. Alonzo T. Jones, *General Conference Bulletins*, April, 1895, p.492, para.6 to p.270, para.3 [GCB1895 267.4]

2. Ellen G. White, *Bible Commentary*, Vol.6, p.1073, para.1

3. Ellen G. White, *The Review & Herald*, October 18, 1898, para.7

4. Alonzo T. Jones, *Advent Review & Sabbath Herald*, December 6, 1898, p.782, para.3

5. Alonzo T. Jones, *Advent Review & Sabbath Herald*, December 27, 1898, p.832, para.1

6. Ellen G. White, *Christ's Object Lessons*, p.60, para.4 to p.61, para.2

7. Ellen G. White, *The Desire of Ages*, p.120, para.1

8. Ellen G. White, *The Desire of Ages*, p.19, para.2

9. Ellen G. White, *The Desire of Ages*, p.753, para.1, 2

10. Ellen G. White, *The Desire of Ages*, p.756, para.2

11. Ellen G. White, *The Desire of Ages*, p.73, para.1

Why the Sanctuary Service was Given to the Israelites

Part 1

1. Ellen G. White, *Selected Messages*, Vol.1, p.337, para.1

Part 2

1. Ellen G. White, *The Desire of Ages*, p.224, para.5

Annihilating the Confusion

1. Ellen G. White, *God's Amazing Grace*, p.259, para.4

2. Alonzo T. Jones, *General Conference Bulletins*, February 23, 1893, p.361, para.3 to para.4
   [GCB1893 214.3-4]

3. Ellen G. White, *Steps to Christ*, p.62, para.2

4. Ellen G. White, *Patriarchs & Prophets*, p.46, para.2

5. Ellen G. White, *The Desire of Ages*, p.710, para.1

6. Ellen G. White, *The Desire of Ages*, p.805, para.3

7. Ellen G. White, *The Desire of Ages*, p.668, para.3

Feeling After God

1. Ellen G. White, *Signs of the Times*, September 10, 1896, para.3, 4

2. Ellen G. White, *The Desire of Ages*, p.794, para.4

3. Ellen G. White, *Testimonies*, Vol.5, p.651, para.2 to 652, para.1

4. Ellen G. White, *The Faith I Live By*, p.123, para.5

5. Ellen G. White, *Manuscript Releases*, Vol.8, p.221, para.1

6. Ellen G. White, *In Heavenly Places*, p.104, para.2

7. Ellen G. White, *The Upward Look*, p.72, para.4

8. Ellen G. White. *Child Guidance*, p52, para.1

9. Ellen G. White, *Child Guidance*, p.46, para.3 to p.47, para.1

10. Ellen G. White, *Sermons & Talks*, Vol.1, p.132, para.1

Are My Sins Forgiven?

1. Ellen G. White, *Steps to Christ*, p.62, para.2

2. Ellen G. White, *Our High Calling*, p.52, para.3

3. Ellen G. White, *Christ's Object Lessons*, p.251, para.1, 2

4. Ellet J. Waggoner, *Present Truth*, UK Edition, August 16, 1894, p.513, para.7

5. Ellen G. White, *In Heavenly Places*, p.23, para.3

6. Ellen G. White, *The Adventist Home*, p.47, para.2

Revisiting 1888

Part 1 - Progression of Light

1. Alonzo T. Jones, *General Conference Bulletins*, February 23, 1893 p.361, para 3, 4
	[GCB1893 214.3-4]
2. Ellen G. White, *Manuscript Releases*, Vol.16, p.104, para.3
3. Ellen G. White, *Manuscript Releases*, Vol.16, p.107, para.2
4. Ellen G. White, *Manuscript Releases*, Vol.16, p.105, para.2 to p.105, para.2
5. Ellen G. White, *Manuscript Releases*, Vol.11, p.257, para.2
6. Ellen G. White, *Manuscript Releases*, Vol.11, p.283, para.3
7. Ellen G. White, *1888 Materials*, p.1814, para.4
8. Ellen G. White, *1888 Materials*, p.608, para.2
9. Ellen G. White, *1888 Materials*, p.954, para.3
10. Ellen G. White, *Manuscript Releases*, Vol.5, p.219, para.1
11. Ellen G. White, *Selected Messages*, Vol.3, p.172, para.1
12. Ellen G. White, *Selected Messages*, Vol.1, p.19, para.1
13. Ellen G. White, *Selected Messages*, Vol.1 p.21, para.3 to p.22, para.2
14. Ellen G. White, *1888 Materials*, p.281, para.1
15. Ellen G. White, *1888 Materials*, p.1689, para.1
16. Ellen G. White, *Selected Messages*, Vol.1, p.19, para.1
17. Ellen G. White, *Patriarchs and Prophets*, p.364, para.2
18. Ellen G. White, *Testimonies*, Vol.5, p.664, para.3 to p.665, para.2
19. Ellen G. White, *Testimonies to Ministers*, p.91, para.2
20. Ellen G. White, *1888 Materials*, p.133, para.2
21. Ellen G. White, *1888 Materials*, p.1814, para.4
22. Ellen G. White, *Signs of the Times*, April 18, 1900, para.9
23. Ellen G. White, *1888 Materials*, p.1689, para.1
24. Ellen G. White, *Christ's Object Lessons*, p.127, para.4

Part 2 - The Law

1. Ellen G. White, *Testimonies to Ministers*, p.91, para.2
2. Ellen G. White, *Testimonies to Ministers*, p.92, para.2
3. Ellen G. White, *1888 Materials*, p.560, para.4
4. Ellen G. White, *Selected Messages*, Vol.1, p.388, para.1
5. Ellen G. White, *Selected Messages*, Vol.3, p.168, para.2
6. Ellen G. White, *Manuscript Releases*, Vol.5, p.219, para.1
7. Ellen G. White, *Patriarchs and Prophets*, p.364, para.2
8. Ellen G. White, *Manuscript Releases*, Vol.17, p.217, para.1
9. Ellet J. Waggoner, *The Everlasting Covenant*, p.330, para.3
10. Ellet J. Waggoner, *The Everlasting Covenant*, p.330, para.4
11. Ellet J. Waggoner, *The Everlasting Covenant*, p.331, para.2
12. Ellet J. Waggoner, *The Everlasting Covenant*, p.332, para.1
13. Ellet J. Waggoner, *The Everlasting Covenant*, p.291, para.2
14. Ellet J. Waggoner, *The Everlasting Covenant*, p.332, para.2
15. Ellet J. Waggoner, *The Everlasting Covenant*, p.333, para.1
16. Ellet J. Waggoner, *The Everlasting Covenant*, p.333, para.2
17. Alonzo T. Jones, *General Conference Bulletins*, February 23, 1893, p.361, para.3-5
	[GCB1893 214.3-5]
18. Ellet J. Waggoner, *The Everlasting Covenant*, p.303, para.2
19. Alonzo T. Jones, *General Conference Bulletins*, February 27, 1893, p.411, para.6 to p.413, para.1
	[GCB1893 246.3-248.6]

20. Alonzo T. Jones, *General Conference Bulletins*, February 27, 1893, p416, para.5 to p.417, para.3
    [GCB1893 254.4-256.1]

Part 3 - Righteousness by Faith

1. Stephen Haskell quoted this testimony in 1899. It is quoted in full on page 188 of this book. He referenced it from memory as a statement from Ellen White published in the General Conference Bulletin of 1892. However, there was no General Conference session in 1892. This quotation remains to be verified by the White Estate. The author of this book has used this quote because he believes it is a genuine statement from the pen of Ellen G. White due its similarity in writing style and spirit of thought with all her other writings. There are a number of similar quotes by Ellen White that also state that the time would have been short had the church received the message of Righteousness by Faith in 1888. In consideration of the rapidity in which the first and second angel's messages went to all the corners of the globe in the 1840's, the technological developments in communications that had taken place in the world since that time, and the Blair Bill that was before the Senate in 1888, two years is not an unreasonable time for the proclaimation of the Gospel and the Second Advent of Christ. Also taking into account the fact that the pure message of righteousness by faith has an immediate effect in the life, we can see that God is indeed quite capable of fulfilling His promise: "For he will finish the work, and cut it short in righteousness: because a short work will the Lord make upon the earth." Romans 9:28.
2. Alonzo T. Jones, *General Conference Bulletins*, February 27, 1893, p.411, para.6
    [GCB1893 246.3]
3. Alonzo T. Jones, *General Conference Bulletins*, April, 1895, p.492, para.6
    [GCB1895 267.4]
4. Ellen G. White, *Faith & Works*, p.18, para.1
5. Alonzo T. Jones, *General Conference Bulletins*, February 27, 1893, p.413, para.1
    [GCB1893 248.6]
6. Alonzo T. Jones, *General Conference Bulletins*, February 23, 1893, p.361, para.4
    [GCB1893 214.4]
7. Alonzo T. Jones, *General Conference Bulletins*, February 23, 1893, p.363. para.4, 5
    [GCB1893 218.2-3]
8. Alonzo T. Jones, *General Conference Bulletins*, February 23, 1893, p.363, para.3
    [GCB1893 221.9]
9. Alonzo T. Jones, *General Conference Bulltins*, February 24, 1893, p.378, para.5
    [GCB1893 221.9]
10. Alonzo T. Jones, *General Conference Bulletins*, February 24, 1893, p.378, para.6 to p.379, para.1
    [GCB1893 222.1-223.1]
11. Ellen G. White, *Bible Commentary*, Vol.6, p.1073, para.1, 2
12. Ellen G. White, *1888 Materials*, p.1165, para.1-5
13. Ellen G. White, *Faith & Works*, p.18, para.1, 2
14. Alonzo T. Jones, *The Advent Review & Sabbath Herald*, January 24, 1899, p.56, para.2-6
15. Ellen G. White, *Steps to Christ*, p.62, para.2
16. Ellen G. White, *Steps to Christ*, p.50, para.1 to p.52, para.2
17. Ellen G. White, *Christ's Object Lessons*, p.61, para.2
18. Ellen G. White, *Bible Training School*, June 1, 1915, para.1
19. Ellen G. White, *The Review & Herald*, October 18, 1898, para.7
20. Ellen G. White, *Selected Messages*, Vol.3, p.145, para.1
21. Ellen G. White, *1888 Materials*, p.281, para.1

Part 4 - Light for Our Generation

1. Alonzo T. Jones, *General Conference Bulletins*, February 23, 1893, p.361, para.4
    [GCB1893 214.4]
2. Ellen G. White, *Early Writings*, p.67, para.2
3. Ellen G. White, *The Great Controversy*, p.612, para.2
4. Ellen G. White, *Christ's Object Lessons*, p.127, para.4
5. Ellen G. White, *Faith & Works*, p.18, para.1
6. Ellen G. White, *The Review & Herald*, October 18, 1898, para.7

7. Alonzo T. Jones, *General Conference Bulletins*, February 27, 1893, p.412, para.3
    [GCB1893 247.3]
8. Ellen G. White, *Steps to Christ*, p.62, para.1
9. Alonzo T. Jones, *General Conference Bulletins*, February 22, 1893, p.344, para.17, 18
    [GCB1893 203.9-10]
10. Ellen G. White, *Steps to Christ*, p.62, para.2
11. Ellen G. White, *Bible Training School*, June 1, 1915, para.1
12. Ellen G. White, *The Desire of Ages*, p.390, para.5
13. Alonzo T. Jones, *General Conference Bulletins*, February 19, 1895, p.233, para.8 to p.234, para.1
    [GCB1895 133.4-134.1]
14. Alonzo T. Jones, *General Conference Bulletins*, February 21, 1895, p.269, para.6-8
    [GCB1895 144.3-5]
15. Alonzo T. Jones, *General Conference Bulletins*, February 22, 1895, p.299, para.1 to p.301, para.9
    [GCB1895 146.2, 150.7-151.3]
16. Ellen G. White, *Christ's Object Lessons*, p.311, para.4
17. Ellen G. White, *The Desire of Ages*, p.668, para.3
18. Ellen G. White, *Testimonies*, Vol.5, p.267, para.2
19. Ellen G. White, *Selected Messages*, Vol.2, p.57, para.1, 2
20. Alonzo T. Jones, *General Conference Bulletins*, February 27, 1893, p.417, para.4
    [GCB1893 256.2]

Christ My Right-doing
1. Ellen G. White, *Christ's Object Lessons*, p.61, para.2
2. Ellen G. White, *The Desire of Ages*, p.123, para.4
3. Ellen G. White, *The Desire of Ages*, p.123, para.3, 4
4. Ellen G. White, *Chist's Object Lessons*, p.311, para.3, 4
5. Ellen G. White, *Steps to Christ*, p.62, para.2
6. Ellen G. White, *Faith & Works*, p.100, para.1
7. Ellen G. White, *Spirit of Prophecy*, Vol.4, p.299, para.2
8. Alonzo T. Jones, *General Conference Bulletins*, February 22, 1895, p.298, para.1 to p.299, para.1
    [GCB1895 146.1-2]
9. Alonzo T. Jones, *Advent Review & Sabbath Herald*, October 24, 1899, p.684, para.19 to p.685, para.2
10. Ellen G. White, Mind, *Character and Personality*, Vol.2, p.691, para.3
11. Ellen G. White, *Steps to Christ*, p.51, para.1
12. Ellen G. White, *Selected Messages*, Vol.1, p.337, para.1
13. Alonzo T. Jones, *General Conference Bulletins*, February 21, 1895, p.270, para.1, 2
    [GCB1895 145.1]

A Call to Immediate Action
1. Ellen G. White, *Testimonies*, Vol.5, p.381, para.1
2. Ellen G. White, *Testimonies*, Vol.5, p.393, para.2
3. Ellen G. White, *The Great Controversy*, p.606, para.1
4. Ellen G. White, *Testimonies*, Vol.5, p.393, para.2
5. Ellen G. White, *Testimonies*, Vol.5, p.393, para.2, 3
6. Ellen G. White, *Testimonies*, Vol.5, p.464, para.1
7. Ellen G. White, *Testimonies*, Vol.5, p.465, para.1
8. Ellen G. White, *Christ's Object Lessons*, p.415, para.5
9. Ellen G. White, *Christ's Object Lessons*, p.419, para.2
10. Ellen G. White, *Testimonies*, Vol.5, p.380, para.2
11. Ellen G. White, *Daughters of God*, p.19, para.1

12. Ellen G. White, *Testimonies*, Vol.5, p.383, para.3

13. Alonzo T. Jones, *General Conference Bulletins*, February 7, 1893, p.181, para.12-14
    [GCB1893 137.7-138.1]

14. Alonzo T. Jones, *General Conference Bulletins*, February 23, 1893, p.361, para.3, 4
    [GCB1893 214.3-4]

15. Ellen G. White, *The Great Controversy*, p.609, para.1

16. Ellen G. White, *The Great Controversy*, p.612, para.1, 2

17. Alonzo T. Jones, *General Conference Bulletins*, February 22, 1895, p.298, para.1 to p.299, para.1
    [GCB1895 146.1]

18. Alonzo T. Jones, *General Conference Bulletins*, February 22, 1895, p.302, para.11 to p.303, para.8
    [GCB1895 153.2-155.1]

CPSIA information can be obtained
at www.ICGtesting.com
Printed in the USA
FSOW04n1235270717
36604FS

9 780994 558510